# SELF-MANAGEMENT
# FOR COLLEGE STUDENTS

# SELF-MANAGEMENT FOR COLLEGE STUDENTS

## The ABC Approach

Edward J. O'Keefe

Marist College

Donna S. Berger

Marist College

PARTRIDGE HILL PUBLISHERS

PHP

HYDE PARK, NY

Requests for permission to make copies of any part of the work should be mailed to Partridge Hill Publishers, Partridge Hill Rd., Hyde Park, NY 12538.

ISBN:  0-9637801-0-7
Library of Congress Catalog Card Number: 93-85780
First edition

Notice:

*Self-management for College Students:  The ABC Approach* was previously titled *The ABCs of Self-management.*

Cartoon characters courtesy of Jim Cooper's Graphics Galore, Louisville, Kentucky.

Cartoon script quotations:

page  91     Mark Twain (American author)
page  115    Samuel Butler (English author)
page  150    Woody Allen (American film writer & director)
page  242    a variation of a quotation by Oliver Wendell Holmes
              (American writer & physician)

# TABLE OF CONTENTS

4   **METHODS FOR CHANGING AFFECT, BEHAVIOR, AND COGNITION**

5   **TO BE A COLLEGE STUDENT**

6 **TIME MANAGEMENT**

# 7   PROCRASTINATION

# 8 ASSERTIVENESS

# FOREWORD

Welcome to college whoever you may be and wherever you may be starting college. Welcome, especially, to new students at Marist College for whom this text was originally inspired and intended. I offer this foreword from my perspective as a university educator who has been involved for more than two decades designing special freshman seminars/freshman orientation courses to help teach new college students how to be successful and fulfill their hopes, dreams, and ambitions as a result of a college experience. In the course of my work, I have trained hundreds of college teachers and administrators at my own university, the University of South Carolina, to teach our freshman orientation course, University 101. I have also worked with thousands of higher educators, for example, at Marist College, who share my interest in making student success happen by design, rather than leaving it to chance, as it was left to chance for me when I was a new college student centuries ago in 1961!

As I read the manuscript for the book that you are about to read, I couldn't help but be reminded of a riddle posed by an educator whom I respect, Dr. Herman Blake, Vice Chancellor for Undergraduate Education at Indiana University/Purdue University at Indianapolis. I've heard Herman ask students to solve the following riddle which I would like to pose to you in this foreword. It goes like this: What is a ten-word sentence with twenty letters, each word having no more than two letters, which poses a question which provides a proven success formula for your success in college? Think about it. Think of all the two-letter words you know. Combine twenty letters into ten separate words. It will give you the key to success in college. Rather than prolong your speculation, let me provide the answer. The message is: "If it is to be, it is up to me." That's really what this book is all about. The authors call it "Self-management." They will teach you about the ABCs of self-management.

The authors of this text share with me the belief that we can't make students do anything that is really important. Ultimately, students have to want to do it for themselves. We realize that many of you have come out of high school experiences where you were forced to do things, whether it was go to class at certain times, go to the bathroom at certain times, speak only when given permission. We, the authors of this book and I, realize that if you're going to be successful, you're going to have to have the motivation to make things happen for yourself. They're going to talk to you a lot about self-motivation. I know what that's all about. I went off to college for other people's reasons, principally, my parents. I didn't become successful in college until I had my own reasons for being there, which were quite different from my parents. I have great respect for the authors of this text who have a long history at Marist College of making college students, like you, wherever you may be, successful.

This book is going to get you to think about your feelings which the authors will call your "affect," your "behavior," and your "thinking" (what your authors will call "cognition"). More importantly, they're going to get you to think about the all important inner connections among feelings, thinking, and behavior. We believe that if you give this book the serious consideration it deserves, that it will provide for you a powerful basis of insight into the mental interplay and dynamics of feelings, thinking, and behavior. You say, "insight, so what, who needs that?" Well, insight is the basis of any kind of important life change. And making that successful first-year college transition may well be the most important basis of change in your entire upwardly mobile American life.

This book has been written for use in a variety of courses which in American higher education are known as freshman seminars, student success courses, self-development courses. They go by lots of different names. But, basically, this book has been written for people like you, who want to take charge of their education and their life. I didn't have a course like this when I was in college and the first report card I got, which unfortunately was mailed home to my parents, included 3 'F's, 2 'D's, and an 'A'. The authors of this book and I don't want you to have that kind of experience. Your careful use of this book may prevent that.

The authors of this book also believe that many college students get into avoidable difficulties by what they call "negative thinking." They are going to help you unlearn negative thinking. It's really understandable that many of you might think this way because you've been bombarded with hundreds of commercial messages each day which may give you negative thoughts about yourself. Do you have bad breath? Do you now have the man or woman of your dreams? Is there something the matter with you that's keeping you from getting that long sought after promotion? If only you will buy this product, then your dreams will come true.

This book will not encourage you to engage in such magical, fanciful thinking. It's going to provide some very concrete, time-tested, and research-tested strategies for successful college student behavior. It's going to help you learn how to make positive predictions for your own behavior, and it will teach you how to fulfill those predictions. I once had a student who said to me, "Professor Gardner, I am not who I think I am, and I'm not who you think I am; I am who I think you think I am."

I urge you to read this book carefully and let it send you an all-powerful message about who the authors think you can become if you take seriously and practice the exercises, activities, strategies, and advice contained herein.

They are going to talk to you about time management. I believe once you can manage your time, you can manage anything in college. They're going to talk to you about procrastination, that deadly enemy of many potentially successful college students, which is even more threatening than all the killer courses that you may face.

They're going to help you learn how to be assertive so you can successfully cope with the challenges of the college bureaucracy and curriculum. They're also going to work through issues of your self-esteem because they know, just as I know, that how we see ourselves is inextricable from our ability to be more open to learning experiences. Most importantly, they're going to offer you proven strategies to enhance your academic motivation. In turn, that's going to greatly increase your probability of achieving **your** goals, not mine or the authors' goals, for college.

So, welcome to college and welcome to *Self-management for College Students*. I predict that if you give serious time and energy to working through this valuable text, you're going to be much more successful in college. That's precisely what the authors want. Best wishes and enjoy your A, B, Cs!

John N. Gardner
Director
The Freshman Year Experience
University of South Carolina

# PREFACE

*Self-management for College Students* presents a comprehensive approach to self-management that can be used to increase academic and personal achievement. The level of motivation we experience, our study habits, how we spend our time, our view of ourselves, others, and the environment will greatly influence our success in college and beyond. It is for these reasons that thinking skills, motivation, study methods, time management, procrastination, assertiveness, and self-esteem are the major topics in this text. Within the context of these general topics we also touch upon important themes such as values, human rights, prejudice, and violence.

The book is structured in two parts. The first four chapters establish the foundation and methods upon which the second part of the text is based. Self-management is introduced as a generic skill that rests upon our ability to manage our own affect, behavior, and cognition — our ABCs. Topics related to self-management such as assertiveness and study skills are usually discussed as separate and distinct areas of human functioning with different methods applied to each. It is here that we depart from other approaches to self-management. The ABCs provide a systematic approach to self-management, for regardless of what aspects of our lives we would like to enhance, our feelings, actions, and thoughts are essential ingredients. They also serve to integrate seemingly disparate subjects and thereby make it easier for us to find common methods for dealing with them.

While the first four chapters are aimed at general areas of interest, the second part of the text focuses on topics relevant to being a college student. Each topic is understood in terms of the self-management model. Whether we are talking about self-esteem or academic motivation, the theoretical framework and general methods for change remain constant.

Thus, approaching self-management from the vantage point of the ABCs serves a very practical purpose. Since they are the elements common to all areas of growth, managing our ABCs enables us to manage many other areas of interest. Feedback from our students indicates they have found a variety of ways to use their knowledge of the ABCs to their own benefit. We hope that everyone who reads this book will have a similar experience.

# ACKNOWLEDGMENTS

First and foremost we are indebted to Harvey L. Berger, a very special contributor who has worked on all aspects of this book from its inception. His technical and editorial skills and his patience through the long hours as publisher of this book have been invaluable. The special care Harvey took in creating everything from the cover design and table of contents to the glossary and index could be matched by few publishers. Without his commitment of personal time and labor, *Self-management for College Students: The ABC Approach* would not have been possible.

Eleanor Kordon ("Mom" to one of us) helped in more ways than can possibly be mentioned here; however, her input on the exercises and cartoons as well as her proofreading skills are deserving of special mention. The proofreading talents of George Kordon (also known as "Dad") were just lately revealed to his family. We are particularly grateful to him for pointing out that not everyone knows what a "couch potato" is. Marilyn O'Keefe's support in taking on added responsibilities to free up one author is greatly appreciated. Her help in proofreading was another important contribution to the text.

The enthusiasm, encouragement, and feedback from Marist College Learning Center staff and instructors has inspired us over the years. The thoughtful commentary and advice of the director, Barbara Carpenter, have been especially helpful. We are also grateful to course instructors, Andrea Raphael-Paskey and Marianne Toscano, for all their ideas and suggestions that helped in producing this text. Other notable supporters have been Patricia Laffin, Linda Parks, Victoria Sarkisian, Jane Sylvester, and Ann Winfield.

We are grateful to our friends and colleagues who volunteered their time to proofread. We thank Janet Lawler, John Miller, Rosemary Molloy, and in particular Harriet St. Germaine not only for proofreading the final draft at the eleventh hour, but for enlightening us with respect to some grammatical oddities.

The students who reviewed and helped in the revisions during the early stages of the text's development are deserving of special mention. Yahairah Aristy, Stacy Bradley, Joseph Calabrese, Jessenia Guzman, Melinda Sage, and Doug Sanders made some very valuable contributions. Their insights and suggestions have found their way into many chapters of *Self-management for College Students*. It is with great pride and pleasure that we thank these students.

We would like to acknowledge that many of our ideas were shaped by the work of psychologists, Arnold Lazarus and Albert Ellis. The writings of Davis, Eshelman, Fanning, McKay, and Waitley have also been very helpful.

Finally, we would like to thank John Gardner, founder of the University 101, for sensitizing us to the unique needs of college students. John provided the initial spark from which this text eventually emerged and his personal support over the years continues to be an inspiration to us.

# A NOTE TO STUDENTS

We encourage you to make this text your own and find new and creative ways of applying the principles discussed in *Self-management for College Students*. Many of our students have done so and we are pleased by their success.

With the exception of the study skills methods in Chapter 5, it is best to read the first four chapters in sequence before reading Chapters 5 through 10 because the latter part of the text builds upon principles introduced in the first four chapters. Chapters 5 through 10, however, need not be read in sequence. Your teacher may opt to emphasize certain topics in the book more than others or skip a chapter or two. If a chapter topic of interest to you is not covered in class, we suggest you read the chapter and do the exercises on your own.

As pointed out in Chapter 1, self-management is a systematic approach to development and change, but it is also an art that takes practice. To get a head start and enhance your learning of the material, you may want to take advantage of the features of the text outlined below.

1. **Case Studies** introduce each chapter. Reading the case study before reading the chapter will give you an idea of what the topic is about. Analysis of the case study after a careful reading of the chapter will help you apply your learning to a real life situation and increase your understanding of the chapter content.

2. Words in ***bold italics*** throughout the text are listed in the **Key Words and Concepts** box at the end of the chapter in which the term or phrase was first described or defined. Students can use the key as a guide for review.

3. The end-of-chapter **exercises** provide practical applications of the principles and methods introduced in the chapter. You may want to review these exercises before each class. Many teachers assign them as homework or use them for in-class activities, role plays, discussion, etc.

4. The **shaded margins** on the textbook pages provide a space for annotations and notes.

5. The **Glossary** supplies concise explanations of many terms and concepts introduced throughout the text.

6. The **Index** is a useful cross reference that will help you to find the pages in which  terms and concepts are discussed throughout the text.

7. **SQ4R** (a reading and study method), **note-taking** strategies, and other study skills are introduced in Chapter 5. To learn the material in this text and in other classes more quickly, you may want to use some of these  methods right away.

We hope you enjoy reading *Self-management for College Students.* What is even more important is that you benefit from having read it.

Edward J. O'Keefe
Donna S. Berger

*Central to the dawning of self-knowledge are our unique dreams and values — these are powerful forces that lend substance and purpose to our lives.*

# CASE STUDIES

To become familiar with concepts used in Chapter 1 (ABCs, ABC interactions, firing order, and ABC spirals), read the case studies in the boxes below and then read the chapter. After completing the chapter, analyze each case study *separately* by following Steps 1 through 4. Be sure to label your answers (step 1, step 2, etc.) and answer *all* parts of each step.

STEP 1    Does the case study reflect an upward or a downward ABC spiral?

STEP 2    AFFECT: Identify the feelings (emotions and sensations) that comprise this spiral.

BEHAVIOR: Identify the behaviors that comprise this spiral.

COGNITION: Identify the thoughts that comprise this spiral.

STEP 3    Which ABC component listed in STEP 2 is the *trigger* of the firing order that began the ABC spiral?

STEP 4    Describe the firing order by citing from the case study and labeling each part of your answer A, B, or C.

---

"I can't take this anymore. I expected college to be difficult, but not like this!" Jamie thinks as she looks at her roommate and the mess that surrounds her. "Four years," she says to herself, "that's an eternity! I'll never get used to this place!" Jamie sits down and begins contemplating the good old days. Thoughts of old friends, home-cooked meals, and high school come to mind. "High school! I sure missed out on a lot in those classes," she recalls. These recollections lead her to conclude that college won't be any different. Even if there are advantages to a college education, she thinks of how far off they are, when all the disadvantages are here and now. Jamie just can't shake off the sadness, and *feels* as though her life is falling apart. Later that day, when her roommate made a snide comment, Jamie took great pleasure in yelling: "Tell it to the new roommate you'll soon be getting!" Convinced that college isn't for her, Jamie can't imagine any alternative other than dropping out of school.

---

"This is the straw that breaks the camel's back! She eats all our food, doesn't pay for it, and now leaves the garbage on the counter!" Carla thought as she threw an empty potato chip bag into the trash. Getting upset again over this all too familiar scene, Carla suddenly realized that her anger wasn't helping her get her homework done nor resolve the problem. She began to laugh when it occurred to her how much time she was about to waste over an empty potato chip bag. "This weekend will be all study and no play unless I get some work done now, " she said to herself as she opened a book. The weekend came and, as Carla was about to go out, the perfect opportunity presented itself. "Would you believe I've gained five pounds!" her roommate said. Carla looked at her and said with a wry smile: "Why don't you come out with me tonight, and we can talk about a solution that could benefit us both."

# 1 SELF-MANAGEMENT AND THE ABC APPROACH

> No man can reveal to you aught
> but that which already lies half
> asleep in the dawning of your
> knowledge...For the vision of one
> man lends not its wings to another.
>
> Kahlil Gibran (1883-1931)
> Syrian poet, mystic

## THE ABCs OF SELF-MANAGEMENT

Central to the dawning of self-knowledge are our unique dreams and values — these are powerful forces that lend substance and purpose to our lives. Our individual character is given shape as we continually attempt to bring into focus a clearer vision of who we are and where we are going. Still, many of us act as though we are detached spectators, watching the events of our lives drift by. That which is basic to our moment-to-moment experiences — the (A)ffective, (B)ehavioral, and (C)ognitive aspects of our functioning — the *ABCs* —are often uncharted waters. Few of us consider how our own feelings, behaviors, and thoughts can be a constant resource for helping us reach our potential and bring shape to our dreams.

The ABCs are part and parcel of what it means to be human, for we are always involved in some level of affect (feelings), behavior (actions), and cognition (thoughts). To reflect on the ABCs is to reflect on the very substance of life, and to understand and direct these areas of our daily lives is the powerful force of *self-management.*

When Lou Holtz, the famous football coach said, "The greatest victory you can ever achieve is the victory over yourself," he was talking about self-management. *Self-management* is the ability to take charge of our affect, behavior, and cognition in order to accomplish a desired goal. It is directing oneself in a purposeful manner so that our reality begins to resemble our wish list. At times misunderstood as a mechanical or emotionless process, self-management is dismissed by some people because they misconstrue its meaning and purpose.

3

Self-management is not a mold we fit ourselves into. It is a choice we make — a choice we make about how we are going to manage our motivation, our time, our study habits, our personal relationships, and any other aspect of our lives. Viewing each day as something that we *make happen* as opposed to something that *just happens* is what differentiates a self-managed person from others.

At its most basic level, self-management is a decision about how we are going to direct our feelings (A), behaviors (B), and thoughts (C) at those times we deem it desirable. By managing our ABCs, we better manage ourselves. Far from turning us into passionless robots, self-management enables us to derive more meaning and pleasure from everyday living. As one student aptly put it, "Learning to manage myself made me captain of my life."

Before learning how to better manage ourselves with respect to the topic areas to be discussed in later chapters, we first need to differentiate among our own affect (A), behavior (B), and cognition (C). Once we can make these distinctions, we will be able to see how our feelings (A), behaviors (B), and thoughts (C) interact. We are then equipped with the fundamentals to improve our self-management skills in any area we choose.

## (A)ffect = Feelings

The 'A' of the ABCs stands for ***affect***, which includes emotions and sensations, those aspects of ourselves that we label or describe as *feelings*. When we say "I feel angry, or tense, or nauseous," we are talking about affect.

Affect can be interpreted as *positive* (pleasant), *negative* (unpleasant), or somewhere in between. Most of us are motivated to increase pleasant affect and decrease unpleasant affect. We will discuss the two different types of affect, *emotion and sensation*, and make a distinction between those that are helpful and those that are harmful.

The close connection between emotions and sensations is probably why we frequently use the common word "feeling" to describe them. "Feeling" angry (emotion) and "feeling" tired (sensation) both fall under the generic category of affect (A). Nevertheless, it is important to distinguish emotions from sensations because if they become problematic, there are different ways of dealing with them.

## Affect As Emotion

Although it is difficult to define emotion, we all know what emotions are when we experience them. Happiness, joy, anger, annoyance, depression, sadness, anxiety, and fear are emotions we all have felt at one time or another. For our purposes, **emotion** will be understood as a pleasant or unpleasant internal physical state that can be brought about by our thinking and can motivate us to act. Happiness, joy, and contentment are usually considered *positive emotions* because they are pleasant and can motivate constructive behavior. Anger, sadness, and anxiety are considered *negative emotions* because they are unpleasant and can motivate inappropriate actions. Being happy may motivate us to be friendly to people; being anxious may motivate us to be rude.

## Appropriate and Inappropriate Negative Emotions

While most of us would prefer to experience pleasant emotions, negative emotions are not necessarily inappropriate unless they are extremely intense or persistent and lead to behaviors that are self-defeating or hurtful to others. We will refer to emotions that are unpleasant but appropriate (annoyance, fear, sadness, etc.) as *appropriate negative emotions*; we will refer to emotions that are unpleasant *but* inappropriate (rage, anxiety, or depression, etc.) as *inappropriate negative emotions.*

*Appropriate negative emotions* may be unpleasant, but they can be useful. Annoyance, for example, can alert us to a possible problem that needs to be addressed. We may get irritated with our roommate for leaving clothes scattered all over the room and decide to discuss the situation before it becomes a major problem. Similarly, being fearful of receiving another low grade in a course we are failing may be appropriate and help motivate us to work more diligently.

*Inappropriate negative emotions* are not only unpleasant, but they can be destructive. Rage usually prevents problems from being resolved and can make them still worse, as for example in becoming so angry with a "messy" roommate that we destroy the relationship. Similarly, constant anxiety and worry over a failing grade is not only an uncomfortable feeling, but it may cause us to avoid the work that needs to be done, and compound the problem.

Inappropriate negative emotions interfere with our ability to manage ourselves. When we experience extreme anger, anxiety, or depression, our self-control and coping skills are lost, or at least diminished, for a period of time. We may say or do things we later regret and then find it difficult to undo the damage.

### Affect As Sensation

*Sensation* is affect (A) that is experienced primarily as a physical response generated by our external and internal senses. Thus, in addition to emotions, affect refers to sensations that we often call feelings. When we are feeling (A) run down, tired, fatigued, "wired," nauseous, or tense, we are experiencing physical sensations. Although strong emotions are often accompanied by physical sensations such as dizziness, "butterflies" in the stomach, or a pounding in the chest, sensations differ from emotions. For example, we can feel the sensation of being fatigued or "hyper" without feeling emotions of sadness or annoyance.

Just as there are positive and negative emotions, there are *positive* (pleasant) and *negative* (unpleasant) *sensations*. Usually the sensations that accompany relaxation are pleasant; those that accompany sickness are unpleasant.

### Appropriate and Inappropriate Negative Sensations

Appropriate and inappropriate sensations can be understood in terms similar to what has been said about appropriate and inappropriate negative emotions. **Appropriate negative sensations** are physically accurate responses to a particular event, as for example "feeling" pain when touching a hot stove. **Inappropriate negative sensations** are intense or persistent physical responses to mild stimuli that result in harm to oneself or others. For example, severe muscular tension or heart palpitations that result from being called on in class are inappropriate negative sensations because they are overreactions to a situation in which no physical danger exists. Inappropriate negative sensations can inhibit and prevent us from reaching our potential.

## (B)ehavior = Actions

The 'B' of the ABCs stands for *behavior* (B), which is an observable act that can be seen or heard. We are always engaging in behavior. Shouting, running, and jumping are behaviors, as are whispering, sitting, and standing still. Activities we label fun tend to be easier to engage in than those we label work. Going to a party as opposed to going to the library would be a case in point for many of us.

We may say we want to do something, but then find it difficult to translate talk into action. Certainly some behaviors are more difficult to learn or develop than others. Running a four-minute mile presents a greater challenge than a walk around the block. Yet, knowing how (C) to do something does not necessarily result in action (B). Many students want a 3.0 grade point average and know (C) how to get it, but fail to act (B) in ways that will help them attain higher grades.

Behaviors help define us as human beings, for our interests and values are reflected in our actions (B). The way we act and the activities we choose to engage in have a tremendous bearing on all areas of life, including our relationships, our academic and professional careers, and our personal well-being.

All of us want to acquire, maintain, or increase certain behaviors; we might also like to stop, alter, or decrease other behaviors. Interacting well with people is a behavior many of us would like to develop; smoking is a behavior some of us would like to stop. Behaviors that we want to increase can be thought of as *positive behaviors*, those that we want to decrease can be thought of as *negative behaviors*. Since most behaviors are learned, they can also be unlearned. Identifying the behaviors we want more or less of is the first step in introducing a change.

## (C)ognition = Thoughts

The 'C' of the ABCs stands for *cognition,* which is another word for thought. *Cognition* spans the gamut of ideas, beliefs, perceptions, and images that we have about ourselves, others, or the world in general. Planning, analyzing, interpreting, and daydreaming are all cognitive processes. Sometimes we think in words as when we talk to ourselves in trying to solve a problem. This is called *self-talk*. At other times we think in images as when we picture the outcome of a plan.

7

*Positive cognitions* are productive, helping to increase our motivation and drive. *Negative cognitions* can be disruptive, helping to diminish positive motivation and drive. Thinking (C) about how proud we will be when we achieve an 'A' in a difficult course can be highly motivating. Reflecting (C) too much on the low grades we received in high school could have the opposite result. Some negative thoughts are warranted and useful because they may signal that something is wrong: "That car is coming toward me at 70 miles an hour!" Other negative thoughts are actually distortions of reality or unsupported assumptions that create problems where they do not exist: "That professor believes all women are 'air heads' — I can't learn from him."

As will be described in Chapter 2, *mind reading, blaming, global labeling, and filtering* are thinking processes that misconstrue or exaggerate events and tend to lead to inappropriate negative affect and behavior.

**The Implications of Negative Versus Positive Thinking**

Negative thoughts that distort reality are generally counterproductive because they breed other negative cognitions. They can preoccupy our minds and deter us from focusing on more positive aspects of life. An illustration of how negative and positive thoughts can have a distinctly different impact on our feelings and behaviors is provided below.

> Jane and Brian are in the same literature class. They both received 'D' grades at mid-semester. One day, the instructor informed the students that they must rewrite their reaction papers on Alice Walker's book, *The Color Purple*, by the next class. Jane thinks (cognition) that there should be more time to do the assignment and that the teacher is unfair. As a result, she feels angry (affect) at the instructor. She interprets (cognition) the teacher's comments on her paper as a personal insult and concludes (cognition) that he dislikes her. That evening, she decides (cognition) to go out with a few friends to let off steam and skips the rewrite (behavior).
>
> Brian also would like to have more time to do the paper over, but he thinks (cognition) that the instructor gave the assignment because some students could use the extra credit. Brian figures (cognition) that this is a chance to improve his grade and feels eager, even somewhat ex-

cited (affect), about getting started. He interprets (cognition) the teacher's comments on his paper as an accurate assessment of his work and thinks that the professor is trying to help him. When Brian's friends try to talk him into going out, he tells them (behavior) he has work to do and that he will catch them another time. He spends most of the evening rereading parts of the book and rewriting sections of his paper (behavior).

Note how these two students think about (C) the same situation differently. Their interpretations (C) prompt very different feelings (A) and behaviors (B). Jane views (C) the assignment as an inconvenience; Brian interprets (C) it as an opportunity. He thinks about the assignment in a way that motivates productive feelings and behaviors. The difference between these two ways of thinking has far-reaching consequences; in this instance, perhaps a failing grade on the one hand and a passing grade on the other. This subject will be discussed in greater detail in Chapter 2. In the meantime, however, we might come up with personal examples of how our thinking (C) about a situation influences our feelings (A) and behaviors (B).

## A Common ABC Error

Since many of our emotions are prompted by our thoughts, affect (A) and cognition (C) can be easily confused because of this close association. The confusion is compounded further by language, for we often express thoughts (C) as if they were feelings (A). A comment such as, "I feel stupid" would be more accurate if it were phrased, "I think I am stupid" because it is a judgment (C) about oneself, not a feeling (A). People frequently express their evaluation or judgment (C) of themselves or a situation as if it were a feeling (A). For example, the statement, "I feel like it's my fault," would be more appropriately stated, "I believe it is my fault."

Our everyday language contributes to misunderstandings about what feelings are. Motivation, time management, study skills, the quality of personal relationships, and many other areas of our lives are not only dependent upon managing behavior, but on managing affect and cognition as well. Therefore, it is important not to confuse affect and cognition because to better manage ourselves, we first have to understand what needs to be managed.

When we mistake a thought for a feeling, we limit our capacity to deal effectively with many situations. For example, if we claim that our motivation is minimal because we *feel* that a teacher does not like us, we leave ourselves very little to work with. In mistaking this belief for a feeling, we focus on our feelings (A) when it is our belief (C) about the teacher that is at the heart of our motivational problem. In recognizing that what we called a feeling is actually a thought, we can then decide if we want to change our point of view (C).

## ABC INTERACTIONS

Although affect, behavior, and cognition can be viewed as separate components of human functioning, they are interrelated aspects of the whole person (Rudestam, 1980). Once we are able to distinguish them from one another, we can begin to explore the interrelationships among the ABCs, which collectively represent the foundation of our self-esteem, social relationships, education, and all areas of academic and personal development.

An *ABC interaction* refers specifically to the impact of each ABC component upon another. It is an ongoing cause and effect relationship in which affect, behavior, and thought influence one another. For example, a driver who thinks (C) other motorists should not tailgate may get annoyed (A) when another car is too close and slam on the brakes (B). Thoughts like "this is unfair" or "nobody should ride on my tail" (C) occur very quickly, and may cause the driver to get tense and angry (A), and then hit (B) the brakes. Obviously, this interaction among the ABCs could continue. The driver might look in his rearview mirror (B) and see that the other motorist is still tailgating. Subsequent ABC interactions would depend upon how the driver feels, behaves, and thinks in response to this situation. He might think, "What nerve!" get even angrier (A), pull the car over (B), etc.

## Firing Order of the ABCs

We can think of ABC interactions as a continuous, ongoing process in which each component influences another in a domino sequence. However, if ever we want to change the way we are feeling, acting, or thinking, perhaps because we are not motivated to study, we can isolate ABC interactions and describe the *firing order* (Lazarus, 1989). This will determine what needs to change to get ourselves motivated.

To specify the ***firing order*** of an ABC interaction is to identify which component (A, B, or C) sets the sequence in motion and the order that the other components follow. The ABC component that begins the ABC interaction is the ***trigger*** of the firing order.

The previous example of the driver reveals a C > A > B firing order: the cognition (nobody should ride on my tail) prompted the affect (tension and anger) that in turn motivated the driver's behavior (hitting the brakes). Here, cognition (C) was the trigger or component that set off the ABC interaction.

How or what we think (C) may trigger a feeling (A), and this feeling may influence how we act (B). Or, we may do (B) something that triggers a thought (C), and this thought may cause us to feel (A) a certain way. Experiencing strong emotions (A) may trigger thoughts (C) that lead to specific behaviors (B). On other occasions, doing something (B) may trigger sensations (A) that influence our thinking (C). Each of these firing orders is illustrated by examples below.

1. When the phone rings, Cynthia thinks: "That must be my friend calling" (C). She feels happy (A) and runs (B) to answer the phone.

2. Yvette introduces herself to someone she does not know (B), thinks well of herself for doing so (C), and feels comfortable (A) as she talks to him.

3. James wakes up feeling sad (A), begins to focus on all that is wrong in his life (C), and mopes around his room the rest of the day (B).

4. Andy drinks a bottle of tequila, swallows the worm (B), begins to feel queasy (A), and decides (C) to leave the party before the worm "shows up."

In the first example, the firing order is C > A > B. In the second, it is B > C > A. In the third and fourth, the firing orders are A > C > B and B > A > C respectively. In describing the firing order for each example, we have systematically identified the component that triggered each ABC interaction and the ABC components that followed in its wake. The trigger of the firing order in the first example was the thought, "It must be my friend on the phone"; in the second it was behavior (introducing oneself to a stranger); in the third it was affect (feels sad); and in the fourth it was behavior (drinking the tequila and swallowing the worm).

Since experience tells us that a firing order can be much more complex than these simple examples demonstrate, if we want to determine the trigger and firing order of our own ABC interactions, we ask ourselves two questions:

- Which ABC component began the ABC interaction?

- In what order did the other ABC components follow?

*Knowing the trigger of our ABC interactions suggests which component to address first if we desire a change.* Understanding how the ABCs interact enables us to interrupt the interaction. Applying this knowledge helps us gain control over our ABC interactions, which is basic to self-management.

## Upward and Downward ABC Spirals

Once we are in the habit of recognizing ABC interactions, we will notice that one ABC interaction can lead to others. This progressive series of ABC interactions can take the pattern of a *downward or upward spiral.*

### Downward ABC Spirals

A *downward ABC spiral* occurs when a series of ABC interactions become increasingly counterproductive and lead to a negative experience. The following example will serve to illustrate a downward ABC spiral.

Ed has decided (C) to put off his research paper for now and go home for the weekend to see his girlfriend. He is "psyched" (A) as he plans (C) to skip his Friday classes in order to leave Thursday afternoon. While visiting his girlfriend (B), he keeps telling himself (C) that he will begin his research paper on Saturday or Sunday. However, before he knows it, Monday morning arrives, and as he walks into his first class, the teacher is reminding the students that their research papers are due in two days. Ed feels a bit anxious (A). As he thinks (C) about how to get the paper done, he doesn't participate (B) in the class discussion or take notes (B). He is feeling so uptight (A) that he rushes out of class without handing in one of his other assignments (B). Thoughts of failure (C) and a feeling of panic (A) lead him to write part of his report by copying (B) from a couple of books without giving credit to the authors. Two weeks later, Ed finds out that he failed the course for plagiarizing his paper.

An analysis of the ABCs in this situation would reveal that a series of ABC interactions led to a negative experience for this student. This downward spiral is symbolically represented below.

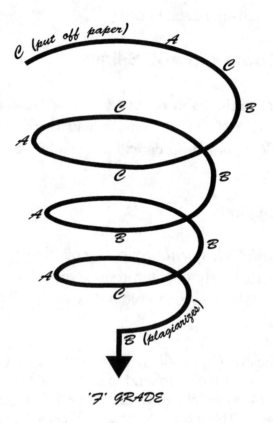

In this example the decision (C) to put off his research paper and go home appears to be the trigger of the firing order. This decision initiated a series of ABC interactions. Whether the situation improves or worsens after this episode will depend on how this student now feels, acts, and thinks with respect to school.

## Upward ABC Spirals

An *upward ABC spiral* occurs when the interaction of the ABCs leads to increasingly productive or positive experiences. Here is an example.

> Jim attends (B) a theater club meeting as a favor to his friend and discovers (C) that the club is not a bunch of "snobs" like he thought. Although he has always been very nervous (A) speaking in front of people, he tries out for a part (B) with only three lines because he likes one of the girls in the play. During rehearsals he discovers (C) that he is actually quite comfortable (A) on stage. He also learns (C) that it is easier to be calm and relaxed (A) in front of a group when playing a role than when speaking as himself. He realizes (C) that he could use the method of *acting as if* to improve his presentation skills. Two weeks later while giving an oral report in class, he thinks (C) of the students as his audience, *acts as if* (B) he were on stage, and is quite calm (A). This was the first 'A' grade he ever received for public speaking.

A review of this student's ABC interactions shows that the ABCs spiraled upward, resulting in a series of positive experiences.

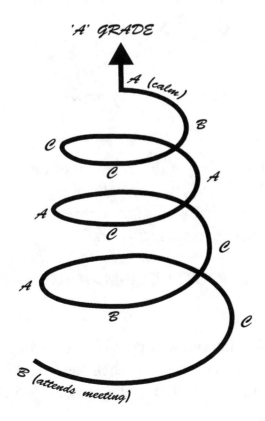

The trigger in this instance appears to be behavior (attending the theater club meeting). This behavior produced new thoughts and feelings that led Jim to seek other opportunities to enhance his public speaking skills. It should be noted that the exact sequence of ABC interactions is subject to interpretation.

### Turning ABC Interactions into Upward Spirals

We can use our knowledge of the ABCs to redirect a downward spiral or to bring about an upward spiral. What begins as a negative experience can quite often be converted to a positive one by just managing our ABCs. When we find, for example, that we are "not in the mood" to study, our knowledge of ABC interactions and firing order can help us to pinpoint the specific feelings, behaviors, and thoughts involved and alter them if we choose. Since changes in one mode (A, B, or C) can alter the other two, a change at any point of an

ABC interaction can change the direction of the interaction and the ensuing spiral. In this way, we can prevent problems from occurring, keep them from escalating further, redirect downward turns, and initiate more positive experiences overall.

## WHY LEARN ABOUT SELF-MANAGEMENT AND THE ABCs?

In a television interview, a popular rock group was asked what led them to break up in the midst of their success. Without going into the details of drug and alcohol problems, one member simply said:

16

"We got in our own way." The band made a comeback after recognizing that the major threat to their continued success was themselves.

Getting *out of our own way* is in part what the ABCs of self-management is about. It is also about the success that comes with winning that victory over ourselves, which Lou Holtz says characterizes the members of his best teams. Understanding the distinctions among affect, behavior, and cognition as well as their interactions, their firing order, and their spirals, and knowing how to apply methods for change are basic to self-management. In subsequent chapters, we will apply these concepts and principles to self-motivation, time management, study habits, assertiveness, and self-esteem and learn ways to change each ABC component when desirable. We will see that the ABCs are the common denominator for change or growth in any area of interest to us.

## KEY WORDS AND CONCEPTS

**ABCs**
**ABC interactions**
**affect**
**appropriate negative emotions**
**appropriate negative sensations**
**behavior**
**cognition**
**downward ABC spiral**
**emotion**
**firing order**
**inappropriate negative emotions**
**inappropriate negative sensations**
**positive and negative behaviors**
**positive and negative cognitions**
**self-management**
**self-talk**
**sensation**
**trigger**
**upward ABC spiral**

## SUGGESTED READINGS AND TAPES

### Self-Management

Johnson, R.C. (1987). *The achievers: The art of self-management for success*. New York: E.P. Dutton.

Schmidt, J.A. (1976). *Help yourself: A guide to self-change*. Champaign, IL: Research Press.

Watson, D., & Tharp, R. (1989). *Self-directed behavior. Self-modification for personal adjustment* (5th ed.). Monterey, CA: Brooks/Cole.

Yates, B.T. (1985). *Self-management: The science and art of helping yourself*. Belmont, CA: Wadsworth.

### ABCs

Rudestam, K.E. (1980). *Methods of self-change: An ABC primer*. Monterey, CA: Brooks/Cole.

### Interaction Effect and Firing Order

Lazarus, A. (1989). *The practice of multimodal therapy*. Baltimore: Johns Hopkins University Press.

# EXERCISE 1.1

## IDENTIFYING THE ABCs

### Affect (A)

Affect, another word for feelings, refers to emotions and sensations. It can be thought of as a physical state that we experience in response to internal or external events, which at times motivate us to act. The following list is comprised of emotions and sensations(A) that are often experienced by college students. Underline the feelings that frequently apply to you.

| | | |
|---|---|---|
| Joyful | Unhappy | Fatigued |
| Annoyed | Bored | Calm |
| Sad | Restless | Tired |
| Depressed | Lonely | Stressed |
| Anxious | Contented | Hyper |
| Fearful | Frustrated | Upbeat |
| Panicky | Excited | Butterflies |
| Energetic | Tense | Nauseous |
| Envious | Angry | Blah |
| Guilty | Numb | Queasy |
| Happy | Tingling | Elated |
| Jealous | Irritable | Wired |
| On edge | Relaxed | Strung out |
| | | Others _____ |
| | | _____ |

What feelings would you like to experience at school more often?

_____

_____

_____

What feelings would you like to experience at school less often?

_____

_____

_____

Describe any situations in which you feel calm or relaxed.

_____

_____

_____

20

# Behavior (B)

Behaviors are observable acts or activities that we engage in, things we do or say, or overt responses we make. The following list contains behaviors that college students often engage in. Underline the ones that frequently apply to you.

Watching TV
Speaking up in class
Writing a resume
Drinking too much
Arriving late
Reacting quickly
Withdrawing from friends
Smoking
Acting aggressively
Studying
Cutting class
Standing up straight
Writing notes
Criticizing others
Shaking

Taking drugs
Going to the library
Getting up early
Lounging around
Overeating
Acting compulsively
Looking people in the eye
Dancing
Giving compliments
Cleaning the dorm/apartment
Watching the clock
Talking to professors
Dating
Others _____
_____

What would you like to do more of?

_____
_____
_____

What would you like to do less of?

_____
_____
_____

What would you like to begin doing?

_____
_____
_____

What would you like to stop doing?

_____
_____
_____

# Cognition (C)

Cognitions are thoughts, beliefs, ideas, perceptions, or images we have about ourselves, about others, or about the world in general. Some thoughts or beliefs that college students experience are listed below. Check off the ones that apply to you.

___ I am creative.
___ I am in good physical condition.
___ I have the ability to succeed in college.
___ I am unattractive.
___ Life is empty, a waste.
___ Most people are smarter than I am.
___ I have little control over my life.
___ It is my responsibility to make other people happy.
___ I daydream too much.
___ Concentrating on school work is tough.
___ I don't know why I am in school.
___ My career plans are clear.
___ When I don't know something, I should pretend that I do.

Underline the words that you might use to describe yourself:

intelligent, confident, useless, worthwhile, evil, ambitious, sensitive, incompetent, loyal, trustworthy, regretful, worthless, a nobody, crazy, immoral, happy-go-lucky, considerate, unattractive, unlovable, persevering, inadequate, forgetful, confused, ugly, stupid, attractive, naive, honest, conflicted, easily distracted, fun to be with, friendly, indecisive, interesting to talk to, well organized, competent

What beliefs about yourself would you like to strengthen?

_____
_____
_____

What beliefs about yourself would you like to weaken?

_____
_____
_____

This exercise was adapted from the *Multimodal Life History Questionnaire*, Lazarus, A. (1989).

## EXERCISE 1.2

### Distinguishing Between A and C

Write an A or C in the space provided to identify whether the statement reflects an example of affect (A) or cognition (C).

____ Jose thinks that people are basically kind hearted.

____ Sue feels that most people are selfish.

____ Benjamin realized that he made a mistake.

____ Cynthia didn't believe a word he said.

____ Pedro is elated.

____ Dominic is planning to travel abroad some day.

____ Susan feels stupid.

____ Allison feels she deserves a raise.

____ Roberta feels she can't do it.

____ Bill knows that he'll make a poor presentation.

____ Ingrid wants to graduate with a 3.5 grade point average.

____ Aretha feels that her teacher was unfair.

____ George felt cheated.

____ Shannon is down in the dumps.

____ Mercinth is tense.

____ Jim feels his girlfriend has lost interest in him.

____ Sam concluded that the car was too expensive.

____ Pauline feels that the car is just the right price.

____ Richie has a headache.

____ Beth is distracted.

____ John is really charged up.

____ Tamara daydreams in class.

____ Bob keeps telling himself that he can't do well in math.

____ Natalie feels as though her life is falling apart.

____ Amy feels like she's being used.

## 2

A strong case can be made for the notion that feelings and behaviors often stem from how we think and what we think.

# CASE STUDY

Before reading Chapter 2, read the case study in the box below. After completing the chapter, analyze the case study by following Steps 1 through 4.

STEP 1    Describe Bill's overall problem.

STEP 2    AFFECT:    Identify the feelings (emotions and sensations) contributing to the problem.

BEHAVIOR:    Identify the behaviors contributing to the problem.

COGNITION:    Identify examples of distorted thinking and dysfunctional beliefs that are contributing to the problem and label them by name.

STEP 3    Which ABC component listed in STEP 2 is the firing order *trigger* of Bill's problem?

Describe the firing order of the ABCs. If there is a *downward ABC spiral*, describe it.

STEP 4    Choose one of Bill's distorted thoughts and dispute it. Choose one of Bill's dysfunctional beliefs and dispute it.

After seeing his girlfriend Yvette with another guy, Bill was so furious that he called her on the phone at two in the morning. "So, you've found a new boyfriend! You conveniently forgot to mention that the *friend* you were meeting was Tom!" he said sarcastically. Before Yvette had a chance to respond, Bill yelled: "You're such a liar! I don't care if I ever see you again!" and then he slammed down the receiver.

Bill had a jealous streak and it put a strain on his relationship with Yvette. He expected that she would call him, but he didn't hear a word. "I'm going to stand my ground — I'm not calling her when she's the one who should apologize to me," he decided. Days later, when he still hadn't heard from Yvette, Bill finally gave in and called. His worst thoughts came true — Yvette wanted to break up. "None of this is fair," he thought, "I didn't do anything and she's acting as if I'm in the wrong!" Thinking about all he had done for her — the expensive birthday present, the dinners out — he began to *feel* as though he had been used.

Since that day three weeks ago, Bill has been moping around watching TV and thinking about Yvette. The things he used to enjoy — practicing his music, going to class, even playing soccer — have lost their appeal. He's so upset that he isn't sure he can make it through the semester. As time went on, Bill began to doubt whether he was ever good enough for Yvette in the first place. "Yvette is so bright and has so many different interests. It's no wonder she wants to date someone else. I've got nothing to offer her and I'm certainly nothing without her," he thought. Now, he blames himself for the break up. " I'm a fool for letting her go — maybe if I had done more of the things she wanted to do we'd still be together. Maybe if I hadn't hung up on her. Maybe if..."

# 2 THINKING ABOUT THINKING, FEELINGS, AND BEHAVIORS

Men are disturbed not by things but the views which they take of them.

Epictetus (c. 55-c. 135)
Stoic philosopher, teacher

Remember, happiness does not depend on who you are or what you have; it depends solely on what you think.

Dale Carnegie (1888-1955)
Author, lecturer

## COGNITION AS THE TRIGGER

A strong case can be made for the notion that feelings and behaviors often stem from how we think and what we think. Epictetus observed over two thousand years ago that our emotional state is not caused by external events, but by the internal "view" we take of them. In other words, it is what we choose to believe or think about events that causes us to feel happy or sad, not the events themselves. The 'C' at the base of the logo on the cover of this text suggests that cognition often triggers our feelings and behaviors.

From antiquity to present day, many philosophers and psychologists have argued that if we are feeling good and behaving appropriately, we are probably thinking positively; and if we are feeling bad and behaving inappropriately, we are probably thinking negatively. This causal connection may seem obvious, but what appears to be common sense is not so common in practice.

## THE LANGUAGE OF THE ABCs

If we listen carefully to the language used to describe the source of feelings and behaviors, we find that people speak as though feelings and behaviors are caused, not by internal thoughts, but by external events. Comments such as these are familiar to most of us:

Monday mornings bring me down.

Fridays make me feel really good.

Rainy days depress me.

My boyfriend makes me happy.

My girlfriend gets me so angry.

That professor annoys me.

Tests make me nervous.

Public speaking makes me tense.

Math stresses me out.

Such comments imply that emotions and sensations (A), and possibly related behaviors, are caused and controlled by other people and outside events. However, when we think critically about them, we realize that the day of the week, the weather, the boyfriend or the girlfriend cannot control our affective response or our behavior. Fridays cannot actually be the cause of our feelings and behaviors because Fridays only exist as a mental concept — a label we associate with a specific time period. Similarly, rainy days do not depress us because if they did, we would always be depressed on rainy days and that is simply not the case. On some rainy days, we are undoubtedly quite happy.

Since the source of our feelings and behaviors is not found in external events, it must be internal. That is, we generate our feelings and behaviors ourselves. If we wanted to be precise and accurate about this process, we would say things like:

I upset myself on Monday mornings by thinking about the week ahead, and then I avoid everyone.

I excite myself on Fridays by anticipating the weekend, and then I party with friends.

When I see that it is raining, I let my thoughts get me down, and when I am down, I just go to bed and sleep.

I make myself happy when I am with my girlfriend by imagining our life together and when I am happy, I do more of the things she likes.

I allow my thoughts about what my boyfriend has done to get me angry, and then I yell at him.

I become annoyed when I think about the way my professor teaches, and I skip her class a lot.

When I think about failing, I make myself nervous and shaky on tests, so I rush through them.

I make myself tense when I give a speech by thinking that I am boring the class, and as a result, I end the speech quickly.

All of these statements, which few of us use in casual conversation, describe the causal connections among the ABCs. They indicate that we control our thoughts, feelings, and behaviors. They also suggest that people and outside events only influence us when we allow them (Ellis, 1969).

Our everyday language usually ignores the influence of our thoughts on our feelings and behaviors. By making comments such as *"this place makes me nervous" or "my roommate drives me crazy,"* we disregard our responsibility for our responses to events and other people. Although we may see no need to correct inaccuracies in our language, research has found that our speech not only reflects, but influences our thinking. Illogical speech can perpetuate and strengthen habits of illogical thought, which in turn can have a negative impact on how we feel and act. In particular, illogical speech and thought can produce inappropriate negative affect (see Chapter 1) and together they can have a major impact on motivation, self-esteem, and other important areas of our lives. An understanding of positive and negative thinking styles will help us to appreciate how this comes about and how speech and thought influence our well-being.

## POSITIVE VERSUS NEGATIVE THINKING

We have all heard about the power of positive thinking (Peale, 1952), and it is not news to most of us that we would be happier, have better relationships, and perhaps even live longer if we were to think in more positive ways. Conversely, we also know that negative thinking can generate discontent and misery, destroy relationships, and cause physical illness. And, as might be expected, while positive cognitions produce positive affect, negative cognitions produce negative affect.

### Positive Thinking

*Thinking positively* means focusing on our personal assets and strengths, as well as what is good in others and the world. When we think positively about ourselves and believe in our ability to succeed, we generally feel comfortable, and act in ways that bring us closer to our goals. Positive thoughts and images about our abilities dramatically increase our chances to succeed, for believing that success is possible is a prerequisite for most achievements.

Positive thinking is also a way of thinking that is accurate and balanced. As Martin Seligman (1991) points out in his book *Learned Optimism*, convincing ourselves to believe upbeat statements in the absence of factual evidence can be misleading. Optimism, he explains, "is about accuracy," and it is learned through the "power of non-negative thinking" (p. 221).

Thinking positively does not mean we are oblivious to our limitations, those of others, or the negative aspects of life. Nor does it mean that we should not keep a critical and watchful eye open for potential problems. Anticipating difficulties as we pursue our goals enables us to avoid them or cope better if they do arise. It is a consistent pessimistic attitude, one that dwells on the negative to the exclusion of the positive, that can be a problem.

## Negative Thinking

*Thinking negatively* means focusing on our liabilities and weak-nesses, the problems we have, and the bad that exists in other people and the world around us. By dwelling solely on the negative, we develop a pessimistic attitude that can be quite debilitating. In our constant search for gloom and doom, defeat and failure, we are usually quite successful in finding them.

People who think negatively about themselves and have little confidence in their ability to achieve are often ill at ease and fre-quently act in a self-deprecating manner. Believing that victory is forever beyond their grasp and that defeat is imminent often results in excess stress and failure-producing behaviors.

## Why Focus on the Negative?

If we want to feel and act in ways that lead to the accomplishment of our goals, we need to increase positive and decrease negative thinking. And, since we control our thinking, we are all capable of doing just that. So why is it that so few of us "accentuate the positive" as a once popular song suggests? Why do we focus on the negative when positive thoughts could motivate us to achieve more? While the answers to these questions are complex, a partial explanation is that we are unaware of our negative thinking and its effect on us. Thinking negatively, over time, can become so ingrained, so much a habit, that it occurs almost automatically in response to any event.

To think positively is to be wary of inappropriate negativity — in ourselves and in others. Recognizing and refuting the inaccuracies of *inappropriate negative thinking* are basic to thinking more positively, more realistically. Therefore, if we are ever dissatisfied with our feelings and behaviors, we need to beware of pessimistic "self-talk" because it may be the source of our dissatisfaction.

# INAPPROPRIATE NEGATIVE THINKING

One of the most serious effects of negative thinking is that it nurtures the development of illogical thoughts and irrational beliefs. When we constantly focus on the negative, it becomes more and more difficult to think clearly and reason logically. Inappropriate negative thinking takes hold, gains strength, and as a result, we experience inappropriate negative affect that can interfere with the achievement of our goals.

## The *How* of Inappropriate Negative Thinking: Distortions

One type of inappropriate negative thinking relates to *how* we think, the way in which we interpret reality and reach conclusions. When our thinking process is illogical or distorted, our interpretation will be incorrect and the emotions that follow will be inappropriate. An interpretation based on logical and realistic thinking might still prompt unpleasant emotions, but at least they would be appropriate.

The following interpretation of a classroom event illustrates how we can distort reality and upset ourselves as a result.

> An instructor, who typically exhibits a professional demeanor, hurries into his English class and slams the door behind him. With an angry-looking scowl on his face, he throws a batch of midterm examinations on the desk, then picks up his grade book and writes on the board in huge letters, MIDTERM GRADES.
>
> Joe, a student sitting in the second row, watches this scene and thinks (C) that the professor must be enraged about the poor test results. He concludes (C) that it is only a matter of minutes before the professor will begin to berate the class. Thinking (C) about the prospect of hearing bad news, Joe becomes increasingly nervous (A), tense (A), and scared (A) as he glances at the class grades on the board. The professor looks at Joe for a moment. As Joe slumps down (B) in his chair to hide behind the student in front of him, he thinks (C) to himself "What an icy stare. Here comes the verdict." Suddenly, in a loud, bellowing voice, the professor says: "About the mid-term grades..." He then proceeds to tell the class that he is pleased with the grade distribution and apologizes for being late. As he passes back the exams, he explains that he had trouble

starting his car, was caught in a traffic jam for over an hour, and got a speeding ticket on his way to class. Joe looks down at the 'B' grade on his midterm exam, breathes a hefty sigh of relief, calms down, sits up, and smiles.

In situations like this, most of us only realize *after* we have calmed down that we merely distorted or misinterpreted the events and that all the fear and tension we experienced was unnecessary. However, much can be learned from this simple example if we understand how Joe's thoughts caused the feelings and behaviors. The mistake made by this student was thinking and concluding that the professor's scowl was related to class performance on the test. As a result of this interpretation, he upset himself. This type of distorted thinking is referred to as "personalization." *Personalization* is the tendency to associate most outside events with ourselves. The student in our example also thought he knew why the professor was upset. Trying to interpret what someone else is thinking is another direct route to misinterpretation called *mind reading*. If, in addition, he believed that he would be singled out by the professor for his poor test grade and that he would then fail the course, this train of thought could quickly escalate to the conclusion that he would have to retake the course, change majors, and perhaps even drop out of college. This type of distorted thinking is called *catastrophizing*. It is a way of thinking that exaggerates the consequences of events and easily leads to panic because it suggests that the future is doomed.

Now it is true that on occasion our personalization, mind reading, or catastrophizing may be a correct interpretation, and it could be argued that anticipating the worst softens the blow. More often than not, however, the conclusions we jump to will be erroneous, but we pay an emotional price nonetheless. Frequently, this emotional response leads us to act in ways that create more of a problem than the one we anticipated in the first place. As such, what begins as a distorted thought can become a self-fulfilling prophecy that serves to reinforce and strengthen the distortion.

**33**

## Common Distortions in Thinking

*Distortions in thinking* are one of the most common means by which people cause themselves unnecessary upset. One distorted thought can quickly trigger another, and in a matter of minutes we can find ourselves in a slump when no real justification for these negative emotions and sensations exists. Below is a list of common distortions borrowed from McKay, Davis, and Fanning (1981). We have added examples for easy reference.

### Filtering

You take the negative details of a situation and exaggerate them, while filtering out all positive aspects. You can only see the bad, none of the good.

Example:

I could be having a great time at this party if only my girlfriend were here.

### Polarized Thinking

You think in extremes; there is no middle ground. People and events are either good or bad; you are either brilliant or stupid; etc.

Example:

America — love it or leave it.

### Overgeneralizing

You reach a general conclusion based on a single incident or piece of evidence. If something bad happens once, you expect it to repeat itself over and over.

Example:

Make one mistake on this job and nobody will ever let you forget it.

## *Mind Reading*

You know what people are thinking and why they act the way they do, even though they have not told you. In particular, you assume you know what people are thinking about you.

Example:

> *Your Lips Tell Me "No No," But There's "Yes Yes" in Your Eyes* (a popular old song title)

## *Catastrophizing*

You expect disaster. You notice or hear about a problem and start "what ifs": "What if I fail this course, what if...?"

Example:

> If I took up skiing, I'd probably break my leg, miss work, be fired, and end up on the unemployment line.

## Blaming

You hold other people responsible for your problems, or you go to the other extreme and blame yourself for everyone else's problems.

Example:

> Maybe if I had been raised differently, I wouldn't be in this predicament now.

## Shoulds

You have a list of ironclad rules about how you and other people should, must, or ought to act. People who break the rules anger you and you feel guilty if you make an error.

Example:

> The waiter ought to be able to figure out that I'm in a hurry and take my order right away.

## Global Labeling

You generalize one or two qualities into an overall negative judgment. You tend to label people, using a single trait to describe the whole person or generalizing the actions of a few individuals to an entire group.

Example:

> I could tell he was "weird" as soon as he opened his mouth.

## Personalization

You think that everything people do or say is some kind of reaction to you. You also compare yourself to others, trying to determine who is smarter, better looking, etc.

Example:

> I don't belong in college; other students are much better prepared than I am.

## *Being Right*

You continually try to prove that your opinions and actions are correct. Being wrong is unthinkable and you will go to any length to demonstrate that you are right.

Example:

How dare you question my opinion; I'm the teacher!

## *Emotional Reasoning*

You believe that what you "feel" must be true — automatically. If you "feel" stupid and guilty, then you must be stupid and guilty. (It should be noted that these are thoughts, not feelings.)

Example:

I feel guilty so I must have done something wrong.

Whenever our feelings or behaviors are not what we would like them to be, we first want to check and see if we are engaging in *distorted thinking*. Once able to recognize these distortions, we can prevent illogical thinking from occurring or correct it when it does occur (see Chapter 4).

## The *What* of Inappropriate Negative Thinking: Dysfunctional Beliefs

Another type of inappropriate negative thinking has to do with *what* we believe, the basic assumptions we make about reality. Beliefs are fundamental to our philosophy or perspective on life in general; they can predispose us to think about ourselves, others, and the world from a particular point of view. Dysfunctional beliefs underlie the distortions just discussed, but they can be more difficult to identify than these moment-to-moment thoughts because we may not reflect upon them very often.

## Dysfunctional Beliefs

Dysfunctional means not (dys) functional — something that is not working for us. ***Dysfunctional beliefs*** are beliefs that work against rather than for us. They work against us because they result in affect and behavior that undermine our aspirations and goals. Over time, they can result in a constricted and unfulfilled life.

Dysfunctional beliefs predispose us to distort the facts of a situation. For example, the belief that we are controlled by external events may prompt us to blame others for the difficulties we experience. Some dysfunctional beliefs are clearly irrational; they violate the rules of logic and have no empirical evidence to support them. Other dysfunctional beliefs, while not necessarily irrational, are self-defeating because they prevent us from reaching our potential or simply lead to unhappiness and despair. For example, the belief that people cannot change can become a self-fulfilling prophecy for the person who holds it. Or, the belief that the value of our actions depends upon approval from others may cause us to feel sad and rejected whenever approval is not given (Lazarus & Fay, 1975).

## Functional Beliefs

Just as beliefs can work against us in very subtle ways, other beliefs can work for us. These are referred to as functional beliefs. ***Functional beliefs*** result in affect and behavior that support the achievement of our goals and enable us to lead a healthy and productive life. For example, if we believe that by working hard we will have just as much chance as anyone to be successful, we will be more motivated to persist in the face of adversity. Similarly, the belief that we control our responses to events rejects the notion that we are helpless victims, and can motivate us to be assertive and take action.

## Distinguishing Between Functional and Dysfunctional Beliefs

Before we can fully appreciate the impact of functional versus dysfunctional beliefs on feelings and behaviors, we must recognize and distinguish between them. Some criteria to identify functional and dysfunctional beliefs are as follows:

## Functional beliefs

- are based on factual evidence.

- are founded on logical reasoning.

- produce positive emotions, sensations, and behaviors.

- support an individual's goals.

## Dysfunctional beliefs

- have no factual evidence to support them.

- are founded on illogical reasoning.

- produce inappropriate negative emotions, sensations, and behaviors.

- undermine an individual's goals.

Each of these criteria warrants further explanation.

*Our beliefs are more likely to be functional when we check our facts before drawing conclusions.* Functional beliefs are supported by factual information. Rumor, hearsay, and conjecture are avoided — we do not base our beliefs simply on what someone has said.

Examples:

Functional

I know a lot of students avoid this class, but I'll form my own opinion after determining how closely we follow the course syllabus.

Dysfunctional

I'm sure this class is not for me because my roommate had a bad experience with the professor last semester.

*Our beliefs are functional if they are developed through a process of logical reasoning that we can demonstrate or verify.* Our beliefs are more apt to be functional when distorted thinking is eliminated and rules of logic are used in reaching conclusions.

Examples:

Functional

I believe that taking challenging courses is more important than gaining a high gpa by taking a lot of easy courses. Research shows that many employers hire college graduates who take courses outside of their majors.

Dysfunctional

I know someone who took a lot of easy courses and got a great job after graduation. If it worked for her, it can work for me.

*Our beliefs are functional if they generate pleasant emotions and sensations that add to the enjoyment of life and contribute to long-term survival and happiness.* Beliefs that lead to short-term pleasures can also be functional, but if they sabotage our long-term goals they are dysfunctional.

Examples:

Functional

I believe it is important to find a variety of ways to have fun, so I make a real effort to enjoy whatever I'm doing whether it's partying, working, or studying.

Dysfunctional

Having fun and feeling relaxed means going out and getting drunk with my friends. My motto is: "Live, drink, and be merry for tomorrow you may die."

*Our beliefs are functional if they are positive not negative, constructive not destructive, and motivate us toward, not away from, our goals.* The belief *"I can do it"* is functional because it keeps us working toward our objective, and therefore increases the probability of success. The belief *"I can't do it"* is dysfunctional because it inhibits action and therefore increases the probability of defeat. Although it could be argued that both beliefs might actually be true, it is usually to our advantage to accept a functional belief over a dysfunctional one. For as Henry Ford once said: "Whether you believe that you can or you believe that you can't, you're right."

Examples:

Functional

I believe that I would do well in upper level math courses if I took the prerequisite classes and worked hard.

Dysfunctional

I can't handle math — never could and never will. I just don't have a knack for it.

## Common Dysfunctional Beliefs

We all have "favorite" dysfunctional beliefs. Listed below are some common ones along with examples of how they can surface in our everyday lives (Davis, Eshelman, & McKay, 1988).

### *Approval*

Your happiness, contentment, and hopes for success are completely in the hands of other people. You must be loved and respected by all the significant people in your life or you are not worthwhile.

Examples:

If someone disagrees with me, I immediately begin to doubt my own judgment.

It would be awful if my friends did not like my hairstyle or the way I dress.

## Perfectionism

It is not good enough to be competent and knowledgeable. You have to be perfect at everything you do and if you can't win, you don't play.

Examples:

> I should know how to act in all new situations: with professors, in classes, and with students in the dorm.

> If I can't do it right the first time, I don't do it at all.

## Fairness

There is a system of checks and balances. What's right is right. You know what is just and get resentful and angry whenever your idea of justice is not upheld.

Examples:

> After all the work I did on that paper, it's not fair that I got a 'D.' I deserve at least a 'C.'

> Given everything I've done for her, it's not right that she wants to see other guys.

## External Control

You think outside events and other people are responsible for your feelings and behaviors. You're just a victim of fate.

Examples:

> It's my parents' fault that I am so miserable.

> That teacher made me so angry that I couldn't go to that class anymore.

## Avoidance

You believe it is best to avoid anything unpleasant, difficult, or demanding. If something is new, challenging, different, or risky, you cannot help but be frightened, scared, or anxious.

Examples:

College should be pleasant and comfortable. It shouldn't challenge my thinking or disrupt my life.

My philosophy is: "Nothing ventured, nothing lost!"

## Expectations

If you do good, you should be rewarded. Similarly, society and the world at large should meet your expectations. You feel bitter when these expectations are not met.

Examples:

I gave him an expensive birthday present, so he should do the same for me.

I got my degree; therefore, the company should hire me for an upper level position at a high salary.

## Determinism

You believe that people's present ABCs are determined by their past — people are the way they are and cannot change. "I can't" statements often reflect a belief in determinism.

Examples:

I can't help it. That's the way I am; that's the way I was raised; and that's the way I'll always be.

Once a failure, always a failure.

One reaction to this list of beliefs might be: "What is all the fuss about? It is nice to have the approval of others and an easy life. It would be great to be perfect, to have things turn out the way I expect, and for life to be fair." This reaction is understandable; however, in sorting out whether a belief is helpful to us, it is important to make a distinction between what is and what we wish were true. Believing that something *should* or *must* be the way we think it should be or must be, does not change reality and may inhibit us from taking constructive action. Reflecting on our criteria for functional and dysfunctional beliefs, we recognize that the examples above fit into the dysfunctional category. Each belief is either unsupported by facts, the result of illogical reasoning, a potential source of negative emotions and behaviors, or antagonistic to achieving a goal. Therefore, if we are ever upset about something over which we have no control, we might ask ourselves if our beliefs are contributing factors. If we discover they are part of the problem, changing the dysfunctional beliefs will help (see Chapter 4, Parts One and Three).

By ridding ourselves of dysfunctional beliefs, we reduce unnecessary emotional turmoil. The difficulty, of course, is that while we may know which beliefs work for or against us, it is not always apparent which are rational or irrational. Thus, it might be best to approach beliefs from a practical standpoint and consider which beliefs about life help us to feel positive and which ones result in inappropriate negative feelings. A simple rule of thumb is to ask ourselves if a belief is helping us to achieve our goals and dreams or holding us back.

## THE DIE MODEL

The *DIE Model*, which is a variation of an approach from Albert Ellis (1969), provides a structure for the concepts introduced in this chapter. Part One of the model simply outlines the way in which an emotional response ("the blues," anger, anxiety, or any strong feeling) stems from our thoughts. Since behaviors are influenced by emotions, it could be inferred that many behaviors (crying, arguing, trembling) also stem from our thoughts. Parts Two and Three of the model, which are detailed in Chapter 4, demonstrate how distortions and dysfunctional beliefs can be changed.

DIE is an acronym for *data, interpretation*, and *emotional response*. **Data** refers to any person, external circumstance, or event that is an occasion for a positive or negative emotion. **Interpretation** refers to our thoughts or beliefs (C) about the data. **Emotional Response** refers to the emotions (A) resulting from our interpretation of the data. The following example of a young man who sees his girlfriend with another man outlines the basic components of the model:

## Data

What are the *objective* facts?

Example:

Last night, I saw my girlfriend with another man in the mall.

## Interpretation

What are the *subjective* thoughts or beliefs about the data?

Example:

She is with another man; therefore, she is cheating on me and it's all over between us. It's not fair.

## Emotional Response

What emotions result from the interpretation?

Example:

Anger, anxiety, depression

Note that the young man's interpretation leads him to feel very upset. A different interpretation would undoubtedly result in a different emotional response. For example, the interpretation that his girlfriend is merely talking to a man with whom she has no romantic interest would not result in such an inappropriate emotional response and his feelings toward his girlfriend would not be negative.

If the young man wanted to change his feelings, the DIE Model would suggest that he either alter the situation, his thoughts, or both. Obviously, he cannot change the fact (data) that his girlfriend was talking to another man. He may find it equally difficult to prevent her from talking to other men in the future. Yet, if his thoughts were not distorted and dysfunctional in the first place, he would not be upset. If he did not think that *because* his girlfriend is with a man, she *must be* cheating, he would not have become angry and depressed about what he saw.

The order in which we experience the components of the DIE Model may seem different from the order presented above. In reality, emotions come on so fast it seems as though we experience the emotion before the interpretation because when we are upset (angry, anxious, sad, etc.), we tend to associate its cause with the data (event or situation). Finding that the situation is very difficult, if not impossible, to change leads us to examine our interpretation of the data. Critically evaluating the experience reveals that our interpretation (self-talk, thinking, or beliefs) is what actually caused the emotional response (affect).

This simple example has profound implications for all of us. It is usually very difficult to control other people and external events, but when dissatisfied with a situation we can choose to view it differently. As was emphasized throughout this chapter, *we* produce our thoughts about events, and therefore, *we* can control our emotional response by critically examining and altering our interpretations. If an interpretation is distorted or dysfunctional, we can logically dispute it. Once disputed, these cognitions can be replaced with a rational or functional interpretation (See Chapter 4, DIE Model).

While the DIE Model does not deny the benefit of trying to change a situation (data), it focuses most attention on our interpretation because our control over events may sometimes be limited, but our *thinking is always under our control*.

## KEY WORDS AND CONCEPTS

**approval**
**avoidance**
**being right**
**blaming**
**catastrophizing**
**Data**
**determinism**
**DIE Model**
**distorted thought**
**dysfunctional belief**
**emotional reasoning**
**Emotional Response**
**expectations**
**external control**
**fairness**
**filtering**
**functional belief**
**global labeling**
**Interpretation**
**mind reading**
**overgeneralizing**
**perfectionism**
**personalization**
**polarized thinking**
**shoulds**
**thinking negatively**
**thinking positively**

## SUGGESTED READINGS AND TAPES

### Cognitive Control of Affect (Functional and Dysfunctional Beliefs)

Davis, M., Eshelman, E.R., & McKay, M. (1988). *The relaxation and stress reduction workbook* (3rd ed.). Oakland, CA: New Harbinger Publications.

Dyer, W. (1976). *Your erroneous zones.* New York: Avon Books.

Ellis, A. (1969). *The essence of rational psychotherapy: A comprehensive approach to treatment.* New York: Institute for Rational Living.

Kranzler, G. (1974). *You can change how you feel.* Eugene, OR: RETC Press.

McKay, M., & Fanning, P. (1991). *Prisoners of belief: Exposing and changing beliefs that control your life.* Oakland, CA: New Harbinger Publications.

### Cognitive Distortions

McKay, M., Davis, M., & Fanning, P. (1981). *Thoughts and feelings: The art of cognitive stress intervention.* Oakland, CA: New Harbinger Publications.

McKay, M., & Fanning, P. (1988). *Combatting distorted thinking.* Oakland, CA: New Harbinger Publications (audio cassette).

**EXERCISE 2.1**

**MATCHING EXERCISE FOR DISTORTED THINKING**

Match the sentence on the left with the type of distorted thinking it exemplifies.

___1. If I do not do well on this exam, I will probably fail the course, my gpa will will drop below a 2.0, and I will be kicked out of college.

A. Global Labeling

___2. My roommate should keep the room clean.

B. Filtering

___3. After the bad experience I had presenting in Dr. Smith's class, I will never be able to give another speech.

C. Catastrophizing

___4. You are either my friend and agree with me or you are no friend of mine.

D. Shoulds

___5. She is nodding as though she likes my ideas, but I know she really thinks I'm stupid.

E. Blaming

___6. He was a loser from the first day he showed up drunk and rowdy.

F. Overgeneralization

___7. This relationship could be a really good one, but he does not express his feelings enough.

G. Polarized thinking

___8. We would not be in debt so much if you would stop wasting money on clothes.

H. Mind Reading

# EXERCISE 2.2

## MATCHING EXERCISE FOR DYSFUNCTIONAL BELIEFS

Match the sentence on the left with the dysfunctional belief it reflects.

____1. I can't get an 'A' on this paper because it's already late, so I'm not going to bother with it at all.

A. Expectations

____2. I was really excited about taking the job, until Angie made a flip comment about the company and said I was silly to take it.

B. Fairness

____3. After all the studying I did for that exam, it isn't right that I got a failing grade.

C. Approval

____4. It's because of my room-mate that I am so upset and am dropping out of college.

D. Determinism

____5. I won't get up in front of the class to give a speech because I get nervous.

E. External Control

____6. You would think that after all I did for her, she'd at least have the decency to do me this one little favor.

F. Avoidance

____7. There is no use in trying. That's the way I am and that's the way I always will be.

G. Perfectionism

# EXERCISE 2.3

## DIE MODEL EXERCISE

A description of a situation or event is presented below following the format of Part One of the DIE Model. After reading through each example and considering the information provided under DATA, INTERPRETATION, and EMOTIONAL RESPONSE, fill in the blanks with a plausible interpretation and/or emotional response. Then, compare your responses to those of other students. Note the relationship between affect and cognition and the individual differences reflected in the class responses.

1.   **DATA:**

My roommate left clothes, books, and papers scattered throughout the dorm room.

**INTERPRETATION:**

My roommate is an inconsiderate slob. He always does things I don't like. It's not fair that I have to live in this pigsty.

**EMOTIONAL RESPONSE:**

_____

_____

_____


2.   **DATA:**

It's Friday night; my friends are all going out; and I have a paper due Monday. I'm staying home.

**INTERPRETATION:**

_____

_____

_____

**EMOTIONAL RESPONSE:**

I'm happy!

51

3. **DATA:**

I received an award for the highest grade point average this semester.

**INTERPRETATION:**

_____

_____

_____

**EMOTIONAL RESPONSE:**

I'm "bummed" out.

4. **DATA:**

My teacher announced that I must do a 20 minute class presentation next week.

**INTERPRETATION:**

_____

_____

_____

**EMOTIONAL RESPONSE:**

_____

_____

_____

## DIE MODEL CASE STUDIES

This exercise is intended to familiarize you with the steps of Part One of the DIE Model. Read the case studies below and answer the questions in the space provided.

**CASE ONE**

Carlos and his girlfriend, Maria, had been planning for some time to go to a family reunion at Carlos' parents' house. Carlos was looking forward to introducing Maria to his family and friends back home. On the morning that they had planned to leave, Maria announced apologetically that she could not go, but she didn't explain why. Carlos was very angry. He thought of all the times that he had gone out of his way to do things that Maria wanted to do, and how inconsiderate she was to ruin his weekend. Now, Carlos is thinking about breaking up with Maria. He is convinced that she must not care about him or their relationship if she could treat him so unfairly.

**DATA:**

What were the objective facts associated with Carlos' emotional response?

_____
_____
_____

**INTERPRETATION:**

Describe the subjective thoughts (distorted thoughts and dysfunctional beliefs) that may have prompted Carlos' emotional response.

_____
_____
_____

**EMOTIONAL RESPONSE:**

What emotions were experienced as a consequence of Carlos' interpretation?

_____
_____
_____

**CASE TWO**

Next Monday, Camile is scheduled to make a presentation in class. When the teacher first announced the assignment, Camile panicked. Even as Monday draws near, she has not begun to prepare or practice her presentation. She is so nervous about speaking in front of the class that she gets uncomfortable even thinking about it. Camile knows her presentation will be a total disaster. She sees herself fumbling with her notes, shaking, and stumbling over her words as the other students snicker and laugh at her. She pictures herself looking stupid and "losing face" with her friends, who have always thought that Camile had her act together.

**DATA:**

What were the objective facts associated with Camile's emotional response?

_____

_____

_____

**INTERPRETATION:**

Describe the subjective thoughts (distorted thoughts and dysfunctional beliefs) that may have prompted Camile's emotional response.

_____

_____

_____

**EMOTIONAL RESPONSE:**

What emotions were experienced as a consequence of Camile's interpretation?

_____

_____

_____

## CASE THREE

Vince plays college football and has a dream of some day becoming a professional athlete. The last game of the season for the conference championship was lost when Vince dropped a pass in the end zone. Vince is devastated. He really feels bad because he has convinced himself that everything is against him. He thinks that he let his teammates down, that they must hate him, and that a clod like him doesn't deserve to remain on the team. He has even contemplated quitting school rather than face his teammates or the fans after such a terrible blunder. Besides, his dream of playing professional football is "down the tubes" for good.

### DATA:

What were the objective facts associated with Vince's emotional response?

_____

_____

_____

### INTERPRETATION:

Describe the subjective thoughts (distorted thoughts and dysfunctional beliefs) that may have prompted Vince's emotional response.

_____

_____

_____

### EMOTIONAL RESPONSE:

What emotions were experienced as a consequence of Vince's interpretation?

_____

_____

_____

## 3

*Given a choice of two roads to travel, our decision to take one road over the other implies that we are motivated to move in that direction.*

# CASE STUDIES

Before reading Chapter 3, read the case studies in the boxes below. After completing the chapter, analyze the case studies by following Steps 1 through 4. (Be sure to do each case separately.)

STEP 1      Describe the motivational problem.

STEP 2    AFFECT:     Identify the feelings (sensations or emotions) that are moving the student *away from* the course.

                 BEHAVIOR:    Identify the behaviors that are contributing to the motivational problem.

                 COGNITION: Identify the beliefs that are moving the student *away from* the course. Identify any cognitions that are dysfunctional or distorted.

STEP 3      Which ABC component listed in STEP 2 is the *trigger* of the firing order? Describe the firing order using examples from the case study. Explain why there is the potential for a *downward ABC spiral*.

STEP 4      How would changing each of the ABC components enable the student to become *motivated toward* the course?

---

**John views his art class as a complete waste of time and is annoyed that he is required to take this class. He cannot understand why a computer science major like himself should have to sit through lectures on art history that he finds so boring. "After all," he says, "I'm not going to need to know anything about Dali or Picasso when I become a systems analyst — so what's the use?" John has missed quite a few classes and has not kept up with the assignments. He finds the readings difficult, gets bored when he reads, and believes that he just isn't cut out for all this abstract stuff. When John does go to class, he rarely participates. Instead, he passes the time by watching the clock and counting how many minutes are left before it's time to go. Sometimes the teacher notices that John is not paying attention and calls on him. When this happens, he gets angry at the teacher for putting him on the spot.**

---

**In high school, Karen found math to be the most difficult subject she had to take. She always felt anxious and nervous, and has avoided math courses ever since she entered college. Although she knows math would be of use to her in any job she might get, she has decided that she doesn't have what it takes to do mathematics and chose a major with this in mind. Then something unexpected happened. Karen found out from her advisor that even though she is a communication arts major, she still has to take two math courses to get her degree. As soon as she was told, she felt her heart racing and she got panicky. She even considered transferring to another college rather than take another course in mathematics. When it came time to register for classes the first semester of her junior year, Karen still hadn't taken any math classes. Each semester she told her advisor, "I'm going to take a couple of electives and register for that math course next time around." Now it is senior year, and Karen is angry because she has to take two math courses in order to graduate.**

# 3 MOTIVATION

Two roads diverged in a wood, and
I took the one less traveled by,
And that has made all the difference.

Robert Frost (1874-1963)
American poet, teacher

## THE ABCs OF MOTIVATION

The word *motivation* comes from the Latin word *movere*, which means "to move." Given a choice of two roads to travel, our decision to take one road over the other implies that we are motivated to move in that direction. Stated plainly, motivation is *to move in a direction of our choosing.*

Psychologists such as Abraham Maslow and B. F. Skinner have researched the topic of motivation in depth. While Maslow contends we are motivated *internally by personal needs* we have yet to fulfill, Skinner claims we are motivated by *external rewards and punishments*. Each theorist attempts to ascertain the basic factors that motivate people, and practical experience suggests that both of them are correct. At times, we seem to push ourselves in a given direction, and at other times we seem to be pulled. For this reason, motivation is popularly described as *those forces acting on or within us that initiate behavior and give it direction.* Thus, motivation seems to stem from two sources.

Although we are influenced by external rewards and penalties, we are motivated by these external factors only when they are internalized. That is, we only move when we "feel" (A) like moving and "decide" (C) to move. *Motivation*, then, can be defined as an inner state that initiates behavior (B) and gives it direction. Since this inner state is an interaction between affect and cognition, motivation can be represented symbolically as $A \times C = B$.

Affect and cognition make distinct contributions to motivated behavior. Yet, as we will see, behavior can impact feelings and thoughts as well, and thereby indirectly influence motivation. Before discussing the role of affect and cognition, however, it is first necessary to distinguish between positive and negative motivation.

## Positive and Negative Motivation

When we are motivated *toward* something because we associate it with positive affect and cognition, we are ***positively motivated***. For example, we might be with someone at a party because we think highly of the person and have a strong emotional attachment to him or her. When we are motivated *away* from something because we associate it with negative affect and cognition, we are ***negatively motivated.*** Using a similar example, we might be with someone at a party only because this enables us to avoid staying home, thinking about an old boy or girlfriend, and feeling lonely.

Often our actions result from a combination of positive and negative motivation. For example, some students' motivation for being in college may be as much a desire to get away from home as it is to pursue learning. In a given instance, one form of motivation may be predominant, but since the behaviors produced often look the same, only we can determine which type of motivation is primary in our everyday lives by understanding the internal factors at work. The distinction between our positive and negative motivation is an important one to make because to manage our motivation, we first need to know which type of motivation is chiefly responsible for our actions.

## AFFECT AND MOTIVATION

As we have already discussed, we tend to move toward or be motivated in the direction of that which we associate with *good feelings* (positive affect) and move away from that which we associate with *bad feelings* (negative affect). On the one hand, a night out with friends might be an activity we are positively motivated toward because we associate it with having fun and being happy (positive affect). On the other hand, we may be negatively motivated away from studying because we feel anxious or frustrated (negative affect) at the very thought of it or because we do not anticipate feeling good while doing it.

## Affect and Positive Motivation

The following examples of positive motivation illustrate how affect influences behavior toward something.

> I am taking this course because I am excited (A) about gaining a new perspective on religion from the instructor.

> I call my friend because I enjoy (A) the conversations we have.

> I jog every day because I feel invigorated (A) when I do.

> I listen to music because it gives me a "rush" (A).

> I work hard because afterwards I am happy (A) about the accomplishment.

In the first four examples, positive affect is experienced before, during, and perhaps even after the behavior. In the last example, good feelings are anticipated once the work is completed.

## Affect and Negative Motivation

Negative motivation is reflected in the following situations because affect influences movement away from something. The behaviors enable the person to avoid, reduce, or escape from something unpleasant.

I am taking this class because it doesn't require an oral presentation, which I really get nervous about (A).

I paid the bill because I was afraid (A) of losing my credit.

I only study for exams when the stress (A) is really high and I can't handle the pressure anymore.

I turned on the radio to drown out the noise from next door, which was giving me a headache (A).

I was so annoyed (A) with his constant complaining that I walked out of the room.

In the first example, moving away from the class that requires public speaking feels good, or at least is expected to feel better than moving toward it. We might become nervous (feel bad) when the professor announces a ten-minute speech requirement. If this nervousness is severe, we may get rid of it by moving away from this class (dropping the course) and taking a different one. In the second example, the fear of losing credit is avoided by paying the bill. In the third and fourth, stress and a headache are reduced by studying and turning on the radio. In the last example, the person escapes the complaints by walking out of the room.

To manage motivation, we first determine whether our affect motivates us positively or negatively. Do we move toward our goals, feeling good as we do so? Or, do we move away from things and only feel good as a consequence of no longer feeling bad?

## COGNITION AND MOTIVATION

We tend to move toward or be motivated in the direction of that which we associate with positive cognition and move away from that which we associate with negative cognition. For example, we might join a political party because we believe in its platform or we may be apolitical because we believe that all political parties are corrupt.

## Cognition and Positive Motivation

The cognitions associated with positive motivation are likely to fall into three broad categories:

1. **We believe the goal is worthwhile.** We believe there is an internal or external value, benefit, payoff, or reward associated with the objective or goal itself. The motivation for our behavior is to achieve the goal.

   Examples:

   > I know that the extra hours I work on my internship will really help to advance my career.

   > I go to church on Sundays because I value religion in my life.

2. **We believe the cost is worth it.** We believe the benefit to be gained from achieving the goal is greater than the cost involved in trying to attain it. The motivation for our behavior is to gain the benefit.

   Examples:

   > Spending more time with my family makes turning down the promotion worth it.

   > Taking careful notes can be exhausting at times, but improving my mind is very fulfilling.

3. **We believe we can do it**. We believe we can achieve the goal and receive the benefit. The motivation for our behavior is to experience proficiency and competence.

   Examples:

   > I am working hard in my new position because with my background, I believe I can get the job done and receive a bonus.

   > I continue to concentrate on this math problem because I know I will solve it and be proud of myself when finished.

We are positively motivated when we *believe* that the activity we are engaging in is worthwhile because:

- the activity takes us closer to a goal we value

- the activity benefits us more than any cost associated with it

- the activity will be rewarded by the achievement of the goal

Belief in the worth and value of the activity and belief in ourselves are key, for these beliefs give meaning and purpose to our actions, enable us to persist, and produce good feelings.

## Cognition and Negative Motivation

When we are negatively motivated, we move away from an object, person, or event that we associate with negative cognitions. These cognitions are likely to fall into three categories:

1. **We believe the outcome isn't worthwhile.** We believe there is little or no value, benefit, payoff, or reward associated with an outcome. The motivation for our behavior is to avoid an unrewarding outcome.

   Example:

   > I submit my first draft of a paper because I believe revising is a waste of time.

2. **We believe the cost isn't worth it.** We believe the outcome has some value, but the cost of achieving it far outweighs the benefit to be gained. The motivation for our behavior is to avoid paying the cost.

   Example:

   > I submit my first draft of a paper because it would take five revisions to improve from a 'D' to a 'C' and it's not worth it.

3. **We believe we can't do it**. We believe we cannot achieve the goal and receive the benefit. The motivation for our behavior is to avoid experiencing a perceived deficiency or the possibility of failure.

Example:

> I submit my first draft of a paper because I am a poor writer and know I can't improve it.

The cognitive aspects of negative motivation are somewhat complex, and therefore require further explanation and illustration. We are negatively motivated when we believe that the activity we are engaging in (for example, handing in the first draft of a paper) is only worthwhile because it moves us away from something we think has little or no value (for example, doing the revision). This "movement away" can result from one or more of the three cognitions mentioned above. In the first example, if a well-written paper is not something we value, taking time and effort to revise our paper will not be viewed as something worthwhile. We are motivated to hand in the first draft because this action keeps us from doing something we view as worthless (revising). In the second example, a well-written paper is perceived as costing too much (five revisions). As such, revision is not perceived as worth doing because the cost is seen as exceeding the benefit. So, we are motivated to hand in the first draft because this action saves us from doing five revisions for which the payoff is only a 'C' grade. In the third example, if a well-written paper is not something we believe we can accomplish by revision, revising will not be seen as worthwhile. So, we are motivated to hand in the first draft because this action keeps us from experiencing the frustration that accompanies trying something we believe we cannot do.

We are negatively motivated when we *believe* that the activity we are engaging in is worthwhile because:

- the activity enables us to avoid or escape an outcome that is not valued or rewarding

- the activity enables us to avoid a cost that is greater than any benefit

- the activity enables us to avoid failing to achieve an objective

Belief in the worth and value of escape and avoidance is key. Any positive feelings produced are the result of reducing negative ones. The following examples of negative motivation drawn from different situations illustrate these same three beliefs:

> I watch the "soaps" in the afternoon to have something to do while my friends work out because I think exercise is pointless.

> I began a diet and quit eating junk food because listening to my family's complaints about my eating habits was too much to take.

> I chose this major only because I couldn't hack any of the other majors.

Understanding the cognitions associated with positive and negative motivation provides us with a starting place for change. If we want to become positively motivated toward some activity or goal, we know what cognitions have to be developed or strengthened. If dissatisfied with negative motivation in some aspect of our life, we can change the cognitions that are the source of it.

## Benefits of Positive Motivation

We might be asking: "What difference does it make if we are positively or negatively motivated? As long as we get the job done, who cares? What does it matter whether we pursue a college degree because we enjoy and value learning or because we don't want to stay home or end up with the same job we had during high school? As long as we get the degree, who cares what motivates us?" These questions are legitimate. It may not matter what motivates us *if* the only alternative is no achievement (such as no college degree). If negative motivation is the *only* way we know to get ourselves to move, then it is better than no movement at all. However, given the choice between positive and negative motivation, positive motivation is decidedly better for all the reasons outlined below.

*Positive motivation is goal-directed.* It keeps the behavior directed toward a specific goal that is valued, worth the cost, and achievable. The cognitions that support negative motivation point us away from something, but not necessarily toward a specific goal.

Example:

> If we are positively motivated to obtain a college degree, we will keep working until we attain this objective. Yet, if we *only* want a degree to avoid poverty, this negative motivation would be short-lived if other options became available. We might quit college if we were offered a pro basketball contract or won the lottery.

*Positive motivation is enjoyable.* The affect that supports it makes the activity a more enjoyable one, and therefore, one that is likely to persist. Conversely, the negative affect that supports negative motivation can make an activity unpleasant, and therefore unlikely to persist over time. We will engage in an activity more often if we are "turned on" by it rather than if it temporarily "turns off" our fears.

Example:

> Feeling excited and pleased as we participate in class will probably lead us to speak up more often, even if we get occasional stares from others. However, if anxiety

under the professor's gaze is all that prompts our participation, this negative emotion can become associated with the activity and lead us to really dislike speaking up in class.

*Positive motivation is instructional.* The self-talk associated with it instructs us about what behaviors need to occur to reach our goal. With the self-talk of positive motivation, we tell ourselves *what to do*, whereas with the self-talk of negative motivation, we tell ourselves *what not to do*. The self-talk of positive motivation provides more information on the actions that will enable us to reach our goals.

Example:

> If we are positively motivated to be healthy, we would instruct ourselves to "eat nutritious food, exercise regularly, get enough sleep, practice relaxation," etc. If we are negatively motivated, our self-instructions might be to "avoid fatty foods, stop being a 'coach potato,' don't stay up late, reduce stress," etc.

## BENEFITS AND COSTS OF NEGATIVE MOTIVATION

For all the reasons given above, we should strive to develop positive motivation for as many activities in our lives as possible. Yet, negative motivation is not always problematic. When we move away from something, we obviously move toward something else. In doing so, we may accomplish something worthwhile. Negative motivation may even shift into positive motivation. How often have we done something grudgingly, just to escape the penalty for not doing it, and then found that we enjoy and even benefit from doing it after all? We may have eaten our first lobster just to quiet our parents, found it tasty, and now eat it because we enjoy it. Or, we may have read an article only because it was required, found the topic interesting, and read another article for pleasure. In spite of the positive result, when we are negatively motivated, the driving force or purpose of our behavior is to move us away from something (our parents' prodding, for example); the movement toward something else (the lobster, for example) occurs only by default. The driving force is a combination of negative affect and negative cognition ($A \times C$), a combination that, while sometimes beneficial, is more often detrimental to the achievement of our goals.

Rather than understanding our negative motivation, we might think it sufficient to know when we are not motivated toward something, call it "a lack of motivation," and leave it at that. However, if we ever want to become motivated toward something, knowing what feelings and beliefs must change can be of benefit. Also, an analysis of our negative motivation helps us understand why certain unwanted behaviors continue to occur. For example, although we want to stop smoking, we may continue to smoke because it reduces our anxiety in social situations. Merely saying "I lack the motivation to stop" says nothing useful. Realizing that we are fleeing anxiety, rather than simply "lacking motivation" to quit, can help us to find another way to reduce anxiety and manage this habit.

## MOTIVATIONAL PROBLEMS AND SOLUTIONS

What few people realize is that we are always motivated to some degree, in some direction. Having motivational problems does not mean we are without motivation; it may mean we are dissatisfied with the level of our motivation, the values reflected in our motivated behavior, or the direction of our motivation.

### Energy Level

At times we seem to be energized to move in a particular direction, whereas other times our energy level seems low. When we are "charged up," we generally refer to this as *high motivation*, which is associated with intense feelings and strong beliefs. When we are lethargic, we generally refer to this as *low motivation*, which is associated with weak feelings and ambivalent or "wishy washy" beliefs. Often these two types of motivation occur in combination. Low motivation for movement in one direction (studying, for example) is frequently accompanied by high motivation for movement in some other direction (partying, for example).

If we are dissatisfied with our level of motivation (high or low), knowing what affect and cognition need to be enhanced or changed can help us address the problem. For example, if our motivational level is low due to fatigue or illness, then rest or seeing a physician may be the answer. Although high motivation is not generally perceived as a problem, it can be if it is high negative motivation.

## Personal Values

When we consider our day-to-day activities, we may become dissatisfied with some of them as well as the values they reflect. We may not like that we are motivated to sleep a lot, spend money on things we do not need, or hang out with old friends. We might prefer to be motivated to work more, spend less, and make new friends. Under such circumstances, we need to learn how to change the values toward which we are motivated.

### Personal Values and Negative Motivation

If we engage in a behavior frequently, we might conclude that we value this activity and the goal to which it is directed. This may in fact be true, but when we think about our actions, we may determine that we do not value the activity highly, do not enjoy it that much, and fail to understand why we keep doing it. For example, we may continue to party and watch TV a lot even though we see little value in these activities and derive little pleasure from them.

Negative motivation can explain why we continue to do things we do not value. Although we do not value the activity, we probably value the role it plays in helping us to escape or avoid something else. We may not really value partying, but instead value the fact that it keeps us from thinking about all the work we have to do. Similarly, watching TV may provide a distraction from doing something viewed as unpleasant (revising a paper perhaps), and is therefore of some "value" to us. Thus, knowing how negative motivation functions in our daily lives helps clarify our values (C), which sets the stage for managing our motivation.

### Personal Values and Positive Motivation

It is possible to be dissatisfied with the values reflected in our actions even though they are positively motivated. We may really enjoy an activity, see great value in it, and be quite proficient at it, but wish we were not so highly motivated in this regard. Our dissatisfaction could stem from a suspicion that more worthwhile activities and goals could be occupying our time. If we knew what they were, we might be more highly motivated toward them than the ones we currently pursue. At the risk of oversimplification, the solution to this problem lies in educating ourselves — learning what people have discovered to be of lasting value since they first reflected on the meaning and purpose of life. In educating ourselves, we clarify our values, change old ones, and acquire new ones.

## Change of Values

In the course of our lives, all of us will experience a lack or loss of motivation toward a goal that was once highly valued and desirable. This can happen with anything we label "work," particularly if it is thought to be keeping us from something we value more, such as "play." For example, we may once have been highly motivated to achieve at work, but if we become bored and disinterested, the motivation may shift from positive to negative. We then stay on the job not because we enjoy and value it, but because we value what it keeps away, what it keeps from happening, such as unemployment or threats to our self-esteem. At such times, we need to rekindle excitement and interest by again finding value in what we are doing, if we wish to experience all the benefits of positive motivation.

## Fear of Failure

Many of us are negatively motivated and spend our lives trying to *avoid failure* rather than *achieve success*. This is sometimes referred to as **fear of failure** or "running scared." For example, we may take a job or remain in one, not because we enjoy and value it, but because it is available or easy. We may avoid a more challenging position because we are unable to handle the tension and anxiety (A) that accompanies the thought (C) of possible failure. Since keeping the available or easy job reduces the negative emotions associated with risk, behavior that avoids risk is rewarded and strengthened. Of course, in avoiding the risk of failure that comes with a more challenging job, we may never learn that we could have done the job and enjoyed the feelings accompanying that success (Fensterheim & Baer, 1977).

## MANAGING MOTIVATION

To overcome all the motivational problems just discussed — lack of energy, change in values, fear of failure — we have to manage the affect and cognition that support them. And, to become positively motivated toward a goal for which we are negatively motivated, we need to get rid of any negative feelings (anxiety, anger, depression) and negative cognitions associated with the goal. So, to be positively motivated, we manage A and C.

### Managing Motivation: The DIE Model

The DIE Model ( introduced in Chapter 2) can be used to identify the thoughts and feelings that are diminishing positive motivation or strengthening negative motivation. The following example of a student's thoughts and emotional response after receiving a low grade demonstrates how thoughts and emotions can lead us *away* from a particular class.

### Data

What are the objective facts?

Example:

I received a 'D-' on my medieval history research paper.

### Interpretation

What are the subjective thoughts or beliefs about the data?

Examples:

I don't see any point in reading about the Middle Ages any more.

Now I'll have to work like crazy just to get a 'C.' It's not worth it.

I just can't do well in this course. I've always been poor at history and this history teacher seems to have it in for me.

## Emotional Response

What emotions result from the interpretation?

Examples:

I feel bored when reading about the Middle Ages.

I 'm really annoyed that I have to work so hard.

I get anxious and uptight whenever I study history.

The *interpretation* (C) and emotional response of this student reduces motivation toward the course, the teacher, the assignments, and the subject in general. If the *data* (the 'D-' grade) were interpreted differently, the emotional response would differ as well. For example, if the student interpreted the grade as an accurate assessment of his work, tried to find some benefit in learning about the Middle Ages, and thought about ways to improve his writing in the future, he might still be displeased with the grade, but his upset would not be so intense. Also, his *emotional response* would not be directed at the class or the teacher, and therefore, his motivation toward the course would not necessarily suffer.

It is important to note that there is no evidence to support the student's interpretation. The loss of positive motivation was due to the student's *self-talk* (interpretation), which was of his own making. He *chose* to accept a negative interpretation as fact, upset himself greatly, and in the process caused himself to lose positive motivation. If he wanted to remain motivated toward the course, he could have chosen to interpret the situation differently. Had he avoided catastrophizing, overgeneralizing, blaming, and other distorted thoughts and dysfunctional beliefs, he might have been motivated to ask the professor for help and come to feel better about the class.

Take as another illustration, the case of the two students described in Chapter 1 who had radically different views about rewriting their reaction papers. One student was happy (emotional response) because he interpreted the assignment as an opportunity to raise his grade. The other student was angry (emotional response) because she interpreted it as an indication that the professor was trying to give the

**73**

students a hard time. The students perceived the same event quite differently and their interpretations led to very different emotional responses. Obviously, their motivation for the assignment differed as a result (Ellis & Harper, 1975).

These simple examples have significant implications. They suggest that our motivation (or a change in it) is heavily dependent on our thoughts and feelings and that by managing cognition and affect, we manage our motivation.

## Managing Motivation: Changing Language

In Chapter 2, it was emphasized that our language not only reflects but influences our thinking. So, if we want to be positively motivated, we need to speak about our goals in a manner that supports them.

A quick way to determine the extent to which we speak positively or negatively is to listen to the way we talk about our activities. If the self-talk contains more negative words and phrases than positive ones, negative motivation probably predominates. These statements would reflect negative motivation:

I exercise so I don't get fat.

I study so I don't fail.

I have a boyfriend so I won't be lonely.

I speak up in class to avoid being called on.

These statements pertain to the same activity, but they would reflect positive motivation:

I exercise to be heathy and feel good.

I study to learn.

I have a boyfriend because I enjoy his company.

I speak up in class to improve my communication skills.

Once we have identified the language in need of change, it is simply a matter of practicing *positive self-talk* to reinforce and strengthen positive cognitions. Positive motivation will follow.

## Managing Motivation: Changing B

While motivation primarily results from affect and cognition that initiate behavior and give it direction (A x C = B), behavior itself can be a source of motivation. For example, after we have done something (B) that is important to us, we usually feel good (A) and think well of ourselves (C). In such instances, behavior can set off an upward motivational spiral by triggering positive affect and cognition. The following statement, which is a variation of one made by E. Robert Jones, captures this idea:

> It is sometimes easier to act your way into a new way of thinking and feeling, than it is to think and feel your way into a new way of acting.

Because of the nature of ABC interactions, the feelings and thoughts that stem from our behaviors in turn motivate new behaviors. For example, we may believe we cannot master statistics and feel uptight in our statistics class. To reduce this anxiety and doubt, we work extra hard in the class and end up doing well. The hard work produces a grade that leads us to think better of our ability, and reduces the negative feelings associated with statistics. By working hard (B) in the statistics class, we learn (C) we can do it and feel (A) good about it, so we become interested (C) and enthusiastic (A) about taking another statistics class (B). Even though we start out negatively motivated (with doubts and fears), positive motivation can result as the thoughts change to "I can do it" and feelings of enthusiasm emerge.

Getting ourselves to engage in any behavior that brings us closer to our goal is important, regardless of the reason for doing so, because the behavior can set an upward spiral in motion. For example, at first our reason for engaging in academic activities (going to the library, participating in class, revising written assignments, etc.), may be to impress the teacher, rather than learn from these activities. Yet, after a while, we may begin to discover (C) the benefits of being a learner, realize (C) the cost is minimal, come to believe (C) that success is probable, and feel (A) more relaxed and comfortable in class. These positive beliefs and feelings could result in more academic activities, greater benefits, better feelings, all of which are part of a *positive upward motivational spiral* that ultimately improves our self-esteem.

The problem, of course, is figuring out how to get ourselves to take action without waiting for thoughts and feelings to "kick in." In other words, how can we initiate new behaviors without first managing our thoughts and feelings? The behavior modification techniques discussed in Chapter 4 address this problem by showing how we can use environmental factors to influence behavior directly. By applying these techniques to manage our behavior, we could motivate ourselves without focusing exclusively on affect and cognition.

While this brief review of upward spirals demonstrates the connection between concepts discussed in Chapter 1 and motivation, it is also intended to reinforce the interconnections among all the topic areas in this book. Since self-management is a unified process, as we proceed, these fundamental principles will be used to integrate topics that would otherwise appear to be unrelated.

## KEY TO MOTIVATIONAL CHANGE

The key to motivation is changing the ABC components in the desired direction. If we want to increase positive motivation toward a particular goal, we need to minimize or change the negative thoughts and feelings associated with that goal. In Chapter 4, the steps of DIE Model are expanded to show how thoughts and emotions can be changed. Practice in using this method helps reduce negative thoughts and feelings that interfere with positive motivation, and generate thoughts and feelings that increase positive motivation. Other techniques for changing cognitions and affect are also introduced in Chapter 4. Specific applications to academic motivation are discussed in Chapters 5 and 10.

Although our emphasis has been on controlling motivation by changing negative feelings through a change in thinking, it is possible to rid ourselves of negative feelings that interfere with positive motivation by "turning on" positive feelings directly. The positive feelings that result from relaxation techniques described in Chapter 4 are useful antidotes to reduce sensations such as fatigue, tension, and stress as well as emotions such as anger and anxiety that minimize positive motivation. As already mentioned, a systematic approach to changing behaviors is also introduced in Chapter 4. Thus, if motivation is ever a problem for us, these methods, used individually or in combination, can be used to change the level and direction of our motivation.

**KEY WORDS AND CONCEPTS**

**A x C = B**
**fear of failure**
**high motivation**
**low motivation**
**managing motivation**
**motivation**
**negative motivation**
**positive motivation**
**positive self-talk**
**positive upward motivational spiral**

## SUGGESTED READINGS AND TAPES

### Motivation (General)

Petri, H.L. (1981). *Motivation: Theory and research.* Belmont, CA: Wadsworth.

Waitley, D. (1991). *The psychology of human motivation.* Chicago: Nightingale-Conant (audio cassettes).

### Academic Motivation

Brim, G. (1992). *Ambition: How we manage success and failure throughout our lives.* New York: Basic Books.

Ellis, D. (1991). *Becoming a master student.* Rapid City, SD: College Survival Inc. (Chaps. 4 and 6).

### Fear of Failure

Barry, R.G. (1975). Fear of failure in the student experience. *Personnel and Guidance Journal, 54,* 190-203.

**EXERCISE 3.1**

**ABCs OF MOTIVATION**

1. What goal or objective are you attempting to accomplish at this point in your life?

   _____
   _____
   _____
   _____

2. What specific behaviors do you engage in regularly to help you reach this goal?

   _____
   _____
   _____
   _____

3. Write down any self-talk that occurs when you engage in these behaviors. (The self-talk will provide clues to A and C.)

   _____
   _____
   _____
   _____

4. What feelings are part of your motivation that initiates these behaviors (AxC=B)?

   _____
   _____
   _____
   _____

5. What cognitions are part of your motivation that initiates these behaviors (AxC=B)?

   _____
   _____
   _____
   _____

6. Is your motivation for this goal or objective primarily positive or negative? Explain how you reached this conclusion.

   _____
   _____
   _____
   _____

## EXERCISE 3.2

## NEGATIVE MOTIVATION

1. Identify a past behavior that was based on negative motivation.

   _____
   _____
   _____
   _____

2. Identify the affect and cognition that contributed to this negative motivation.

   Affect:

   _____
   _____
   _____
   _____

   Cognition:

   _____
   _____
   _____
   _____

3. Explain why positive motivation for this behavior would have been more beneficial for you than negative motivation.

   _____
   _____
   _____
   _____
   _____
   _____
   _____

## EXERCISE 3.3

## FROM NEGATIVE TO POSITIVE MOTIVATION

1. What school-related behavior have you engaged in grudgingly at first, but later came to value or enjoy?

_____

_____

_____

_____

2. What were the feelings and thoughts that contributed to your being negatively motivated at first?

Affect:

_____

_____

_____

_____

Cognition:

_____

_____

_____

_____

3. What were the new feelings and cognitions brought about by this behavior that changed your motivation for this activity from negative to positive? How did the behavior change your feelings and thoughts about the activity?

_____

_____

_____

_____

_____

_____

## EXERCISE 3.4

### ABC FIRING ORDER FOR PERSONAL MOTIVATION

To identify the firing order of your motivation, it is helpful to focus on the specific ABCs that were at work at a point in time when you were highly motivated. Follow the instructions below for the imagery exercise in Part I and then respond to the items in Parts II, III, and IV.

**Part I**

1. Recall a time in your life when you had high motivation to achieve a specific goal. Reflect on the details of that situation (both external and internal factors) and try to put yourself into or imagine yourself experiencing that motivational state. That is, go back in time and try to place yourself into the situation and recreate the motivational state as you experienced it then. This is not easy, but with repeated attempts it can be done.

2. As you observe yourself in this motivational state, determine which ABC component is the trigger. Do you focus primarily on the cognitive elements (for example, thoughts of benefits, costs, or images of achieving your goal)? Or, do you focus primarily on the emotions and sensations at work, such as getting excited, relieving anxiety, or reducing anger? Or, as you see yourself getting motivated, do you focus primarily on the activities or behaviors related to your goal ?

3. If you find that all three ABC components seem to be equally important, which one is absolutely necessary to your motivation? That is, which one is essential or vital to get you moving? The answer to this question may be found by reflecting on the component that seems to have the greatest intensity when experienced, the one that first comes to mind, or is easiest to reexperience.

4. After identifying the trigger, use the same procedure to determine which component follows next in leading you to accomplish your goal. Identify this thought, feeling, or behavior. Then, identify the next component in the firing order.

**Part II**

1. Now that you have recalled the specifics of a situation in which you were highly motivated, respond to each of the following.

   a. Describe the situation briefly.

   _____

   _____

   _____

   _____

   b. Describe the trigger.

   _____

   _____

   _____

   c. Describe the second and third components in the firing order.

   _____

   _____

   _____

   d. Would you say that your motivation was primarily positive or negative? Explain.

   _____

   _____

   _____

**Part III**

Once the firing order has been identified, answer the questions below to gain additional information on each ABC component. Continue to reflect on the situation you just recalled in Part I of this exercise as you answer these questions. Your answers will provide more specific information needed for managing your motivation in the future.

1. For the *cognitions* associated with your personal motivation, respond to the following:

   a. What were the specific payoffs or rewards that were part of your motivation? Explain.

   _____

   _____

   _____

   _____

b. Were these rewards internal (satisfaction) or external (recognition), abstract (love) or tangible (money), individual (diploma) or social (fellowship) etc.?

_____

_____

_____

_____

c. What were the specific costs, if any, of pursuing your goal?

_____

_____

_____

_____

d. What specific abilities did you believe you had that supported your motivation for this goal? Were they physical or mental attributes, individual or social skills, etc?

_____

_____

_____

_____

2. For the *feelings* associated with your personal motivation, respond to the following:

a. Were you moved more by one sense than the others, i.e. sight, sound, touch, smell, or taste?

_____

_____

_____

_____

b. Did positive sensations and emotions such as relaxation, excitement, and happiness move you to action or negative sensations and emotions such as tension, anxiety, and anger?

_____

_____

_____

_____

3. For the *behaviors* associated with your personal motivation, answer the following:

   a. Which of your behaviors had the greatest impact on your motivation? Explain.

   _____
   _____
   _____
   _____

   b. Did vigorous physical activity or more sedate and tranquil behavior play a part in your motivation? Explain.

   _____
   _____
   _____
   _____

   c. Did you find that you were more highly motivated when you worked alone or as part of a team? Explain.

   _____
   _____
   _____
   _____

**Part IV**

1. What have you learned from this exercise that will help you to manage your motivation in other situations? Explain.

   _____
   _____
   _____
   _____
   _____
   _____
   _____

This exercise was adapted from Robbins (1986).

## 4

*Our goals and dreams are deferred until we find strategies that bring them to fruition.*

# CASE STUDY

Before reading Chapter 4, read the case study in the box below. After completing the chapter, analyze the case study by following steps 1 through 5.

STEP 1      Describe the overall problem.

STEP 2      AFFECT:     Identify the feelings contributing to the problem.

                         BEHAVIOR:   Identify the behaviors contributing to the problem.

                         COGNITION: Identify the thoughts contributing to the problem.

STEP 3      Identify the firing order.

STEP 4      Describe the downward spiral.

STEP 5      Describe three different ABC change techniques that could have been used to alter the downward spiral. Explain at what point Jesse could have used each of these techniques to address a specific ABC component.

"I would like you to give a presentation on the team's project to upper-level management." Those words echoed in Jesse's mind as he stood tongue-tied, staring in sheer terror at his manager as she explained how important it is that he make a great pitch. "Why me when there are nine other members of the team? I've never done anything like this before!" he thought. He couldn't imagine himself as a presenter, especially in front of this crowd. He wanted to say, "Thanks, but no thanks!" Instead, he stammered, "Why me?" "Because you relate well with people and are very knowledgeable about the project. Think it over and let me know by tomorrow morning," she said, and walked away.

That night Jesse stayed awake for hours. Thoughts like these kept running through his head: "I can't let her know that I'm scared out of my gourd! I might look bad giving the presentation, but I'd look even worse if I said 'no.' " The next morning Jesse told his manager he'd do it and tried not to tremble as she explained what was expected of him.

Jesse had three weeks to prepare. He was so uncomfortable with the idea of presenting that he tried to put it out of his mind. His manager advised him to rehearse in front of a co-worker, but he was too embarrassed to ask anyone for help. "That won't do any good; they'd just say nice things so I wouldn't feel bad," he thought and dismissed the idea. The night before the big day, Jesse began to rehearse in the privacy of his own room. Stumbling over the intro twice, he got frustrated and gave up. "This is making me more nervous," he thought. "I'll just wing it tomorrow."

After another sleepless night, Jesse looked across his audience and didn't detect a single smile. "How did I ever get myself into this mess? They can tell that I'm a wreck. They know I'm dying up here — this is mortifying," he thought. Hands shaking, Jesse picked up his notes and began reading them word for word. He could feel his voice quivering and every time he looked at his audience it got worse. By the looks on their faces, he knew they were thinking about how bad he was. When he lost his place at one point, he decided to end the agony and cut the presentation short.

# 4 METHODS FOR CHANGING AFFECT, BEHAVIOR, AND COGNITION

What happens to a dream deferred?

Does it dry up
like a raisin in the sun?
....
*Or does it explode*?

Langston Hughes(1902-1967)
American poet

## INTRODUCTION

Our goals and dreams are deferred until we find strategies that bring them to fruition. Dreams can sometimes appear to be so distant that we allow them to just "dry up." Feelings, behaviors, and thoughts will have a lot to do with what happens to our dreams because they are integral components of motivation, time management, study habits, relationships, and self-esteem — those dimensions of ourselves that can help us make dreams become a reality. As emphasized in previous chapters, we can improve in these and other areas by changing the ABC interactions that comprise them. We can increase upward spirals, decrease downward spirals, and achieve at a higher level by using methods for changing affect, behavior, and cognition.

No doubt we have our own ways of managing ourselves and working toward our goals, and we may not do this by following a formal or organized system. If these techniques work without causing harm, we will probably continue to use them. Even so, we might want to consider employing the techniques introduced in this chapter, if we are not doing so already, because research has shown that some techniques for changing the ABCs are more efficient and effective than others. It is also true that certain methods are more effective when targeted for a particular ABC component. For example, relaxation is best suited to change affect, behavior modification to change behavior, and thought stopping to change cognition. However, because of the close interaction among the ABCs, a technique effective with one component will usually impact the others. For example, the calming effect of relaxation can also help us think clearly and act prudently.

Whether we are dealing with a particular problem or just trying to improve our well-being, the ABCs are involved. Once we have identified the precise feelings, behaviors, and thoughts, the interactions among them, and determined the component we want to change first, we can then apply the methods introduced in this chapter. As with any skill, proficiency takes practice, but once mastered and used regularly, these change techniques can improve the quality of our lives dramatically.

> **NOTE:** This chapter has been divided into three sections to make it easier to learn the material. It is recommended that students pause after each section and reflect on how the techniques described might be used before continuing on to the next.

## Section One

## METHODS FOR CHANGING AFFECT

Chapter 1 pointed out that affect consists of *emotions* and *sensations* and that most emotional responses involve some physical sensations. The methods discussed in this section can help change emotions and sensations that present a problem for us.

### Changing Emotions By Using the DIE Model

In Chapter 2, Part One of the DIE Model (data, interpretation, emotional response) illustrated how our interpretation (cognition) can be responsible for our emotional response (affect). It also demonstrated how interpretations based on distorted thoughts and dysfunctional beliefs can result in inappropriate negative feelings. Part Two of the model, which is outlined below, illustrates how to change a negative emotional response by changing the thinking that is causing it. Part Three teaches us how to deal with the negative aspects of reality. Parts One through Three of the DIE Model (adapted from Ellis, 1969) are combined in the example below to show how they can be applied to the problem introduced in Chapter 2.

## Part One:   Data, Interpretation, and Emotional Response

### Data  (*facts*)

What are the *objective facts*?  Write down what happened.  Focus on 4 "Ws" — Who, what, where, when.

Example:

Last night, I saw my girlfriend with another man in the mall.

### Interpretation  (*thoughts or beliefs*)

What are the *subjective thoughts or beliefs* about the data?  Be as thorough as possible in describing the thoughts and beliefs.

Example:

She is cheating on me.  It's all over between us.  It's not fair.

### Emotional Response (*affect*)

What emotions result from this interpretation?

Example:

Anger, anxiety, depression.

# Part Two: Disputation, Exchange, and Practice

## Disputation

We ***dispute*** the distorted thoughts or the dysfunctional beliefs that are part of our interpretation by identifying and challenging them. Here's how to do it:

1. Select the distorted thoughts or dysfunctional beliefs to be disputed. Write them down. It will be helpful to refer to the sections on distorted thoughts and dysfunctional beliefs in Chapter 2 for comparison with the thoughts selected.

   Example:

   > *Personalization*: She's with another guy; therefore, she must be cheating on me.
   >
   > *Catastrophizing*: It's all over between us.
   >
   > *Fairness*: It's not fair that she is with someone else.

2. How is this thought or belief wrong, false, or misleading? Is it specific, accurate, nonjudgmental? Is it balanced? What evidence is there that it is false? Is there any evidence that it is true? How is it dysfunctional (counterproductive)?

   Example:

   > I did see her with that guy (specific), but I could be wrong about the cheating (inaccurate) and I jumped to a conclusion without getting the facts (judgmental) and without hearing her side (unbalanced). There is no evidence that she's cheating and it isn't helping my mood to think that she is (dysfunctional).

## Exchange and Practice

We *exchange* distorted thoughts and dysfunctional beliefs for rational thoughts by replacing them with specific, accurate, nonjudgmental, and balanced thinking.

Example:

> I don't know that she's involved with this guy. For all I know, it could be a friend or a relative. Before I go jumping to conclusions, I'll mention that I saw her and ask her whom she was with. It may have nothing to do with me.

We *practice* the exchanged thoughts and beliefs by persistently rehearsing them in our minds (particularly when the data are present).

Only by persistently practicing *disputation* and *exchange* will a logical thought or functional belief replace the negative interpretation and change the negative emotion. With practice, these cognitive processes become automatic and negative emotions become less frequent. As one student put it: "This model was a little hard to pick up at first, but like anything else it takes practice."

## Part Three:  Coping and Reframing

Identifying and changing distortions and dysfunctional beliefs enable us to counter subjective thoughts that have no basis in fact or are harmful in some way.  However, getting rid of distortions does not  mean that a negative interpretation is false.  After logically assessing a situation, we may find our negative interpretation is correct. *Coping* and *reframing* will help in dealing with this negative reality.

## Coping

*Coping* is focusing on our personal resources and using them to adapt to a negative situation. It is particularly beneficial when dealing with a situation that we cannot change or one that we cannot change in the immediate future. We determine the *worst* thing that could happen and decide how to adjust to it.

Examples:

> She is seeing another guy! What could be worse? She may want to break up with me and never see me again. I'll talk with her about it calmly and assertively. Then we'll have to decide if our relationship is finished or if we'll continue to see each other.

> I have handled worse situations in my life and survived them. I've had relationships in the past that have gone sour and I've gotten over them. As Elton John said, "I'm Still Standing."

## Reframing

**Reframing** is focusing on the positive aspects of negative data. We practice reframing by focusing on some *good* things that could result from a negative reality we are faced with.

Examples:

> If she wants to go out with someone else, that means I'm free to do the same. I might even meet someone I like better.

> This will give me a chance to do some of the things I've been putting off because of all the time I spent with her. Better to have found out about this now before I invested too much in the relationship.

The coping thought process reduces a negative emotional response by strengthening the belief that we can handle a situation without excessive cost to ourselves. By reframing, we think about how we can benefit from the experience. In time, these thoughts can produce positive feelings that will motivate us to act toward the situation in a manner consistent with our goals.

As we attempt to cope and reframe, distorted thinking or dysfunctional beliefs can interfere with the process. For example, filtering may block our recall of past successful coping strategies or lead us to see reframing as "just kidding ourselves." We would then need to dispute these distortions, rather than allow them to undermine our efforts to manage our feelings.

Applying the DIE Model to change the negative thinking and emotions will go a long way in helping us succeed. Some college students have offered these reasons for learning the model:

The model helped me to control my emotions when things seemed to be going badly. I found myself using it a few times when dealing with a bad grade, a disagreement with a roommate, or when something negative occurred. It helped me to get hold of my negative thoughts, feelings, and behaviors and take control of them before they got out of hand.

I use the model in situations that I can't handle. It helps me break down a situation and deal with it in a healthy way.

One time I got into a fight with my girlfriend...I was thinking about not calling her back. Then I stopped and asked myself if that would really accomplish anything. I realized it would just make matters worse and I decided to call and settle everything for the better. I did all this, in a sense, by using the model in my mind.

I use the model to look at motivational problems and to correct them.

This model helped me deal with distorted thoughts in a more sensible way. For example, just recently I found myself being "screwed over" or at least that's how I saw it. I applied this model to the problem and in the long run it helped me solve it.

It helps me change distorted thoughts into positive, confident thoughts.

## Changing Sensations and Emotions By Using Relaxation

Relaxation is an affective change technique we are all familiar with. Friends tell us to relax when we are upset or nervous. Instructors tell students to calm down before a test. Basketball coaches instruct their players to relax on the line before shooting a foul. Professional golfers relax when teeing off, and surgeons relax periodically during a long operation. Relaxation is useful in many situations. As one student indicated, "Relaxation helps me when I give an oral report. I get very nervous so I use it before I get up in front of everyone and while I am giving the oral presentation."

Being extremely tense, uptight, or nervous often interferes with our personal goals and relationships. Several relaxation methods can alter negative sensations, and if used consistently, generate positive sensations. Since sensations usually accompany emotions, relaxation can help us manage our emotions by changing our sensory experience.

Research has shown that we cannot feel physically relaxed and be tense, anxious, or angry at the same time because such feelings are incompatible. In "turning on" a relaxed state, we "turn off" unwanted negative sensations and emotions. Some methods of relaxation will require more time and training than others. Whatever one we choose to learn, it is wise to practice it regularly.

### Deep Breathing Relaxation

Shallow breathing from the upper chest is how many of us breathe, but it is not the most efficient breathing pattern. If we breathe from the diaphragm or lower chest, air is brought into the lower part of the lungs, resulting in a more efficient use of oxygen.

To learn *deep breathing relaxation*, Davis, Eshelman, and McKay (1988) recommend these steps:

1. Sit or stand up straight.

2. Inhale and exhale through the nose.

3. Fill the lower portion of the lungs while inhaling by pushing the abdomen outward and allowing the chest to move slightly forward. Then fill the upper part of the lungs by raising the chest and pulling in the abdomen a bit.

4. Hold breath for a few seconds.

5. Exhale slowly and pull in the abdomen a bit more.

After practicing deep breathing regularly, it can become natural and automatic. However, even if it does not become habit, we can use it whenever we need to relax.

## Progressive Relaxation

We are generally unaware that we tense our muscles all day long. As we become "stressed out," muscles tighten throughout the body as if we were under attack.  Muscles held in a tight, tense manner cause physical discomfort (headache, backache, neck pain, fatigue, etc.). This tension  increases our overall sense of being stressed, which in turn increases muscular tension. Muscular tension then intensifies the physical discomfort and stress  in an escalating cycle.

Progressive relaxation interrupts this cycle, enabling us to cope more effectively.  We first allow ourselves to experience muscle tension by contracting and tensing muscles.  After tensing a muscle, we relax it by "letting go" of the tension and experiencing a pleasant sensation.  Muscles should be tightened enough to feel the tension, but not so much as to strain them.  By practicing this routine progressively with various muscle groups,  relaxation will occur and  tension will be reduced.

Davis, Eshelman, and McKay (1988) recommend the following procedure for ***progressive relaxation*** if we want to achieve deep muscle relaxation quickly:

1.  Clench both fists, tightening forearms and biceps in a sort of "muscleman" pose.  Hold for five seconds. Then release the tension and relax the muscles for twenty seconds.  Repeat this procedure two times.

2. Close eyes tightly. Wrinkle the forehead. Press head as far back as possible, rotate it clockwise and then counterclockwise once. Relax. Repeat two times.

3. Arch back and shoulders, take a deep breath and hold it for five seconds. Exhale and let back and shoulders slump forward. Repeat two times.

4. While seated, straighten and lift legs, bend toes toward face, and tighten thighs and buttocks. Hold this position for five seconds and then release the tension and place feet back on the floor. Repeat two times.

When practicing progressive relaxation, we should note the contrast between sensations of tension and relaxation. In time, we will recognize the first signs of tension anywhere in the body and be able to relax them away before they become uncomfortable or stressful. After we are skilled in these procedures, we can combine various muscle groups and tense and relax the body as a whole. When this stage is reached, the body is set to be relaxed without first having to be tensed. We need only tell ourselves "to relax."

## Other Methods for Changing Affect

Exercise, nutrition, and the *act as if* method, which are briefly described below, are other ways of changing affect. Students interested in a more detailed discussion on exercise and nutrition are advised to read *The Relaxation and Stress Reduction Workbook* (Davis, Eshelman, & McKay, 1988), the book from which some of this material was drawn.

### Exercise

Practical experience tells us that when we are emotionally upset it is good to "work it off" by "working out." Vigorous physical exertion is a natural way for the body to release negative affect such as anxiety, anger, tension, and stress. Even individuals who are depressed experience some relief from a brisk ten-minute walk or jogging in place. After exercise, the body returns to its normal state of equilibrium and we feel relaxed and refreshed. The hormones that are released in the body during exercise are also natural pain killers and mood elevators. Thus, exercise lessens our need for drugs.

People who exercise for at least twenty minutes, three or four times a week, are less prone to respond with negative affect to the stressors encountered each day. A regular exercise routine contributes to our overall physical health, making us less reactive to minor problems. When we are physically "out of it," our tolerance for frustration is low and we generally pay the price affectively.

Aerobic and low intensity exercise are two approaches we might want to consider. **Aerobic exercise** is sustained rhythmic movement of the large muscle groups, particularly those in the legs. Running, jogging, fast walking, tennis, racquetball, and biking are common forms of aerobics that serve to burn calories, reduce fat, strengthen the heart, and improve stamina. **Low intensity exercise** is not as strenuous as aerobics. In addition to toning the body, it increases muscle strength, flexibility, and joint mobility. Calisthenics (sit-ups, knee bends, etc.), isotonics (weight lifting), and isometrics (pushing or pulling stationary objects) are all low intensity exercises.

Exercise is a form of behavior that helps to manage affect and improve health, but behaviors such as exercise have to be managed themselves if they are to be sustained. The technique of behavior modification discussed in Section Two of this chapter can help us to start and maintain an exercise program. Using a short exercise routine to reduce tension, anxiety, and stress will bring immediate rewards. However, the long-term rewards of making exercise a daily routine are improved physical and emotional health.

## Nutrition

To stay physically healthy, we need a proper balance of approximately 40 to 60 nutrients. Without them, we could suffer from malnutrition, but be unaware of it because we may not experience any specific physical symptoms. A poor diet can also result in increased irritability, anxiety, tension, fatigue, as well as insomnia and weight gain. For example, a calcium deficiency can be caused by a lack of dairy products and leafy vegetables. Calcium is needed to counteract the high level of lactic acid that builds up in tense muscles when under stress. The resulting fatigue, anxiousness, and irritability are much greater than they would be if we were eating a balanced diet.

*Proper nutrition* helps us combat illness, avoid weight gain, and decrease stress as well as the negative emotions and sensations associated with it. The following guidelines are recommended to promote good health and nutrition:

1. Eat regular meals.

2. Maintain a varied diet.

3. Eat slowly.

4. Limit fried foods.

5. Limit starchy vegetables (peas, corn, potatoes, etc.) to one per meal.

6. Eat plenty of natural foods, particularly fruits and vegetables.

7. Eat whole grain cereals, breads, and rice.

8. Avoid refined foods that are stripped of their nutrients.

9. Avoid excess fats, sugar, sodium, alcohol, caffeine, snacks.

10. Avoid chemically treated foods.

11. Avoid drugs.

## Act As If

As peculiar as it may sound at first, a rather quick way to change affect is to **act as if** we are feeling the way we would like to feel. This means that we assume the posture, breathing, facial expressions, voice level, mannerisms, movements, etc. associated with the emotions and sensations we want to experience. For example, if we would like to get out of a bad mood, we can act as if we are happy by assuming the posture, facial expressions, and mannerisms of being happy. If we are angry, and want to be calm, we can lessen the upset by acting as if we are relaxed. This technique probably works because of the close connection that has been established over the years between specificfeelings and behavioral responses to these feelings. By changing a behavior that accompanies a feeling, we change the feeling. The reactions of others is another contributing factor. When we are acting in ways that reflect positive feelings, other people often respond positively to us, which in turn makes it easier for us to  acquire the positive feelings.  So, if we find ourselves saying, "I don't feel like it" and we wish we did, *acting as if* we feel like it is a start.

**KEY WORDS AND CONCEPTS**

**aerobic exercise**
**act as if**
**coping (DIE Model, Part Three)**
**deep breathing relaxation**
**disputation (DIE Model, Part Two)**
**exchange and practice (DIE Model, Part Two)**
**low intensity exercise**
**progressive relaxation**
**proper nutrition**
**reframing (DIE Model, Part Three)**

## Section Two

# METHODS FOR CHANGING BEHAVIOR

The conditions present before a behavior occurs (or fails to occur) and the conditions that follow it often influence the behavior. The conditions occurring prior to behavior are called *antecedents*; the conditions that follow it are called *consequences*. Whether the intent is to increase desirable behaviors or decrease undesirable ones, by changing the antecedents and consequences of a particular behavior, we can change that behavior. This method is called behavior modification. Two approaches are described below.

## Behavior Modification Steps

*Behavior modification* is making use of the antecedents and consequences of a behavior to change it. The steps are as follows.

1. *Pinpoint* (specify) the behavior to be changed and the situation in which you want it to change.

   Example:

   > I want to stop getting drunk on weekends with my friends.

2. *Record* the conditions that are present before (antecedents) and after (consequences) the behavior occurs. To discover antecedents, keep a record of the *4Ws*:

   > Who is present?
   > When does the behavior occur?
   > Where does the behavior occur?
   > What is happening when the behavior occurs?

   Example:

   | | |
   |---|---|
   | Who: | My friends, Ray and Janet |
   | When: | Friday nights |
   | Where: | In the local pub |
   | What: | Everybody is partying, talking about sports and school. |

To discover consequences, keep a record of what happens after the behavior occurs. Note anything that is reinforcing the behavior.

Example:

> When I get a "buzz," I talk a lot and easily. Friends pay attention to me. I feel relaxed and comfortable. I laugh and joke around. I get drunk.

*Record* the frequency and duration of the behavior.

Example:

> I get drunk at least one night every weekend. I'm drunk from 9 p.m. until I fall asleep at 2 or 3 a.m.

3. *Analyze* the data collected in Step 2 to see if there is a pattern to the behavior. This is known as a ***functional analysis of the behavior*** in terms of antecedents and consequences.

Example:

> An analysis of data collected on my drinking reveals that I drink most often with two specific people (Ray and Janet) on Friday night, in the local pub, when discussing sports and school. (Note the 4Ws.) The consequences of drinking are that during the early part of the night I get a "buzz," am relaxed, can talk easily, and have an audience. Later on, I get drunk and slur my words.

4. *Determine* what conditions (antecedents and consequences) are influencing the behavior.

Example:

> I think being with friends on a Friday night in the local pub, talking about sports after a tough week in school, increases the chances that I will drink a lot. Getting a "buzz" early in the evening probably leads to more drinking, getting relaxed, talking a lot, and eventually getting drunk.

5. *Decide* what antecedents and consequences to alter in order to change the behavior.

Example of changing antecedents:

> I plan to go out with friends other than my "drinking buddies" on Friday night; or I will go to the movies with Ray and Janet on Friday night; or I will go to the local pub on Friday night with Ray and Janet, but I will only bring enough money for two or three beers and after about an hour, we will go to the movies.

Example of changing consequences:

> I will ask my friends to tell me if I am drinking too much, talking too much, or slurring my words. I will slow the pace of my drinking to one beer an hour, and ask the bartender to "cut me off" early if I am drinking too fast.

6. *Provide systematic rewards* for any improvement as a result of changing antecedents or consequences.

Example:

> After decreasing the number of times I get drunk, I will use the drinking money saved to buy new jeans or tickets to a concert.

7. *Provide systematic penalties* whenever the behavior occurs.

Examples:

> After each night I get drunk, I won't allow myself to party for one week.

> Having given my roommate $20 to hold, I'll tell him to donate it to charity if I get drunk.

8. *Observe* how much the behavior has changed by keeping a record.

9. *Modify* the plan if there is no improvement after two weeks. This might include arranging new types of antecedents to make the desired behavior more probable, or perhaps altering the consequences. Providing different or stronger pay-offs for improvement or penalties for "failure" might work.

## Behavior Modification Steps: Short Form

Analysis of behavior in terms of antecedents and consequences and the use of this information to change behavior is a systematic and comprehensive approach to self-management. However, if we want a systematic, but less comprehensive approach to strengthening existing behaviors, the **contingent use of rewards** will help. It requires that our rewards be "contingent" upon a particular behavior taking place. The steps are as follows:

1. *Pinpoint* the behavior to be strengthened.

   Examples:

   Reading a textbook for a half hour

   Completing an assignment

   Asking my roommate to turn down her stereo

   Writing to my parents

2. *List* enjoyable activities and other things to use as rewards (reinforcers).

   Examples:

   Favorite foods, beverages, etc.

   Favorite activities, events, etc.

   Favorite people, groups, etc.

   Favorite thoughts, images, etc.

   Things I would like to own (jewelry, clothes, etc.)

3. *Reward* yourself immediately *after* engaging in the behavior to be increased or strengthened. That is, make the reward contingent on the behavior.

Suggestions and Examples:

Be sure that the behavior to be increased always occurs before taking the reward. (Study first, then socialize.)

The reward should follow as soon after the behavior as possible.

The stronger the reward, the better.

High frequency behaviors can reinforce low frequency behaviors by having behaviors that are engaged in frequently (eating, for example) follow behaviors that occur less often (studying, for example).

Rearrange the rewards that are already in place (socializing, partying, phone calls, desserts, etc.) so that they reinforce a desirable behavior rather than an undesirable one. We do this by allowing these rewards to occur only *after* engaging in the desired behavior. For example, we could arrange to have a girlfriend call at a set time *after* we have worked on our research paper for an hour. If we haven't done the work, we don't answer the phone.

## Other Methods for Changing Behavior

The methods for changing behavior that conclude this section are discussed in much greater detail in *Self-Directed Behavior* by Watson and Tharp (1989).

### Shaping

The ancient Chinese proverb, "a journey of a thousand miles begins with the first step," indicates how long the method of shaping (also called successive approximations) has been around. **Shaping** is a method of working toward a goal in a succession of incremental steps. To take the first step toward our goal, we begin with a behavior we are capable of, one that is the closest approximation to the final goal. After practicing and mastering this behavior, we raise our standard a bit by moving a step closer to the goal. We continue to approach the goal gradually with each successive step until we reach it. For example, if our goal is to study five days a week for three hours a day, but right now we only study 40 minutes a day, we can begin by studying 45 minutes a day for five days. The next step might be 60 minutes a day. Once mastered, we could increase the amount of time studying to 75 minutes, 100 minutes, and so on. The first steps in shaping are very small, but become larger as we approach the goal. It is imperative to reinforce the achievement of each step, and withhold rewards when the behavior does not occur.

The steady experience of success that occurs with successive approximations strengthens goal-directed behavior. With each success comes an increasing belief in our ability to achieve our goals, which leads to even greater success.

### Imagined Rehearsal

Practicing or rehearsing a new behavior as we want it to occur is the best way to master that behavior. Yet, if we cannot practice, we can use imagined rehearsal. *Imagined rehearsal* is rehearsing a behavior in our imagination. Studies have shown that mentally picturing a behavior (sometimes referred to as mind scripting) can influence the frequency and quality of actual behaviors. People use it to perfect their skills, to resolve problems, and to prepare for challenges.

To use imagined rehearsal effectively, we imagine the behavior in minute detail. For example, to conduct a successful interview with a professor, we would imagine her appearance, expressions, voice, movements, reactions and imagine our actions as we progress through the interview. We might even imagine the interview in a time sequence and concentrate on each segment separately.

One way to get a clear image of ourselves performing a new behavior is to picture our success in a past situation, perhaps one that required similar behaviors. We can then transfer this image to the new situation and imagine ourselves acting as we did when successful.

## KEY WORDS AND CONCEPTS

**4Ws**
**antecedents**
**behavior modification**
**consequences**
**contingent use of rewards**
**functional analysis of behavior**
**imagined rehearsal**
**shaping**

**Section Three**

# METHODS FOR CHANGING COGNITION

The DIE Model, which was introduced earlier, is an effective way to sort out and change distorted thoughts and dysfunctional beliefs. Sometimes, however, negative thoughts and images pop into our minds so quickly they seem to have a will of their own. For example, we may be going along our merry way until a thought about how a friend treated us comes to mind. We then may find ourselves becoming upset and distracted. Or, during a party, we may find ourselves dwelling on a family problem and begin to get tense and anxious. We can change these cognitions on the spot before they take their toll on our feelings and behaviors by using the technique of thought stopping.

*Thought stopping* is a method for curtailing negative thinking by interrupting and stopping it forcefully and dramatically. Two different methods of thought stopping are outlined below.

## Thought Stopping: The On-the-spot Method

If negative thoughts sneak up on us when we can ill afford them, the *on-the-spot method of thought stopping* can block them before they have a major impact. This approach is somewhat of a quick fix and is most effective when coupled with more comprehensive approaches to cognitive change; nevertheless, it can be very useful in any situation in which negative affect is accompanied by negative thoughts.

The procedure is quite simple. As soon as an inappropriate negative thought comes to mind, we yell "Stop!" to ourselves, relax for a few seconds, and switch to an appropriate thought. If done properly, the disruptive thought will disappear, at least momentarily. If we allow the negative thought to continue for long, it will gain in strength and intensity, and become more difficult to shut down. By yelling "Stop!" to ourselves and substituting a more functional thought as soon as we notice the negative thought, we are more apt to stop it before it takes hold of us mentally and physically. Once we have worked ourselves up into a full-blown state of panic, the method takes much longer to be effective.

The following example illustrates on-the-spot thought stopping:

> As Barbara begins her final exam in English, she thinks, "I just have to do well on this test to keep my 'B' average." As Barbara scans the first essay question on *Rappaccini's Daughter*, she realizes that she only vaguely remembers reading it. All that she can remember is that it is a short story by Nathaniel Hawthorne. She begins to think: "I cannot possibly answer this question and it is worth 25 points!" Thoughts of doing poorly on the exam begin to race through her mind. Barbara feels herself starting to panic. Suddenly, she says to herself in an abrupt manner: "Barbara, stop it! Cut out the nonsense and answer the question!" She calms down and relaxes for a moment. As she begins to refocus on the question, the thought creeps in: "I can't bluff on this one." Again, she shouts to herself: "Stop it already; just answer the question as best you can." She takes a deep breath, puts her pen to the paper, and begins to outline what she can recall from the story, thinking to herself, "That's right, the daughter's name was Beatrice..."

Barbara used thought stopping to keep negative thoughts out of her mind long enough to allow positive ones to take over and avoid panic. By interrupting the unwanted thoughts each time they occurred, she weakened the thoughts that were preventing her from recalling the story. Then, by thinking of something more appropriate to the task at hand, the negative thoughts gradually lost ground and the specifics of the story came to mind. Relaxing also aided the process.

This technique is effective only when the negative thought is stopped each time it occurs, and then replaced by a more positive or appropriate thought, as Barbara did in the example by saying "Just answer the question." Of course, if she had never read *Rappaccini's Daughter*, thought stopping would not have helped much. It was effective here because the panicky feeling was preventing her from thinking clearly.

A college athlete explains how he uses this method:

> Out of all of the ABC methods, the one I use most is thought stopping. Whenever I am taking a test or even playing a basketball game, I use this approach so as not to let my thoughts interfere with my work. Say that I was on the verge of making an important basket for my team, my mind would start to tell me that I am about to miss the shot so

don't even bother trying for it. This is where thought stopping comes into play.  I would shout in my mind "I can make that shot." Then I will take the shot, and usually make it, if I have good form.

While thought stopping is used primarily for negative thoughts, at times  pleasant thoughts or images prevent us from doing something we planned.  "I would like to have a beer" or "I would like to quit studying and go skiing" could be considered rather pleasant thoughts.  However, if we had planned to drink less and study more, these thoughts  could lead us away from our goal.  In such a situation, instead of interrupting a negative thought, we would interrupt the pleasant thought and refocus attention on a thought that relates to our goal.

## Thought Stopping: The Practice Method

The *practice method of thought stopping* is used to halt recurrent or persistent negative thinking.  For example, we may find that we generally experience negative thoughts in certain situations, with certain people, or at certain times.  Perhaps the feelings associated with these circumstances are quite similar.  Maybe we get down on a regular basis during exam time or are uneasy around particular people. If we want to develop a more positive outlook and become more comfortable in these situations, we can determine what kinds of thoughts occur, focus on them, and then get rid of them.

**111**

The practice method requires conjuring up the disruptive thought in order to dismiss it from our minds once and for all. If we find ourselves plagued by the same nagging thoughts time and again, the practice method is preferable to the on-the spot method because its effectiveness is more lasting. The steps are as follows:

### Phase I

1.  Sit in a comfortable chair; close your eyes; and bring to mind the thought, image, or words that are bothersome.

2.  When the thought is clearly in mind, forcefully yell "Stop!" out loud to interrupt it. Then say softly: "relax." Relax all muscles and think of something pleasant or neutral.

3.  Repeat the above procedure five times consecutively each practice period. Practice these steps as often as it takes to get to the point where the thought is successfully interrupted each time. If the unwanted thought is not being interrupted, increase the intensity of your voice when yelling "Stop!"

### Phase II

1.  When it is apparent that the thought has been successfully interrupted, practice the same steps above, but this time say "Stop!" to yourself. Again, practice only as long as it takes to get to the stage when the thought is successfully interrupted each time.

2.  Next, practice interrupting the thought by saying "Stop!" to yourself when you first start to have the thought or image. Catch the thought as early as possible; do not wait until it is very clear in your mind before interrupting it.

After completing Phases I and II of the practice method, the on-the-spot method can be used whenever necessary. For rather obvious reasons, the practice method is best used when alone.

# Correcting Cognitive Distortions

Logical and functional thinking is basically nonjudgmental, accurate, specific, and balanced self-talk; the absence of these characteristics in our thoughts and speech is a clue that distorted thinking is involved (Fanning & McKay, 1987). Most of us use certain distortions (see Chapter 2) more than others. We may refrain from overgeneralizing and making snap judgments, but mind read and blame other people on a regular basis. As we become familiar with the different types of distorted thought processes, we will notice them particularly when we are upset. Since the cost of distorted thinking is often painful emotions or ongoing conflicts with family, friends, teachers, and employers, changing such thoughts and avoiding such a high price is well worth the effort.

To correct distorted thoughts, we first identify and label any cognitive distortions, and then change our internal dialogue to reflect the critical thinking patterns represented by the four categories below.

## Nonjudgmental Language and Thought

To be *nonjudgmental* in language and thought requires that we avoid "either-or" thinking and refrain from describing other people or events as good or bad, right or wrong, etc. When we are nonjudgmental, we *stick to the facts* and are careful not to prescribe what others should be doing. Instead of focusing on how people and events *should be*, we focus on the way they *are*.

| Nonjudgmental | Judgmental |
|---|---|
| Carlos has stopped seeing Maria and is dating Louise. | Carlos is a real "creep" for dropping Maria and dating that "air head" Louise. |
| Linda wore a black mini to the party. | To wear a sexy dress like that, Linda must really want to get a guy in the worst way. |

| Nonjudgmental | Judgmental |
|---|---|
| Jane is marrying a man ten years her junior. | Jane should marry someone older and more mature, instead of "robbing the cradle." |
| Mac has a Mohawk haircut. | Mac got that stupid haircut just to fit in with his weird friends. |

**Accuracy in Language and Thought**

*Accuracy* in language and thought involves describing people and events based on the *evidence* available. It requires making a separation between fact and conjecture. Treating assumptions as if they were indisputable facts or using derogatory labels are signs of inaccurate thinking. Mind reading is a prime example of conjecture masquerading as fact. When we want to know what people are thinking, it is better to ask them than to assume we know what they think. *Feeling* something is true does not make it so; these feelings are thoughts that usually have no basis in fact.

| Fact | Conjecture |
|---|---|
| My girlfriend has not phoned me in four days. | My girlfriend must want to break up. |
| My parents told me that they cannot give me any more money and they want me to go to work. | My parents must not care how I do in school if they expect me to hold down a job while I'm at college. |
| Althea said that my best friend told her that I plagiarize term papers. | Althea is a gossip who is just jealous of my good grades. |
| My sister didn't come to the family picnic and my mother was unhappy about it. | My sister didn't come to the family picnic to spite our mother because Mom doesn't like her husband. |

## Specificity in Language and Thought

*Specificity* in language and thought means that we focus on the relevant aspects of a situation without drawing conclusions based on other situations, even if the circumstances are very similar. To be specific, we simply *state what was observed* and avoid elaboration and overgeneralization.

| Specificity | Overgeneralization |
|---|---|
| My girlfriend and I had an argument about sex. | My girlfriend and I never agree on anything. |
| The course did not cover applications in the business world. | All the courses offered in that department are too abstract and theoretical. |
| My son and his roommate leave clothes on the floor. | All college students are slobs. |
| That man is now 50 pounds overweight. | That man will always be fat because he eats everything in sight. |

## Balance in Language and Thought

When we describe people and situations in a balanced way, we *focus on both the positive and the negative* and attempt to avoid a one-sided view. In situations where we have experienced a loss or setback, **balanced thinking** occurs when we acknowledge what has been lost as well as what we still have left and the possibilities that lie ahead. The notion that the glass is not only half empty, but also half full applies here.

| Balanced | One-sided |
|---|---|
| I am not happy about the 'D' in statistics, but I did all right in history. | That 'D' in statistics proves that I do not have what it takes to make it in college. |
| My relationship with my boyfriend is not working, but I have friends and family that are supportive. | My relationship with my boyfriend is falling apart, and I cannot take it because he is everything to me. |
| I may not have a lot of money now because I have to pay for college, but I have the potential to be successful in the future. | I cannot stand being in college. It's like being forever "broke." |
| Sometimes I win, sometimes I lose. | I always get the short end of the stick. |

There are no hard and fast distinctions among these four categories. Some examples could fit in one category as readily as another. The categories merely serve as a quick way to pinpoint and change illogical or distorted thoughts and speech. Distortions, such as those in the right-hand columns above, are often unintentional, automatic, and habitual. Therefore, we have to become more critical of the cognitive processes we use if we wish to develop a more productive way of speaking and thinking. Additional discussion of these concepts can be found in McKay and Fanning (1988).

# Other Methods for Changing Cognition

The methods described below can be very effective, particularly when used in conjunction with the methods for cognitive change already discussed in this chapter.

## Act As If

The **act as if** technique discussed previously for affect is also applicable to cognitions, particularly with respect to beliefs that impact our self-esteem. By acting in a manner that suggests that we already believe that we are worthwhile and competent, we can strengthen this belief and thereby enhance self-esteem. In "playing the role," success is often achieved and *acting as if* becomes *acting as I am.*

Acting as if can also result in a positive response from others, which may foster a belief in ourselves. Using this technique can promote a self-fulfilling prophecy that works to our advantage.

It needs to be emphasized that the acting as if technique (for cognition or affect) is not a substitute for developing genuine skills and abilities. It is most helpful when our thoughts and feelings are keeping us from enjoying our accomplishments or are preventing us from implementing the behaviors of which we are capable.

## Visualization

To change how or what we think, particularly with respect to ourselves, *visualization* (Bry, 1978) is useful. It requires that we train our imagination to "see" in our mind's eye what it is that we want to believe about ourselves. In other words, if we want to believe that we can be a successful student, it helps to vividly imagine ourselves doing what successful students do, and imagine ourselves achieving similar results. If we want to believe that we can make an interesting and informative presentation, rehearsing a successful speech in our imagination and "seeing" a positive response from others can strengthen such a belief.

117

Olympic athletes, corporate executives, and accomplished professionals have attested to the power of visualization in strengthening their thinking and beliefs. The steps that many of them follow can be outlined as follows:

1. Relax.

2. Imagine in clear detail the desired action or result. Call up images of past successes to help.

3. Allow positive feelings to support the image.

4. Use positive self-talk to reinforce the images of achievement and success.

5. Imagine yourself enjoying the rewards of success.

For maximum results, repeat these steps several times a day until the belief becomes strong. Be sure to replay the image of success after achieving any goal. It should be noted that visualizing an action is sometimes difficult. To strengthen our imagination in this regard, the brief exercises at the end of the chapter are recommended. (See Exercise 4.4.)

Visualization is similar to the imagined rehearsal technique discussed under methods for changing behavior. The difference is that visualization is intended to enhance how we think about ourselves, whereas imagined rehearsal is intended to change the actual behavior. Of course, if using imagined rehearsal changes the behavior, what we think about ourselves is bound to change as well. This illustrates once again the interaction among the ABCs and the techniques of self-management.

## KEY WORDS AND CONCEPTS

**accuracy
act as If
balanced thinking
nonjudgmental
on-the-spot method of thought stopping
practice method of thought stopping
specificity
thought stopping
visualization**

## SUGGESTED READINGS AND TAPES

### Change Techniques (General)

Rudestam, K.E. (1980). *Methods of self-change: An ABC primer.* Monterey, CA: Brooks/Cole.

### Relaxation Techniques

Davis, M., Eshelman, E.R., & McKay, M. (1988). *The relaxation and stress reduction workbook* (3rd ed.). Oakland, CA: New Harbinger Publications (Chaps. 3 and 4).

Strobel, C.F. (1978). *Breathing: Basic elements of the quieting response.* New York: BMA Audio Cassettes.

### Changing Behavior

Bry, A. (1978). *Visualization: Directing movies of your mind.* New York: Barnes & Noble Books.

Davis, M., Eshelman, E.R., & McKay, M. (1988). *The relaxation and stress reduction workbook* (3rd ed.). Oakland, CA: New Harbinger Publications (Chaps. 18 and 19).

Friday, R.A. (1988). *Create your college success.* Belmont, CA: Wadsworth (Chap. 18).

Lazarus, A., & Zilbergeld, B. (1987). *Mind power.* Boston: Little, Brown and Company.

Watson, D., & Tharp, R. (1989). *Self-directed behavior. Self-modification for personal adjustment* (5th ed.). Monterey, CA: Brooks/Cole.

**Thought Stopping**

Davis, M., Eshelman, E.R., & McKay, M. (1988). *The relaxation and stress reduction workbook* ( 3rd ed.). Oakland, CA: New Harbinger Publications (Chap. 9).

**Correcting Cognitive Distortions**

Lazarus, A., & Fay, A. (1975). *I can if I want to.* New York: Warner Books.

McKay, M, Davis, M., & Fanning, P. (1981). *Thoughts & feelings: The art of cognitive stress intervention.* Oakland, CA: New Harbinger Publications.

McKay, M., & Fanning, P. (1988). *Combatting distorted thinking.* Oakland, CA: New Harbinger Publications (audio cassette).

**Nutrition and Fitness**

Brody, J. (1981). *Jane Brody's nutrition book.* New York: Bantam.

Davis, M., Eshelman, E.R., & McKay, M. (1988). *The relaxation and stress reduction workbook* (3rd ed.). Oakland, CA: New Harbinger Publications (Chaps. 18 and 19).

Gardner, J.N., & Jewler, A.J. (1992). *Your college experience: Strategies for success.* Belmont, CA: Wadsworth (Chap.5).

Jerome, A., & Fredericksen, L. (1992). Diet mate: Computerized self-management for weight control. *Behavior Therapist, 15,* 257-259.

# EXERCISE 4.1

## CORRECTING DISTORTIONS

For each statement below, determine if it is judgmental, one-sided, an overgeneralization, conjecture, or some combination of these. Then rewrite the statement in the space provided so that is nonjudgmental, balanced, and specific.

1. A student's statement about a roommate: "I knew her in high school and she was such a snob. The people she hung out with were so stuck up. They even dressed alike."

    This statement reflects the distortion:

    _____

    Correction:

    _____
    _____
    _____

2. A professor's comment: "I swear nobody in that class cares about learning; they're only interested in their grades. Why, there's this one student who asks about grades every week."

    This statement reflects the distortion:

    _____

    Correction:

    _____
    _____
    _____

3. A boyfriend's comment to his girlfriend: "You mean you're staying in another Friday night to study! All you do anymore is study; you're turning into a real bookworm."

    This statement reflects the distortion:

    _____

    Correction:

    _____
    _____
    _____

4. A student's advice to another student: "I'm warning you, don't take a course with that professor. He gives athletes a real hard time. When I took his class, I almost failed."

This statement reflects the distortion:

_____

Correction:

_____

_____

_____

5. A student's reaction to an 'F' grade on a paper: "I'm going down the tubes fast. Maybe I should give up while I'm still ahead and drop the class."

This statement reflects the distortion:

_____

Correction:

_____

_____

_____

## EXERCISE 4.2

## IDENTIFYING METHODS FOR SELF-MANAGEMENT

The headings listed across the top of the chart describe different topics for self-management. For each of the headings, indicate whether or not it describes a change that would be of benefit to you by circling **yes** or **no** under each heading. Then, for each **yes** answer, place a check mark in the box that corresponds to a method you might use to initiate this change.

| | Increase Positive Affect | Increase Positive Thinking | Increase Goal-oriented Behaviors | Improve Study Habits | Manage Time Better | Decrease Procras-tination | Enhance Relation-ships | Raise Self-esteem |
|---|---|---|---|---|---|---|---|---|
| **METHODS** | Yes No | Yes No | Yes No | Yes No | Yes No | Yes No | Yes No | Yes No |
| **Reframing** | | | | | | | | |
| **Coping** | | | | | | | | |
| **Progressive Relaxation** | | | | | | | | |
| **Deep Breathing** | | | | | | | | |
| **Exercise** | | | | | | | | |
| **Good Nutrition** | | | | | | | | |
| **Act as If** | | | | | | | | |
| **Behavior Modification** | | | | | | | | |
| **Imagined Rehearsal** | | | | | | | | |
| **Thought Stopping** | | | | | | | | |
| **Correct Distortions** | | | | | | | | |
| **Visualization** | | | | | | | | |

**EXERCISE 4.3**

**IDENTIFYING METHODS FOR CHANGE**

1. Identify an area of potential growth in your life that you have not begun to work on yet. Briefly describe it.

   _____

   _____

   _____

2. Describe the ABCs that would need to be in place to bring this potential to fruition. What kinds of feelings, behaviors, and thoughts would need to occur?

   _____

   _____

   _____

3. What ABC component might serve as the trigger to begin this growth process? Explain.

   _____

   _____

   _____

4. Choose a method(s) from this chapter that could be used "to pull the trigger" and get the process started.

   _____

   _____

   _____

5. Explain why you think this method might help.

   _____

   _____

   _____

# EXERCISE 4.4

## JOURNAL PROJECT

1. Follow through with the plan developed in Exercise 4.3 by attempting to implement the steps you identified.

2. Keep a journal in which you record the progress made as well as the obstacles encountered.

3. Review your journal after one month and determine if you are satisfied with your progress. If not satisfied, what can you do to improve? What other methods described in this chapter might you use? Explain.

## EXERCISE 4.5

## IMPROVING VISUALIZATION

The following exercises not only improve our imaginative skills by increasing our ability to visualize, they are fun to do and take only a few minutes. Set a timer for Chalkboard Letters at four minutes, for Lightbulb Glow at five minutes, and for Room Objects at six minutes. Each time you practice these exercises, you will find that the image remains in your "mind's eye" a bit longer than the previous time.

**Chalkboard Letters**

Get yourself in a relaxed state. Close your eyes and imagine the letter 'A' on a chalkboard. Try to make the picture in your mind's eye as vivid as possible. When successful, add the letter 'B' and picture 'A' and 'B' next to each other. Keep adding letters picturing the entire group together. See if you can increase the number of letters in your imagination with each practice.

**Lightbulb**

Relax, close your eyes and imagine a dim lightbulb suspended in front of you. In your imagination, try to make the bulb glow brighter and then dimmer. Alternate between bright and dim five times. Now imagine the bulb growing brighter and brighter so that it illuminates everything. Then make it grow dimmer gradually until it is turned off. Practice this exercise each day trying to improve the vividness and clarity of the image with each session.

**Room Objects**

Stand in the middle of a room and for one minute look around and observe everything in it. Then shut your eyes and try to picture the room and everything in it. Name out loud every object you can "see" in your imagination that is in the room. Open your eyes and check your accuracy. How many objects did you identify correctly? How many did you miss? Close your eyes again and try to improve your accuracy. Repeat this exercise in a different room each day, until you can identify more objects correctly.

This exercise was adapted from Lazarus (1977) pp. 44 - 45.

# 5

To be a college student means to become a self-motivated learner. As learners, we listen, we question, we communicate. We try to remember, understand, integrate, and apply new knowledge.

# CASE STUDY

Before reading Chapter 5, read the case study in the box below. After completing the chapter, analyze the case study by following steps 1 through 4.

STEP 1　Explain why Ernie was *motivated away* from school work before he changed his study routine.

STEP 2　AFFECT:　Identify feelings that led Ernie to be *motivated away* from academics.

BEHAVIOR:　Identify the behaviors that indicate he was *motivated away* from academics.

COGNITION: Identify any thoughts or beliefs that led Ernie to be motivated away from academics. Are any of these cognitions distorted or dysfunctional? If so, explain.

STEP 3　Which ABC component listed in STEP 2 was the trigger of the firing order? Describe the firing order. If there is a downward ABC spiral, describe it.

STEP 4　What methods or techniques described in this text could have been used to change the trigger and thereby increase Ernie's motivation toward academics? What techniques would alter the other two components?

"Either you've got it or you don't — street smarts I've got, academic smarts I don't," Ernie would say. Growing up, Ernie thought studious types were bores. He never imagined himself a student, but when the opportunity to go to college presented itself, Ernie thought he'd give it a shot. "A college degree is a sure ticket to a high-paying job," he explained to one of his buddies who was puzzled by Ernie's decision to go to school.

Academic life didn't come easy for Ernie — it was a stressful series of deadlines. Just before exams, he would plow through his readings a second time, marking the few remaining spaces that hadn't seen his yellow highlighter. When a paper was due, he would stay up all night if he had to. A push on the computer spell check button was Ernie's idea of revision. One day, a professor asked him, "Why are you in college?" Surprised by the question, Ernie wasn't sure what to say. "Same as anyone else — to get a job," he mumbled. "Do yourself a favor and forget the job; educate yourself first," the professor responded. " You are your career! If you're interested, I've got a book that might help."

*You are your career.* Ernie was struck by the idea. The next day, he asked the professor for the book. "*Learning Strategies*?" he asked in a quizzical way. His professor just smiled and said, "give it a try." That evening Ernie used a study technique from the book, but after an hour, got annoyed with it. He didn't think it was worth it. Then he got a 'B' on the exam, used the method again, and after earning another high grade, used it regularly. At first he thought this systematic study routine was awkward and time consuming, but with each high exam grade, it became easier. Ernie was amazed with his grades, and even more so with the change in him. By the end of that semester, for the first time in Ernie's college career, he was excited to think of himself as having "academic smarts."

## TO BE A COLLEGE STUDENT

I dwell in possibilities -

Emily Dickinson (1830-1886)
American poet

## WHAT DOES IT MEAN TO BE A COLLEGE STUDENT?

To be a college student means to become a *self-motivated learner.* As learners, we listen, we question, we communicate. We try to remember, understand, integrate, and apply new knowledge. Not only do we become increasingly competent in our particular discipline, we also broaden our thinking about ourselves and the world around us. As if all this were not enough, to do any of it effectively, we must think critically, read carefully, and write coherently.

As we move from high school to college, we discover quickly that we have moved from a teaching to a learning environment (Walter & Siebert, 1993), where the responsibility to learn is placed on us. The sooner we learn how to manage ourselves as students, the sooner we begin to see learning, not as drudgery, but as discovery. When this happens, all kinds of new and exciting *possibilities* begin to emerge.

## ABCs THAT SPELL ACADEMIC SUCCESS

A task fundamental to success in college is meeting the challenge of feeling, acting, and thinking like a successful student. Being "bright" is recognizing (C) our strengths as well as our weaknesses and feeling comfortable (A) enough with ourselves to take the steps (B) necessary to reach our full academic potential.

Although extenuating circumstances sometimes influence academic performance, most students who do well academically do so because they are positively motivated to learn. Since our motivation toward learning is something we have control over, we control the quality of our education. This chapter will focus on ABC characteristics that motivate students toward and away from learning. Chapter 10 will provide more detail on how to maintain academic motivation and how to regain it when it is lost. Since thinking and learning are so closely tied, we will begin our discussion with cognition.

## Cognition and Motivation for Learning

We all have beliefs (C) about our capabilities as learners and some ideas about the capabilities of other students. Consider how the following beliefs might influence a student's academic performance:

- There's little benefit or value in my being a good student.

- The costs of being a good student are just too high.

- I'm not a good student. I can't do the work.

These beliefs about learning are expressed indirectly in everyday language or by thoughts such as:

- I don't see why I have to do this assignment. (There's little benefit.)

- I would never take that professor — she assigns homework on the computer and embarrasses students in class. (The cost is too high.)

- I can't hack this class. (I can't do it.)

Such beliefs will motivate students away from a particular course or assignment. They also seem to reflect a preconceived notion that academic work should never be difficult or inconvenient. The more beliefs we have like these, the more negatively motivated we will be with respect to academics. Students who do not believe they have what it takes to learn or believe they have little to gain from learning will not give academic tasks a high priority.

Beliefs about what it means to be a student are a powerful influence on academic performance. Beliefs that promote positive motivation toward academics would include:

- There is value in learning. (There are benefits.)

- Taking risks and paying the price in order to learn are worth it. (The cost is worth it.)

- I can be a successful student. (I can do it.)

A potent force in becoming a successful student is believing it is possible to become one. To become *self-motivated learners*, we work at thinking in positive terms about our role as students and the tasks associated with learning. What separates the positively motivated student from others is the belief that the hard work (e.g. rewriting papers, hours in the library, following a study schedule, etc.) is worth the effort, even in the face of disappointments.

## Distorted Thinking and Motivation for Academics

Much has already been said in Chapter 3 about how distortions in thinking can interfere with positive motivation in general. The same principles apply to motivation for academics in particular. If we are not motivated toward learning but would like to be, we need to avoid thinking about academics in distorted terms. Cognitive distortions about classwork, tests, professors, and studying can interfere with academic accomplishment. Mind reading or blaming our professors or other students; catastrophizing about how much work we have to do; using global labels or polarized thinking with respect to ourselves or our courses promote a negative view of academic pursuits.

The *imperative should* is perhaps the greatest contributor to negative motivation with respect to a particular course. When we hold a list of ironclad rules about how our instructors *should*, *ought to*, or *must* be, we are bound to be disappointed time and again. We can get an idea of how many shoulds we subscribe to with respect to our instructors by checking off the statements we agree with below.

_____ Instructors should be interesting.
_____ Instructors should never keep students late.
_____ Instructors should have all the answers.
_____ Instructors should not call on students.

____ Instructors should not give a lot of work.
____ Instructors should motivate their students.
____ Instructors should be entertaining.
____ Instructors should not lecture.
____ Instructors should care about their students.
____ Instructors should be personable.

No doubt it would be nice if all of our instructors measured up to our personal list of shoulds, but how would we like our instructors to continually measure us against the list below?

Students should make the class interesting.
Students should not prepare to leave class until dismissed.
Students should always be prepared for class.
Students should participate in class without being called upon.
Students should want to work hard.
Students should be self-motivated.
Students should make teaching enjoyable.
Students should be attentive to lectures.
Students should care about their teachers.
Students should be personable.

The more rules we have about other people's behavior, the more we are apt to become angry or frustrated when our demands for conformity are not met. When these feelings are harbored by students or professors, the learning process is compromised. To avoid paying the emotional price that comes with should statements, we might say: *"I would prefer that..."* instead of *"should."*

## Dysfunctional Beliefs and Motivation For Academics

Many cognitive distortions about school are rooted in dysfunctional beliefs about college instructors. Below are some common but *inaccurate assumptions* (referred to as myths by Walter and Siebert, 1993) that some students make about college instructors:

**Assumption:** *I can't learn from an instructor I don't like.*

This statement reflects one of the most common dysfunctional beliefs (determinism) among students of all ages. It is more accurately stated: *"I won't learn from an instructor I don't like."* All too often we say *"I can't,"* when in reality we mean, *"I won't."* Without question it is more difficult to learn from people we do not like, but if we were offered $20,000 to learn from them, *difficult* would become *easy* and *"I can't"* would become *"I will."* We may prefer learning from someone we like, but when we say or think *"I can't,"* we mentally inhibit ourselves. So, if we ever find learning from a teacher we do not like difficult, we might make it easier by considering how much more than $20,000 a college degree is worth.

**Assumption:** *Professors are trained to be effective teachers.*

The reality is that few college instructors ever took courses or received formal training on teaching strategies and techniques. Emphasis in graduate school is generally on scholarly research, not teaching. Therefore, students are bound to encounter poor teaching, but they have the responsibility to learn nonetheless.

**Assumption:** *Professors will be nonjudgmental and unbiased in presenting material.*

While this is an accurate statement for many teachers, it is not true for all. Some teachers may believe that they have discovered ultimate truth, and see no point in discussing opposing views. It is necessary, therefore, to carefully evaluate not only what we read, but also what we hear from instructors in class. A "scholarly" presentation does not mean it has to be accepted uncritically.

**Assumption:**  *Professors have all the answers.*

It would be nice if this were true. Then, we would not have to work at finding answers ourselves. As intelligent as instructors may be, they are not always experts on every topic they teach. Their advanced degree may be in a specialty area with only limited connection to other aspects of their discipline. Most instructors have no problem admitting when they do not have an answer to a question. Yet, when a professor does not answer questions to our satisfaction, it is best to research the topic on our own, rather than use it as an excuse to become disenchanted with the instructor.

**Assumption:**  *Professors personally believe and accept the material they discuss in class.*

Because of time constraints, particularly in introductory courses, instructors must be selective in choosing theories, topics, and ideas to discuss in class. They may even present views they personally oppose. Some instructors play the "devil's advocate" and argue a position to challenge students' thinking and stimulate discussion. If we are ever confused or upset by this, a simple solution is to ask teachers for their personal views. We may not get the answer we want, but at least we have been assertive enough to ask. Whatever the professor's position, it is our responsibility to determine where we stand, after weighing the relevant facts.

The more realistic we are about professors, the more our academic decisions will be guided by accurate information. Also, negative affect will be less likely to interfere with our learning. As Walter and Siebert (1993) point out, myths create problems because disappointment and disengagement frequently follow from false expectations.

### Beliefs that Interfere with Listening

Certain beliefs can interfere with learning because they diminish our motivation to listen to what is being said. We may hear a class lecture or discussion, but actually miss the main points because we assume we know what the instructor is about to say. Our prejudgments can lead us to tune out the message altogether or reject it before considering its merit. All of us have witnessed politicians disagreeing with one another before listening long enough to understand what is being said. The same thing can occur in the classroom when we form premature judgments about a point of view being expressed.

We may have such strong beliefs about a subject that we refuse to listen to ideas that do not fit neatly with what we believe to be true. It is easy to listen to messages that confirm our beliefs and to dismiss messages that are inconsistent with our own point of view (Fisher, 1992).

Unless we consciously attend to information that is communicated to us, we do not process it. To enhance our listening skills, we need to make a concerted effort to become *focused listeners* by consciously directing our attention to the message. We reserve judgment and try to understand the speaker's perspective by mentally outlining what was said. Finally, we refrain from screening out new ideas and work at keeping our minds open to different perspectives.

## Cognitions That Motivate To and Fro: An Example

Two different perspectives on what it means to be a student are illustrated in the following example.

> Anthony and Joe are good friends with much in common. They are both first-semester sophomores; they have the same friends; they live in the same dorm; they even have the same cumulative index. Recently, Anthony has begun to think (C) differently about school. He decided (C) to find something of interest in each of his classes so that he will be more motivated to study. During lectures, he tries to figure out (C) what the professor is emphasizing. He also tries to think (C) of questions to ask in class so that the discussion moves in a direction that interests him. Time goes quickly now because instead of anticipating (C) when class will end, he is genuinely curious (C) about some of the course material. Anthony is beginning to see (C) his efforts pay off and believes (C) that with some tutoring he will be able to improve his grades this semester.
>
> Other students, including Joe, think that part of their role is to bad-mouth professors and complain about the work. Joe is in the same classes as Anthony, but Joe believes (C) that most of the classes are a waste of time. He is bored during lectures. Although he knows (C) that class would be more interesting if he participated, he thinks (C) that he

**137**

has nothing worthwhile to say. Besides, he thinks (C) that students who participate in class are "nerds." Joe believes (C) his only chance to raise his grades will be next semester when he signs up for easy courses or takes professors who grade "fairly" and do not expect so much from their students.

The way these two students think about themselves as students and the beliefs that they hold about learning will have a lot to do with their level of motivation and achievement. Anthony's cognitions would motivate him toward learning, Joe's away from it.

## Managing Motivation: Changing Cognition

Some important points should be noted if we want to be positively motivated as learners:

- We need to recognize how our thinking influences our motivation toward academics.

- We need to think of learning and course work in relatively positive terms.

- We need to be able to change thoughts that deter us from learning.

Thinking like a successful student is usually a prerequisite to becoming one. Yet, it is just as important to be realistic about the work involved. Being a successful learner means considering the benefits as well as sacrifices associated with the learning process. It also involves planning (C) ways to overcome obstacles and learning (C) from mistakes. Being motivated toward academics requires strengthening beliefs in the value of learning as well as in ourselves, while eliminating cognitive distortions and dysfunctional beliefs.

## Affect and Motivation for Learning

If, in the process of learning, we feel excited or happy (A), we will want to be involved in that process. If we feel overly anxious or angry (A), we will not want to be involved. When excited over a new insight from an assigned reading or aroused by an impassioned lecturer, we are experiencing positive motivation for learning. Anxiety associated with homework assignments or anger toward professors who do not lecture well can promote negative motivation.

Most college professors feel "turned on" (A) by their scholarly work and communicate the joy (A) of discovery to their students. However, some have become bored or unhappy (A) with teaching and may communicate this dissatisfaction. The impact of their affective states on their motivation and ours is only a problem if we do not know how to manage our motivation.

### Affect That Motivates To and Fro: An Example

The positive and negative influence of affect on motivation is readily seen in the way people handle stress. Stress is a label many students use to describe a variety of emotions and sensations experienced in school. *Managing stress* is, in part, managing the feelings associated with it. When managed, stress can be used as a source of energy that contributes positively to the achievement of our goals. Allowing stress to escalate can interfere with our performance by motivating us negatively. The two students experiencing stress during a math final described below illustrate this.

> Frank is so "hyper" (A) that he jumps right into the exam before reading the directions through to the end. Breathing rapidly with his foot tapping a mile a minute, he rushes through the exam. Given all the tension (A), he doesn't even notice that he hit the wrong button on the calculator and that his writing is becoming illegible. Because Frank is so anxious (A), he just wants to get the test over with. As a result, he doesn't check his answers, and is the first student out the door.

> As Tracy looks at the exam she begins to feel anxious (A), but figures a bit of tension (A) will keep her alert during the test. Relaxing (A) for a moment, she carefully looks over all the questions in order to decide where to begin. After completing most of the exam, she gets stuck on a problem and notices time is running short. She begins to tense up (A), but calms (A) herself. As she marks off the difficult

**139**

problem, she reminds herself that she has already solved most of the problems and can return to this one later. Completing her last answer with fifteen minutes to spare, Tracy is tempted to hand in her paper without checking it. However, she decides to use her excess energy (A) to review her answers and begins to feel good (A) because she knows she has made full use of the time allotted.

Often we fail to write the correct answer on an exam, not because we do not know it, but because we are too "stressed out" to think clearly. If we allow stress to mount unchecked, as in the first example, stress can interfere with our ability to perform well. When channeled in the direction of our goals, as in the second example, tension associated with stress can be converted into energy that is beneficial.

## Managing Motivation: Changing Affect

Affect (A) is an essential and powerful component of our academic motivation. The specific connection can be expressed as follows:

- Positive motivation increases for courses and course work we associate with positive affect.

- Negative motivation increases for courses and course work we associate with negative affect.

The task confronting students who desire to become positively motivated is to figure out how to get positive affect *in* and negative affect *out.*

**To get positive affect *in:***

- Imagine vividly short- and long-term payoffs for learning.

- Provide tangible rewards immediately after a learning task.

- Focus on payoffs for academic success, not penalties for "failure."

- Use positive self-talk to reinforce abilities.

- Recall past academic achievements.

**To get negative affect *out:***

- Change distortions about academics to specific, accurate, and balanced thoughts.

- Change dysfunctional beliefs or myths about academics by using the DIE Model.

- Interrupt thoughts that cause distress over academics immediately by using thought stopping.

- Practice relaxation in academic situations.

- Get plenty of rest on school nights.

## Behavior and Motivation for Learning

No one is either a good or bad student; nor is anyone always successful or always unsuccessful. Such simplistic labels and overgeneralizations are often used to distinguish between students who really want to learn and those who are less motivated.

Some rather obvious differences between more or less motivated students are seen in their behaviors. Just as professionals act in certain ways before they are considered for promotion, students who do well in college act in ways that enable them to get good grades and advance academically.

We all know students whose behaviors parallel one or more of the those listed below.

Participating in class

Keeping appointments with professors

Getting to class on time

Going to the library

Reading all assignments on time

Revising and proofreading papers

Taking notes in class

Handing in assignments on time

Following a study schedule

Asking questions in class

Meeting with academic advisors

Making excuses about missing classes

Purchasing the texts late in the semester

Slouching in the seat during class

Handing in assignments late

Whispering to others in class

Turning in papers with trim on computer printouts

Turning in papers without stapling the pages together

Missing appointments with professors

Walking out of class during a lecture

We can judge for ourselves which behaviors are those of a student motivated toward academics. In doing so, we will probably reach the same conclusions as our instructors because our actions say a lot about what we value. And, for better or worse, our behaviors make an impression on other people.

**Behaviors That Motivate To and Fro: An Example**

In addition to signaling to teachers whether or not we are positively motivated, behaviors can help increase positive motivation toward learning. The behaviors of the students described below will motivate them in two different directions.

Five minutes before class begins, Millicent takes her seat in the front row (B). Feeling relaxed, and with time to spare, she opens her notebook, fills in the date, begins to review her notes from the reading assignment, and jots down a few questions (B) she wants to raise in class. As class begins, Millicent leans forward a bit, positioning herself (B) in such a way that she can devote her full attention to the lecture. During class, she asks for clarification on any questions (B) she has. As the rest of the students are hustling to leave, Millicent sits for a minute to fill in her notes (B). Walking across campus she feels pretty good, knowing she has learned something new.

Caroline walks into class and hands the teacher an assignment (B) that was due the last class when she was out. After telling the professor her excuse, she slumps into her usual seat (B) in the back of the classroom and waits. As class begins, she whispers (B) to one of her friends, "Do you have a pen I can borrow?" Finally, she settles down, opens her notebook, and begins to doodle (B). At the end of class, she breathes a sigh of relief, packs her books (B) before the professor is finished talking, and realizes how anxious she is to get out the door.

Without knowing anything more about these two students, we might conclude from their behaviors that the first student is positively motivated toward class while the second is negatively motivated. We would probably be correct because our behavior not only reflects, but influences the direction in which we are motivated. Our body language, the way we take notes, and our level of participation will influence how we think and feel in that class. These feelings and thoughts will influence subsequent behaviors. So, if we are not positively motivated, it can be helpful to *act as if* we are because this can encourage positive thoughts and feelings to take hold.

## Managing Motivation: Changing Behaviors

Students who develop skills to enhance learning and take advantage of the resources available to them in college continually improve their academic performance and are generally less "stressed out." The remainder of this chapter outlines strategies for taking notes, reading and studying, preparing for and taking tests, writing and revision, as well as some general information on a very important resource — the computer. How do we get ourselves to do all this? One way has already been emphasized: think and feel in ways that promote the behaviors we want. Another way is to take the Nike advertising slogan seriously and, *Just Do It!* Applying the principles discussed in Chapter 4 will certainly make the doing easier. However, once we begin to experience the results from developing these skills, the built-in rewards will become self-evident.

## Study Habits

*Studying effectively* is more than mere recall of discrete facts; it involves an understanding, integration, and application of knowledge. It also requires that we organize our time, resources, and environment.

Learning material thoroughly enough to be recalled is a process that cannot be rushed. Cramming for tests creates stress and confusion, which prevents us from processing information accurately and achieving the grade of which we are capable.

Studies on learning and memory indicate that students who study systematically in short, well-spaced sessions learn more in less time than students who study "helter skelter" for long periods of time only before exams. Taking a fifteen-minute break with some small reward after each hour of studying works well for many students.

Some of us mistakenly associate studying for hours, propped up in bed with highlighter in hand, as a good study method. These behaviors need to change if we want study time to be time well spent. Behaviors that reflect more effective study habits include:

Sitting at a desk, table, or computer

Using a systematic method for studying, note taking, and revision

Using college resources (library, computer terminals, tutors, advisors, etc.)

Minimizing distractions

Following a study schedule

## Note Taking

Taking notes and reviewing them regularly increases attention, interest, and class participation. Students who take notes usually learn more from lectures and discussions and they have material to study for exams. Whether we are more comfortable taking notes in an outline or topic format, the following steps adapted from the *Cornell Note-taking System* will be useful.

### Preparation

Use a separate notebook for each class.

Bring it to class.

### Before Class

Review notes from the previous class.

### In Class

Date all class notes.

Draw a straight vertical line from the top to bottom of the page approximately three inches from the left-hand side.

Reserve the left-hand side for key words and study questions.

Use the right-hand side of the notebook page for detailed notes.

Leave the backside of all notebook pages blank for notes from other sources (readings, quizzes, etc.).

Use abbreviations when taking notes.

Note key words and summary statements during a lecture.

Copy anything the instructor writes on the board.

Jot down the name and author of books, articles, or page numbers cited in class for future research.

## After Class

Review, rewrite, and organize notes within one day after class.

Make up study questions from class notes and write them on the left-hand side of the notebook page next to the notes that will help answer the question.

Compare notes with those of other students in the class. Write down questions to ask the professor if anything is confusing or unclear.

## Before a Test

Cover up the right-hand side of notebook pages and try to answer all study questions without look-ing at notes.

## Outline Format for Notes

When taking notes using an *outline format*, main ideas and related material presented in class are organized into an outline as shown.

```
        Study questions                Notes
        and key words

  ┌──────────────────────────────────────────────────┐
  │              │  I. ABCs of Motivation to Learn    │
  │   ◯          │  A. Affect that Motivates          │
  │              │    1. Positive feelings motivate toward │
  │              │    2. Negative feelings motivate away   │
  │  What are the ABCs │  B. Behaviors that Motivate   │
  │  of a motivated    │    1. Participation in class  │
  │  learner?          │    2. Note taking             │
  │   ◯          │    3. Effective study habits       │
  │              │  C. Cognitions that Motivate       │
  │              │    1. I can do it                  │
  │              │    2. Learning pays off            │
  │              │    3. Price is worth it            │
  │              │ II. ABC Motivation Techniques      │
  │  ◯ Motivation│  A. Affect - relaxation            │
  │    techniques│  B. Behavior - behavior modification │
  │              │  C. Cognition - DIE Model          │
  └──────────────────────────────────────────────────┘
```

Note that the left-hand side of the page is used for study questions and key terms.

## Topic Format for Notes

When course material is not easily organized into an outline form, a *topic format* can be used in which notes are arranged by topic or theme. If the lecture or discussion diverts from the main topic while we are taking notes, we should drop down a quarter of a page and continue to take notes under a new heading such as "miscellaneous comments." (Just because a discussion or lecture digresses does not mean that the material is unimportant.) Once the discussion reverts to the main point, we merely return to the blank section to record notes. Study questions that correspond to each topic or theme can easily be generated after class.

### Reading and Studying for Exams Using SQ4R

In his book, *Cultural Literacy*, E. D. Hirsch (1987) points out that "reading and writing are cumulative skills; the more we read, the more necessary knowledge we gain for further reading" (p.28). That is, the more we read, the better readers we become. Students who like to read and read critically are better able to keep up with assignments and remember what they have read than those who do not. Their enjoyment of reading enables them to widen their vocabulary and develop stronger reading, thinking, writing, and communication skills.

Although the advantages of reading are many, some students do not read well, dislike it, and get discouraged with lengthy reading assignments. However, students who improve their reading skills eventually begin to enjoy it.

Students who want to improve their reading and study skills will find a method called *SQ4R* very useful. This method will also dramatically improve performance in class and on exams. The basic steps of SQ4R are:

### Survey

Survey each page of the chapter to get an idea of what the chapter is about and what important points are being emphasized. Look over illustrations, diagrams, tables, examples, pictures subtitles, introductions, etc. If there is a summary, read it carefully.

### Question

Generate questions from the surveyed chapter by changing the first sentence, subtitle or main idea of each paragraph or section into a question. Be sure the question cannot be answered by a simple "yes" or "no." Do this for every paragraph or section of the chapter to be read during the study session.

### Read

Read to answer the questions. By doing this, attention will be focused on the important details of each section of the chapter. Read each paragraph purposefully to gain answers to questions that are likely to reappear at quiz or exam time.

### W(R)ite

Write the answer to each question posed. Save the questions and answers for review before a quiz or exam.

### Recite

Recite aloud in your own words the answers to the questions that were generated from the chapter. Do not merely memorize the text. This way, we quickly find out whether we comprehended what was read.

### Review

Review all questions and answers before class and before exams.

When we use SQ4R, we ask and answer questions and find out to what extent we have comprehended what we have read. Posing questions before reading provides us with a motivation for reading: *to find the answers!* We are less likely to gloss over what we read because we become active, rather than passive readers and learners. An added benefit is the ready-made study guide that results from the questions and answers produced.

Many students are not motivated to recite their answers because it places them in a testing situation and they are afraid to find out that they did not comprehend what they read. Nevertheless, it is better to know what we have missed *before* rather than *during* the exam. Therefore, if ever tempted to skip this step, we should consider the consequences. Motivation and our ability to handle discomfort are key.

### Preparing For and Taking Tests

Students who routinely use the note-taking and SQ4R methods described above are continually preparing themselves for tests. They already have much of the material necessary to create a practice test.

### <u>Creating a Practice Test</u>

One of the most effective ways to review for an exam is to take a *practice test* as if it were a real test. Here are the steps:

1. Gather questions generated from notes and readings.

2. Create a comprehensive practice test that would be similar to the actual test.

3. Find a quiet spot and take the test without referring to notes or texts.

4. Check answers and score the test.

5. Create another practice test; include questions answered poorly or incorrectly on the previous test.

6. Continue this process for each practice test until the answers are correct.

## Taking the Test

When we are prepared for tests, we usually do well. However, attention during exam time to the following *test-taking strategies* can help.

1. Read the instructions carefully. Pay attention to key-words and phrases in the question such as: *provide an example, illustrate, relate, define, contrast, compare,* etc.

2. Answer the question asked, *not* the one preferred.

3. Allot a specific amount of time for each section of the exam and keep track of the time.

4. Organize answers to essay questions *before* beginning to write. Begin with an effective introduction and end with a forceful conclusion. The body of the essay should integrate details from lectures, notes, texts, etc.

5. Leave enough time at the end of the exam to check for *spelling, punctuation, coherence, completeness,* and *legibility.*

6. *Relax.* Thorough preparation is usually enough to reduce test anxiety, but if it is a problem, relaxation, and thought stopping techniques are helpful in avoiding an attack of the "nerves."

## Writing: A Process of Exploration Through Revision

In the words of William Faulkner, writing "well" means: "Read, read, read...Just like a carpenter who works as an apprentice and studies the master, read!" The notion that good writers are first good readers is not a novel idea. The ancient Greek and Roman writers were keenly aware that substantive writing was a product of extensive

**151**

reading. Whether it involves exploring the ideas or styles of other writers, researching a topic, or organizing our own thoughts on a subject, *effective writers* begin with an exploration, and this exploration continues throughout the process of revision.

Before we begin writing, we usually read about and reflect on our topic, allowing for a free flow of ideas. As we explore what we want to write, we jot down ideas. Then, we organize our ideas, perhaps using an outline, and write our first draft. However, the *real* writing begins with revision. Hemingway went so far as to say that "the first draft of anything is sh--."

Many students mistake proofreading for revision. **Proofreading** is reading to correct errors in grammar and spelling in the final draft. Since most college students know the mechanics of the writing process, we will focus on the process of revision as a way to transform *writing thoughts* into *thoughtful writing.*

**Revision** is precisely what the word suggests — a *re*-vision — a process by which we take another look at our work, view it critically as the reader, and alter it in accordance with our new view of it. It is *rethinking* and *rewriting* each draft to incorporate this new vision of our work. Experienced writers revise as they write and never consider the first draft to be the last. They rework their own writing, making conceptual and organizational changes as ideas emerge in the writing process. As such, revision aids learning, for new ideas have to be integrated with other material.

A polished piece of writing takes time and sometimes we may be pressed for time. Even so, we should be sure that our paper is communicating the intended message to the reader before handing in the final draft. Effective writers have a clear purpose in mind, and part of that purpose is to communicate and maintain the interest of the reader. Mitchell Ivers (1991) points out in his book *Good Writing* that *effective writers* take on the *pain in revision* so as to save readers that pain in reading. He claims that "looking at your writing with the cold and ruthless eye of a stranger is the only way to see what needs to be edited — edited in as well as out" (p.161). Having a friend or advisor read our paper and asking them the following questions can help us in this process:

- What is the main idea of the paper?

- Is the main idea clearly communicated in the *first paragraph*?

- Does the paper adequately answer all of your questions?

- Is the final paragraph a good *conclusion*?

- Did you stumble over any words or phrases?

- What is your overall opinion of the paper?

- What would improve the paper?

At the very least, we should read our paper aloud and answer these questions for ourselves before handing a paper to a professor to evaluate. The checklist for revision of essays and research papers in the exercise section of this chapter is recommended for students who prefer a more comprehensive and systematic approach to revision.

## Computer Literacy

Because the computer can perform many tasks very quickly, it has become a requirement for basic literacy in the world of academe and work. McFarlan, a Harvard business school professor, points outs that the ability to use a computer will be a "prerequisite — like reading — that you'll just be expected to be able to do" (as cited by McKeown, 1988, p. 7).

We need not, however, be a computer science major to be computer literate. *Computer literacy* is "an understanding of what a computer can and cannot do and ability to make the computer do what is desired" (McKeown, 1988, p. 6). It involves learning enough about the computer to use it as a tool to make our jobs easier and to expand our minds.

The speed and accuracy of the computer can be a real asset to students. Not only can computers store information that can be readily retrieved, it can expedite the process of writing and revising papers as well as perform calculations. Many libraries now have computerized catalogs where students can browse through library holdings by sitting at a computer terminal. Several colleges have indexes such as ERIC (for education), PsycLit (for psychology), ABI/INFORM (for business and management), Life Sciences Collection, General Science Index, Newspaper Abstracts, and a host of others. These indexes are searched to find journal articles relevant for a research topic by merely entering a combination of terms on the computer that specify the area of interest.

As powerful and useful as the computer is, it is no substitute for the human mind. Many a student who has relied solely on a computer to proofread a paper has found out the hard way that grades and learning suffer when the computer is used in place of their own critical judgments. A computer does precisely what it is told to do by us — no more, no less. However, inaccuracies are pervasive when we do not appreciate the computer's limitations as well as its uses.

While an introduction to computers is beyond the scope of this text, students who wish to increase their knowledge of computers would be well advised to enroll in a computer course in the first year of college. An understanding of the applications of mainframe and personal computers to general college studies and specific academic majors can increase a student's chances for success. Today, computers are so essential in dealing with so many day-to-day issues in college and the work force that computer literacy has become a must.

## SELF-MANAGEMENT: A PREREQUISITE TO LEARNING

If we are not a self-motivated learner and decide we really want to be one, we first need to think, feel, and behave in ways that will make this goal a reality. Developing personal and academic self-management skills will be essential. While not an easy task, acquiring such skills is something we are all capable of and the rewards are well worth the effort.

## KEY WORDS AND CONCEPTS

computer literacy
Cornell Note-taking System
effective writers
focused listeners
imperative should(s)
inaccurate assumptions (about instructors)
managing stress
outline format
practice test
proofreading
revision
self-motivated learner
studying effectively
SQ4R
test-taking strategies
topic format

## SUGGESTED READINGS AND TAPES

### Student Motivation and Beliefs about Learning

Walter, T., & Siebert, A. (1993). *Student success.* Fort Worth, TX: Holt, Rinehart, Winston (Chap. 10).

### Study Habits and Test Taking

Ellis, D. (1991). *Becoming a master student.* Rapid City, SD: College Survival Inc. (Chaps. 4 & 6).

### Note Taking

Ellis, D. (1991). *Becoming a master student.* Rapid City, SD: College Survival Inc. (Chap. 5).

Starke, M.C. (1993). *Strategies for college success.* Englewood Cliffs, NJ: Prentice-Hall (Chap. 4).

### Writing

Crews, F., & Schor, S. (1985). *The borzoi handbook for writers.* New York: Alfred A. Knopf, Inc.

Gardner, J. N., & Jewler, A.J. (1992). *Your college experience: Strategies for success.* Belmont, CA: Wadsworth (Chap. 9).

Ivers, M. (1991). *The Random House guide to good writing.* New York: Random House.

### Computer Literacy

McKeown, P.G. (1988). *Living with computers.* New York: Harcourt Brace Jovanovich, Inc.

Starke, M.C. (1993). *Strategies for college success.* Englewood Cliffs, NJ: Prentice-Hall (Appendix).

The object of this exercise is to determine the course(s) for which you are positively or negatively motivated this semester. List all your courses in the left-hand column. Under **AFFECT**, rate the amount of anxiety, anger, and boredom experienced for each class on a scale of 1 to 5, with 1 being the lowest. Under **COGNITION**, rate how important the course is to you and your chances for success. Note that the scale for **COGNITION** is reversed, 1 being the highest (most important) and 5 being the lowest (least important). After completing the ratings, add subtotal A to subtotal C for each course and put that number in the final total square for each course. The courses with the highest totals are very likely the ones for which you are less positively motivated in comparison to the others.

**AFFECT**

(1 = Least  5 = Most)

**COGNITION**

(5 = Least  1 = Most)

| COURSE | ANXIETY AROUSED | ANGER AROUSED | BOREDOM EXPERIENCED | SUBTOTAL A | IMPORTANCE OF COURSE | CHANCES FOR SUCCESS | SUBTOTAL C | FINAL TOTAL |
|--------|-----------------|---------------|---------------------|------------|----------------------|---------------------|------------|-------------|
|        |                 |               |                     |            |                      |                     |            |             |
|        |                 |               |                     |            |                      |                     |            |             |
|        |                 |               |                     |            |                      |                     |            |             |
|        |                 |               |                     |            |                      |                     |            |             |
|        |                 |               |                     |            |                      |                     |            |             |

## EXERCISE 5.2

## CHECKLIST FOR TEST PREPARATION AND TEST TAKING

For each of the following, check the appropriate box to indicate whether or not you typically prepare for and take tests as described.

| Yes | No | Prior to the Exam |
|---|---|---|
| ____ | ____ | I review all notes, reading and homework assignments, etc. |
| ____ | ____ | I make up a practice test from class notes and other materials and quiz myself. |
| ____ | ____ | I answer the practice quiz questions without looking at my notes. |
| ____ | ____ | I refine my answers to quiz questions. |
| ____ | ____ | I use SQ4R or some other systematic study method to review reading assignments. |
| ____ | ____ | I take short breaks between study sessions. |
| ____ | ____ | I follow a weekly study schedule. |
| ____ | ____ | I get plenty of sleep the night before an exam. |

| Yes | No | During the Exam |
|---|---|---|
| ____ | ____ | I read the instructions and questions on the exam carefully before I begin. |
| ____ | ____ | I ask the instructor to clarify questions that I do not understand. |
| ____ | ____ | I determine how I will schedule my time for each part of the exam before I begin. |
| ____ | ____ | I leave myself some time at the end of the exam to review my answers. |
| ____ | ____ | I outline answers to essay questions before I begin to write. |

| Yes | No | |
|-----|-----|---|
| ____ | ____ | I make sure that my answers to essay questions have an introductory and concluding paragraph. |
| ____ | ____ | I try to write legibly. |
| ____ | ____ | I am careful about spelling, grammar, and punctuation. |
| ____ | ____ | If I begin to get nervous on an exam, I use relaxation techniques to calm myself down. |

If you answered **yes** to the majority of items on both parts of the checklist (prior to the exam and during the exam), you should have few problems on exams. However, if you answered **no** to three or more of the items in either section, you could probably improve your test grades dramatically by incorporating more of these strategies into your study and test-taking routine.

# EXERCISE 5.3

## CHECKLIST FOR REVISION OF ESSAYS AND TERM PAPERS

Effective writers take into account a critical reader. The questions posed below can be thought of as questions a critical reader (your instructor perhaps) will ask when reading (and perhaps grading) your paper. For your next essay or research paper, read the first draft a few times, asking yourself the questions below. (You will find it helpful to make notations in the margins of your draft.)

**Yes**      **No**

_____      _____      Does the introduction try to interest the reader in the topic or thesis?

_____      _____      Is the purpose of the paper clearly stated in the introduction?

_____      _____      Is strong evidence, research, or a solid argument used to support the thesis or main idea?

_____      _____      Are important terms defined or explained?

_____      _____      Have the obvious disagreements with the thesis been addressed and refuted in the paper?

_____      _____      Does each paragraph have unity?

_____      _____      Are there transitions between paragraphs?

_____      _____      Do all sentences and paragraphs contribute to the theme or purpose of the paper?

_____      _____      Is the language of the paper appropriate for the audience and purpose for which it was written?

_____      _____      Have inappropriate abbreviations and colloquial phrases that detract from the paper been eliminated?

| Yes | No | |
|-----|----|---|
| ____ | ____ | When read aloud, do the words and sentences flow smoothly? |
| ____ | ____ | Does sentence structure vary throughout the paper? |
| ____ | ____ | Do sentences begin with different words to enhance the paper's readability? |
| ____ | ____ | Has language that sounds too choppy, repetitive, or exaggerated been corrected? |
| ____ | ____ | Are there enough examples to help illustrate the important points? |
| ____ | ____ | Does the conclusion logically follow from the material previously presented? |
| ____ | ____ | Has new information been avoided in the concluding paragraph? |
| ____ | ____ | Is the format for quotations correct? |
| ____ | ____ | Is the format for references correct? |
| ____ | ____ | Does the title of the paper capture the essence of the paper? |
| ____ | ____ | Are the margins, headings, etc. aligned properly? |
| ____ | ____ | Overall, is the final draft the most attractive presentation of the paper that can be provided? |

Negative answers to the questions will serve as a guide for rewriting parts of your paper. After revising the first draft, reread it using the checklist. If your goal is to get an 'A' on the paper, continue this process until you are satisfied with the revisions. Be sure to proofread the final revision carefully and then make corrections.

## EXERCISE 5.4

## LEARNING AND STUDYING APPLICATIONS

1. Read a textbook chapter and apply SQ4R. Do not form questions that can be answered by a simple **yes** or **no**. Also, be sure that the answers to the questions you generate are in your own words.

2. Use one of the note-taking methods in one of your classes. After revising your notes and generating some study questions, type your notes and questions in the format of the note-taking method you used.

3. Following the steps for creating a practice test, design a practice test for one of your courses. Take the test, grade it, and make corrections where applicable.

4. Using the checklist for revision of essays and research papers on pages 160 through 161, revise one of your papers. Compare the first draft with your editorial notations to the revised paper. The revised paper should reflect substantive improvements as a result of checking it against the questions on the checklist. (If you are not currently writing a paper for any of your classes, revise a paper you wrote previously.)

## 6

The concept of time has long intrigued poets, philosophers, and scientists alike. "Time is a measure of motion" and all change and motion occurs "in time," Aristotle once said.

# CASE STUDY

Before reading Chapter 6, read the case study below. After completing the chapter, analyze the case study by following steps 1 through 4.

STEP 1    What evidence is there that Arlene has a time management problem?

STEP 2    AFFECT:    Identify the feelings (emotions and sensations) that are contributing to Arlene's time management problem.

BEHAVIOR:   Identify the behaviors that are contributing to the problem.

COGNITION: What values are reflected in Arlene's behaviors? Do these values relate to her goal?

STEP 3    What key ABC components need to change for Arlene to manage her time and reach her goal? Explain your answer.

STEP 4    How can these changes be brought about?

Arlene says that she places great value on her education. Her goal this semester is to earn a high grade point average. At mid-terms, she had low grades, but she thinks she can raise her grades if her professors are more fair-minded in marking her tests. A typical day for Arlene follows:

It is 10 a.m. The alarm clock is ringing and Arlene rolls over and hits the snooze button. Ten minutes pass, the alarm rings again, and Arlene, still tired, turns it off. Twenty minutes later she gets up, showers, dresses, grabs a bite to eat, and makes it to class a few minutes late. Catching her breath, she takes her seat and anxiously asks another student what assignments were to be read. As she skims through the chapters, she feels a bit nervous and thinks, "I just hope I am not called on." While the class is talking about the readings, Arlene tunes out the discussion and thinks about her plans for the weekend. By the middle of the class, she is so bored that at one point she almost dozes off. After class Arlene had planned to catch up on her coursework, but she is too exhausted from staying out late the night before. So instead, she takes a nap. She had scheduled an appointment with one of her professors just before the class, but waking up too late to keep her appointment, she is now embarrassed to go to class. So she skips it and joins her friends at the mall.

#  TIME MANAGEMENT

When to the sessions of sweet silent thought
I summon up remembrances of things past,
I sigh the lack of many a thing I sought,
And with old woes new wail my dear time's waste.

William Shakespeare (1564-1616)
English poet, playwright

## TIME: A MEASURE OF CHANGE WE CAN MANAGE

The concept of time has long intrigued poets, philosophers, and scientists alike. "Time is a measure of motion" and all change and motion occurs "in time," Aristotle once said. For centuries thereafter, classical physics likened time to a container or receptacle in which change and motion occurred (Abel, 1976). A fifteenth century scientist, Nicolas of Cusa, was one of the first to voice what would later become the mainstay of modern scientific thought when he proposed that space and time are creations of the human mind (Jeans, 1981). The notion that we are the measurers of time and that we give time its meaning has become one of the most discussed topics of modern day philosophy and science.

So too in literature, time and its passage are often presented as creations of human choice and action. With the exception perhaps of love and death, few topics have sparked the poetic imagination more than the illusive nature of time. In Shakespeare's sonnet sequence (a few lines of which are cited above), the first grouping of poems allude to time repeatedly. As literary convention would have it, time is personified as the great enemy against which we have no defense. Youth and beauty are forewarned to guard against the future so as not to feel too harshly the cut of time's sharp scythe. Later in the sequence, a shift in emphasis occurs as the poet-speaker begins to explore ways to conquer the "injurious hand" of time. A protective shield is finally raised as the Bard's own poetry is elevated to immortal words that cannot be silenced by time's passage.

**165**

Shakespeare would not have used the term "time management," but he undoubtedly understood well that looking back at time wasted is painful. Perhaps what inspired him to write the first of his 154 sonnets was the belief that the words of fine poetry would outlive those of the actor.

In a very real sense, time management involves halting the "injurious hand" of time long enough to reflect on those aspects of life that are most important to us and then focusing our time and energy in those areas. If we think of time management as a way to overcome a sense of time wasted by attaining goals that have value to us, managing time suddenly loses any mechanical connotation we might at first be tempted to associate with it.

In recent history, time has taken on new meaning. Shakespeare's image of time as a natural enemy armed with a scythe that wretchedly hacks away our days gave way long ago with the advent of the modern timepiece. Precision in seventeenth century clock-making had made it possible for people to ask each other to be "on time," and by the late eighteenth century the word punctuality itself had changed from its earlier meaning, "a person who insisted on points of conduct," to its current meaning, "to be on time" (Boorstin, 1983, p.72).

Yet, meeting deadlines and being "on time" are only part of time management. More important to managing time well is seeing to it that the way we spend our time parallels to the greatest extent possible the manner in which we *want* to spend it. Time schedules are meaningful only insofar as they enable us to structure our activities so that our goals and values are realized. The degree to which we are on time, the number of minutes or hours we devote to an activity, and the way we divide up our day is measured by us when we work out a time schedule.

## THE ABCs OF TIME MANAGEMENT

Although thoughtful reflection (C) about how much time we waste on unimportant or meaningless activities is sometimes enough to prompt us to set up a schedule, managing time is much more than having a time schedule. It is first and foremost a set of feelings, behaviors, and thoughts that enable us to function in ways that reflect what is important to us and lead to the achievement of our goals. We are managing time well when we derive satisfaction out of the time we have available to us by using it in ways that *we* have judged to be of value.

To manage time is to follow a course of action (B) that is guided by decisions (C) in keeping with pre-established priorities. In other words, *time management* is a continuous series of decisions or choices (C) based on priorities that we feel (A) good about and act (B) upon in order to reach both our immediate and more distant objectives. It, therefore, requires an assessment of how affect (A), behavior (B), and cognition (C) interfere with and contribute to managing our time and reaching our goals.

Whereas some feelings, behaviors, and thoughts help us use time effectively, others are not useful and can sway us from our objectives. Managing time also contributes to the development of new feelings, behaviors, and thoughts. People who manage their time well feel, behave, and think differently than those who manage their time poorly. They view (C) time as something they can control and use to their advantage. They feel less anxiety and stress (A) about deadlines because they generally complete tasks on time. They are apt to engage in pleasurable activities more frequently (B) because they refrain from wasting a lot of time, and tend to do things (B) they enjoy. They are also inclined to think more positively (C) about themselves because their goals are being achieved on a regular basis.

## Time Management and Affect

*I just was not in the mood* (A) summarizes why many of us fail to do (B) things we intended (C) to do. Yet, if we want to manage our time well, we need to be aware of how our own feelings can work for and against us. For example, we may be motivated to draw up a time schedule that includes plenty of study time. We may even feel excited (A) about the prospect of following this new schedule, but then fail to follow it because we are apathetic (A) about doing a particular assignment. Later on, we may become angry or upset (A) at ourselves because now we have to rush to complete the assignment on time. Our annoyance (A) might even be compounded by the anxiety (A) that comes with the realization that our grade will suffer. Unless we understand the cause of our change in mood, we may repeat the same scenario. In this instance, positive affect (excitement) contributed to the formulation of a study schedule, but the lack of positive affect (apathy) was a deterrent to completing the assignment on time. Then, negative affect (anger and anxiety) served to increase the amount of time already wasted. Strong negative feelings are *time wasters*. Negative emotions such as anger, depression, and anxiety are sure ingredients for wasting time. Negative sensations such as fatigue and tension can also interfere with the best of intentions to follow a schedule. A lack of positive affect toward a particular activity also makes managing time difficult. Following a schedule requires effort, and much of this effort centers around managing feelings. So, to manage time, we first identify the feelings deterring us from our goals and learn how to change them so they work *for* rather than *against* us.

## Time Management and Behavior

We act differently when we manage our time well, for time management necessitates the development and maintenance of new behaviors. We spend less time on activities that interfere with our goals and more time on concrete goal-oriented tasks. To do this, we need to reduce time-wasting behaviors. Watching television, taking naps, gazing out the window, and talking on the telephone are common time wasters, unless of course these behaviors relate to our goals. As we get good at time management, we may actually begin to identify some *time savers* and gain free time. By using a daily checklist (B), we can get tasks done more quickly. Doing (B) two things at once can also be a tremendous time saver. For example, listening to lecture tapes while driving to work (B) makes driving time more productive. Similarly, studying (B) with others combines time with friends and study time, making the hours spent studying more fun.

While it may seem obvious that managing time involves managing behaviors, the extent to which these changes touch every aspect of our lives can come as a surprise. Using time effectively impacts our relationships as well as our professional and academic careers. When prepared to do a particular task, we may find it difficult to say "no" (B) to the requests of friends and family or to ask (B) people to leave us alone. Thus, devoting time to goal-related activities requires strengthening skills in other areas such as motivation and assertiveness.

## Time Management and Cognition

A well-conceived time schedule demands a lot of thought both in its planning and execution. The *planning stage* of time management is a series of cognitive steps that center around our personal values, priorities, and goals. The *execution stage* of following the schedule requires additional thinking skills such as making decisions because as we attempt to achieve short- and long-term goals, we need to decide from day to day whether we will follow the schedule.

## THE PLANNING STAGE (C) OF TIME MANAGEMENT

The *planning stage of time management* is a critical, but often ignored, first step in developing a personally meaningful time schedule. We first define our *values* (what is important to us) and our *goals* (what needs to be attained). Then, we try to make some direct connections between our values and goals. Many people mistakenly skip this step because it is not easy to clarify and make our values explicit.

## Values and Goal Setting

The likelihood of success in following a schedule is dramatically reduced if we establish goals that have no immediate relationship to what we value. When college students are asked to specify their goals, a high grade point average is frequently first on the list. Those students who do not attain this goal may have neglected to determine whether a high grade point average has any connection to something they think is truly worthwhile. If we love learning, admire self-reliance, or respect competence, the goal of high grades will be easier to attain once the connection to these values is recognized.

As we establish goals, it is important to consider three questions:

- What do we really value?

- How do our goals relate to these values?

- What are the immediate and future benefits of achieving these goals?

One of the quickest ways to bring our values into focus is to keep a record of how we spend our time and determine what activities predominate throughout a typical week. What we do with our time brings into sharp focus what is truly important to us, for our actions (B) generally say more about what we value than any other measure. We may find that our most time-consuming activities are at variance with, or only indirectly related to, our stated goals. In such a situation, we need to come to terms with what is really important to us. We can then decide if our activities reflect values we actually subscribe to, and if not, either align our goals and our time with our true values or commit to a different set of values.

In planning how to spend our time, we need to

1. Decide (C) what is important to us (what we value).

   Examples:

   Self-reliance (self-management)

   A good education

   Competence in chosen field

2. Identify (C) long-term goals that relate to our values.

   Examples:

   A good job after graduation (specify field)

   A high gpa at graduation (specify index)

3. Identify (C) short-term goals that relate to long-term goals.

Examples:

High semester gpa (state gpa)

High course grades (state them)

Specific grades on exams and assignments
(state for each course)

4. Identify (C) specific activities to meet short-term goals.

Examples:

Go to classes and career-related activities
(which ones?)

Study more (which subjects, where, when?)

Use SQ4R (for which texts?)

Use the library

Do assignments

Take notes (using which method?)

Use review checklists (for which assignments
and exams?)

5. Plan a schedule that includes activities identified.

Examples:

Determine number of hours that need to be allo-
cated for these activities, given a 168 hour week.

Identify any potential conflicts between time allo-
cated for activities and the way time is currently
spent.

Make adjustments in allocation of hours for these
activities if necessary.

**171**

## Conflict Between Values and Goals: An Example

The scenario described below illustrates how values and goals can be in conflict.

> Yolanda's long-term goal is to be a successful accountant. She chose accounting as a major because she was advised that high-paying jobs are available in this field. The course work for her accounting classes is difficult and it is a constant struggle for her to get her work done. Although she has a time schedule that allocates specific hours to do her accounting homework, she dreads reading her intermediate accounting text. Instead of preparing the balance sheets and income statements when the assignments are given, she usually hangs out and talks with her friends.

Yolanda values (C) the money that goes along with getting a high-paying job, but she does not seem to have found a major that she places as much personal value on. She also seems to value her friendships and a social life, but the time spent with friends conflicts with doing course work that will ultimately enable her to enter her chosen field. It is not surprising that Yolanda spends time with her friends rather than doing balance sheets and income statements; accounting work is not something she values as much as socializing.

The long-term goal Yolanda has set for herself may be unrealistic. Being an accountant is only partially related to her values (good job, money, and friends). Since balance sheets and income statements are only important to her as a means to get a job and make money, it is going to be difficult for her to reach her long-term goal of becoming a successful accountant. Her difficulty in doing what is necessary to become an accountant suggests that she not only has a time management problem, but a motivational problem as well.

## Realistic Goals and Activities: Making Values Concrete

Once we have decided what is important to us, the next step is to establish long-term and short-term goals that relate to these values. To bring our *long-term goals* into focus, we try to envision future accomplishments that would indicate to us that we have done something of value to us. To bring our *short-term goals* into focus, we try to envision more immediate accomplishments that would indicate that we have done something related to our long-term goals.

In identifying long- and short-term goals and the activities that will lead to them, we give concrete form to our values. Difficulty in achieving short-term goals usually occurs when we have not narrowed them to specific activities that can become part of our schedule. Consider the following short-term goals set by a psychology major.

- 3.0 gpa for the semester

- 'A' grades in physiological psychology and statistics

- 'B' grade or better on all term papers

These short-term goals will not likely be achieved unless the student specifies *goal-oriented activities*. Until the student identifies what needs to be done as well as when and where it will take place, a commitment to these goals has not been made.

*Realistic goals* bridge the wide gap between more abstract values and the specific goal-oriented activities related to time, date, and place. Thus, in defining our goals, three points should be kept in mind:

- Our long-term and short-term goals must clearly relate to something we value.

- Our short-term goals must be defined in terms of activities or behaviors that occur at a specific place and point in time.

- Dates for the completion of short-term goals must be set so that realistic dates for long-term goals can be determined.

### Values, Goals, Activities: The Makings of a Schedule

The graphic below shows the *relationship among values, goals, activities, and a time schedule*. It illustrates how values and related goals and activities form the basis of a meaningful time schedule. Note how a general value is narrowed to long-term goals and then narrowed still further to short-term goals and specific activities to be incorporated into a time schedule.

Time management begins at the base of the pyramid with a broad definition of our values. This definition narrows as we define goals and specific activities that will be included in our time schedule. The pyramid points toward the schedule to show that living our values and goals means planning carefully how our time is spent. The shades of gray suggest that there are not hard and fast lines of distinction among values, goals, and our daily activities.

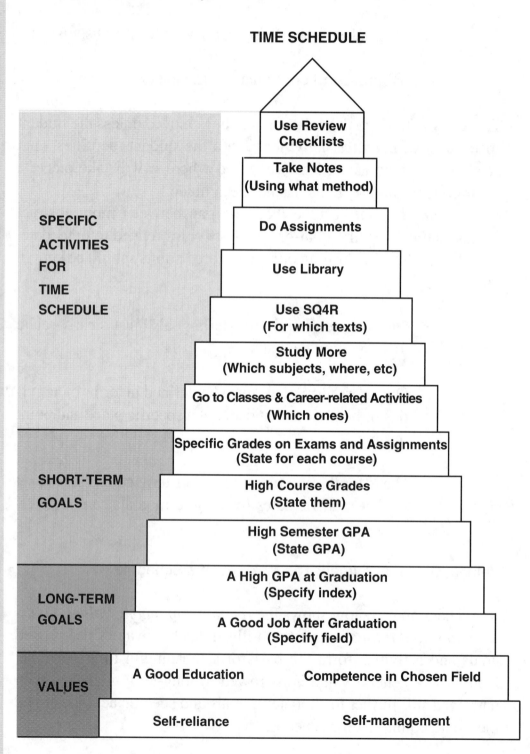

**TIME SCHEDULE**

SPECIFIC ACTIVITIES FOR TIME SCHEDULE

**Use Review Checklists**

**Take Notes (Using what method)**

**Do Assignments**

**Use Library**

**Use SQ4R (For which texts)**

**Study More (Which subjects, where, etc)**

**Go to Classes & Career-related Activities (Which ones)**

SHORT-TERM GOALS

**Specific Grades on Exams and Assignments (State for each course)**

**High Course Grades (State them)**

**High Semester GPA (State GPA)**

LONG-TERM GOALS

**A High GPA at Graduation (Specify index)**

**A Good Job After Graduation (Specify field)**

VALUES

**A Good Education     Competence in Chosen Field**

**Self-reliance     Self-management**

## Personal Characteristics and Goal Achievement

Research indicates that individuals who are *high achievers* do more than simply state their goals. They have certain personal characteristics in common that enable them to achieve. Knowing what these characteristics are can help us identify what we need to do as we strive to manage our time and reach our goals. Robbins (1986) summarizes these qualities as follows.

### Goal Commitment

High achievers have a clear goal or objective in mind and they are committed to it. They know precisely what it is they want to achieve, and can picture the outcome before it occurs. The goal is of their own choosing, not one that another person has defined for them.

We need to be able to state our goals clearly and specifically and be strongly committed to accomplishing them. Without a destination in mind, we are apt to wander aimlessly. Without the determination to reach that destination, we can too easily take a detour at the first sign of trouble.

### Passion for Goals

High achievers actually feel the desire for the goal in their bodies. They are moved passionately toward the goal by just thinking about or picturing it. Their desire to achieve the goal is not simply an intellectual exercise, it is experienced emotionally as well. High achievers are excited, energized, and "turned on" by their goals.

"Nothing great in this world was ever achieved without passion," according to the German poet Goethe. Emotional excitement over a goal helps us to achieve it. If we do not really enjoy what we need to do to reach our goals, we will find them difficult to achieve. To perform at a very high level and to stay committed, we need to choose goals that require activities from which we draw satisfaction and pleasure. If we must continually prod ourselves, attaining the goal will be laborious. The degree of passion we have for a goal is particularly important when choosing a career or making long-term commitments.

## Belief in the Value of the Goal

High achievers are convinced that the goals they seek are of great worth and value to themselves or others. They are confident in their ability to achieve the goal in the face of obstacles, and they often express this commitment both privately to themselves and publicly to others. Their belief in themselves is based on a realistic appraisal of their personal strengths and weaknesses and an awareness of the obstacles they face. As Albert Bandura points out: "People do not much care how they do on activities that have little or no significance for them. And little effort is expended on devalued activities" (1977, p. 132).

Thus, the probability of achieving a goal is directly related to our belief in the value of our objective and in our ability to achieve it. We need to be convinced that the goal sought squares with our basic values. After a thorough and realistic appraisal of our strengths and weaknesses related to a goal, we must be convinced that we have the qualities necessary to attain it. A strong belief in the value of a goal and belief in ourselves enables us to persevere through adversity.

## Strategy for Goal Achievement

High achievers develop a step-by-step strategy or plan of action for accomplishing their goals. They figure out how to organize their resources and use them effectively to bring about the desired outcome. *"If it happens, it happens"* is a thought that *rarely* enters their minds.

To reach the goals we seek, we need to be clear about how we will proceed. Without a plan, our goal is simply a wish. With a written plan that specifies general goals and subgoals to be achieved within a specific time frame along with the activities that will bring them to fruition, our goals become reality.

## High Energy

High achievers are able to work long and hard because they have a large store of energy at their disposal. In part, they are energized by their commitment, passion, and belief in the goal. However, they also refrain from wasting energy on worries, doubts, or fears of failure. They constantly direct their energy toward the achievement of their goals.

Since high level achievement requires a high level of energy, we need to take care of ourselves physically so that our natural energy is continually available. Good nutrition, exercise, rest, and relaxation contribute not only to good health, but are a source of high energy. To guard against wasting time and energy on doubts and fears, we need to manage the distortions and dysfunctional beliefs that contribute to such problems. In doing so, we restore energy that would otherwise be wasted.

## Goal Achievement and Other People

High achievers acknowledge the support and help of others in achieving their goals. They develop the ability to communicate so that they are not alone in their endeavors.

Establishing meaningful relationships can make our achievement more interesting and pleasurable, and thereby increase our passion for a goal. Other people are a valuable resource to draw on when we need help to accomplish an objective. Since very few individuals can achieve their goals without some help, it is important to develop the ability to communicate and relate well with others. Forming positive, mutually supportive relationships with people is usually a necessary ingredient for success.

# THE EXECUTION STAGE: FOLLOWING THE SCHEDULE

The *execution stage of time management* involves putting our plans into action by following a schedule. Keeping our values and goals in mind as we follow a schedule makes the task an easier one. We need to understand, however, that our goals will not necessarily come to fruition all at once; and therefore, we should resist the temptation to create a schedule that mandates all work and no play. A good schedule is flexible, rather than restrictive, and includes relaxation, free time, and play.

Once our values and goals are clear, activities determined, and a schedule created, the stage of "tough" decision-making begins as we attempt to follow the schedule. This is a challenging task because it requires that we continually make hard choices and act upon them.

## Decision Making

*Strong decision-making skills* are based upon strong commitments to our values and goals. Such skills are critical to time management because the choices we make on an hourly basis about how our time is spent determine whether our short-and long-term goals will be achieved. Since we are constantly faced with options that conflict with our time schedule, we need to decide (C) what we will or will not do as these options present themselves.

Deciding (C) how best to handle situations that may deter us from our plans is one of the most difficult aspects of managing our time. Yet, it is important to realize that having a schedule does not mean that we lock-step ourselves into following it at every conceivable moment. We may have good reason not to follow our schedule because something more important has come up. So long as we acknowledge to ourselves that our reason for neglecting our schedule is more important than the goal we set, and we are satisfied with the consequences of our decision, then we have managed our time well.

When we manage our time, we pay close attention to our daily choices; we determine if we want to alter the path that those choices are setting for us; and we continuously ask ourselves whether our actions are getting us closer to our goals. If we frequently neglect the activities in our schedule, a problem is apparent (perhaps a motivational one), and a new time schedule should be devised.

## Dealing with Potential Problems and Pitfalls

Taking decisive action to get ourselves to *move* in the direction of our goals not only requires strong decision-making skills, it requires learning how to deal effectively with difficulties that arise. However flexible our schedule is, we will inevitably find that a host of different goals or new objectives will appeal to us and compete with the goals we have established. We will not feel (A) like following the schedule on some days. Perhaps we are too annoyed, angry, or tired to stick to our plan. The behaviors (B) necessary to follow the schedule may be unappealing to us. We may need to ask our friends to leave our room so that we can study. Or, we may need to ask a professor for clarification on an assignment in order to complete it. We may even begin to doubt (C) our ability to be self-disciplined enough to follow a schedule. Problems such as these are likely to deter us if we do not develop strategies for dealing with them. It is all too easy to convince ourselves (C) to give up (B) at the first bit of discomfort (A) experienced in trying something new. We need to realize that following a schedule can be tough, particularly in the beginning.

The level of difficulty experienced in managing our time is generally proportional to skills needed in other areas. As we develop decision-making skills and the ability to manage our motivation and assertiveness, we can improve our time management dramatically. Reflecting on the following questions will also help to identify factors that may interfere with our ability to follow a schedule.

1. Is the goal identified something we really want to attain? Is the goal in line with our values?

2. Is the amount of time we need to allocate to the goal worth the price we must pay?

3. Are we able to sacrifice short-term pleasure for the long-term gain?

4. Are we able to say "no" to others when they ask us to do something that would interfere with our schedule?

5. Are we able to request that others refrain from doing things that interfere with our ability to follow the schedule and attain our goals?

6. Do we inform friends that we are attempting to organize our time and ask for their support?

7. Are our living quarters organized in a way that helps us do what we set out to do?

8. Do we have available the resources that we need to complete the task at hand?

9. Are we easily distracted from focusing on scheduled activities?

10. Are the more difficult tasks tackled first and the easier ones left for last?

If all the questions above are answered in the affirmative, following a schedule will present no major difficulty. If answers to one or more of the questions are negative, reflection on the question may reveal the source of the problem and suggest a possible solution. For example, a negative response to questions 1, 2, or 3 indicates problems related to values and goals and suggests that values clarification and goal setting exercises may be helpful. Negative responses to questions 4, 5, and 6 indicate problems in a social context and suggest the need for assertiveness training, whereas negative answers to questions 7 and 8 would reveal a need to make our living quarters more organized and functional. If answers to 9 and 10 are negative, it may mean that short-term pleasures have priority over long-term gains. The obvious point here is that time management, like every aspect of self-management, requires skills related to many other areas of our lives.

## How to Get Started

The following steps will be helpful in beginning a time management program.

Step 1  Determine how time is spent currently by keeping a time record of all activities for one week.

Step 2  Review the record at the end of the week to assess the activities to which time was allotted; group these activities into general categories (eating, studying, working, attending classes, sleeping, socializing, etc.).

Step 3    Focus on values. Specify long-term goals that relate to these values.

Step 4    Choose the most important long-term goals and break them down into short-term goals.

Step 5    Narrow the short-term goals to specific activities that need to occur in order to reach these goals. Compare these activities with how personal time was spent during the past week. Then, either alter the long- and short-term goals so they are more realistic or commit to the activities that reflect the preferred values and goals.

Step 6    Draft a time schedule by allocating time to these activities.

Step 7    Post the schedule in a visible place and follow it for one week. Then, make adjustments in the schedule based on experiences during the course of the week.

The exercises at the end of this chapter will also be useful in planning and executing a strategy for managing time in a personally meaningful way.

**KEY WORDS AND CONCEPTS**

execution stage of time management
goal-oriented activities
goals
high achievers
long-term goals
planning stage of time management
realistic goals
short-term goals
strong decision-making skills
time management
time savers
time wasters
values

## SUGGESTED READINGS AND TAPES

### Time Management (General)

Ellis, D. (1991). *Becoming a master student.* Rapid City, SD: College Survival Inc. (Chaps. 4 and 6).

Lakein, A. (1973). *How to get control of your time and your life.* New York: Signet.

### Time Management (Student)

Gardner, J. N., & Jewler, A.J. (1992). *Your college experience: Strategies for success.* Belmont, CA: Wadsworth (Chap. 2).

Walter, T., & Siebert, A. (1993). *Student Success.* Fort Worth, TX: Holt, Rinehart, Winston.

Friday, R.A. (1988). *Create your college success.* Belmont, CA: Wadsworth (Chap. 12).

### Values Clarification

Gardner, J. N., & Jewler, A.J. (1992). *Your college experience: Strategies for success.* Belmont, CA: Wadsworth (Chap. 13).

Simon, S.B., Howe, L.W. and Kirshenbaum, H. (1978). *Values clarification: A handbook of practical strategies for teachers and students.* New York: A and W Visual Library.

# EXERCISE 6.1

## TIME RECORD

1. Using the Daily Record form on the next page, keep track of the time you spend on activities related to each of the following categories for 7 consecutive days:

   Classes (time in classes, labs, etc.)
   Studying (homework, reading, assignments, etc.)
   Meals (breakfast, lunch, dinner, snacking)
   Exercise (jogging, working out, etc.)
   Sleep (including naps)
   Personal Chores (laundry, house cleaning, etc.)
   Work ( paid employment or internships, etc.)
   School Activities (sports, clubs, extra-curricular activities)
   Free Time (socializing, relaxing, TV, or whatever)

2. At the end of the week, record below how many hours you spent in each category.

| Category | Hours Spent |
|---|---|
| Classes | _____ |
| Studying | _____ |
| Meals | _____ |
| Exercise | _____ |
| Sleep | _____ |
| Personal Chores | _____ |
| Work | _____ |
| School Activities | _____ |
| Free Time | _____ |
| Total Hours | 168 |

# DAILY RECORD

| | MON | TUE | WED | THU | FRI | SAT | SUN |
|---|---|---|---|---|---|---|---|
| 7 - 8 AM | | | | | | | |
| 8 - 9 | | | | | | | |
| 9 -10 | | | | | | | |
| 10-11 | | | | | | | |
| 11-12 | | | | | | | |
| 12- 1 PM | | | | | | | |
| 1 - 2 | | | | | | | |
| 2 - 3 | | | | | | | |
| 3 - 4 | | | | | | | |
| 4 - 5 | | | | | | | |
| 5 - 6 | | | | | | | |
| 6 - 7 | | | | | | | |
| 7 - 8 | | | | | | | |
| 8 - 9 | | | | | | | |
| 9 -10 | | | | | | | |
| 10-11 | | | | | | | |
| 11-12 | | | | | | | |
| 12- 1 AM | | | | | | | |
| 1 - 2 | | | | | | | |
| 2 - 3 | | | | | | | |
| 3 - 4 | | | | | | | |
| 4 - 5 | | | | | | | |
| 5 - 6 | | | | | | | |
| 6 - 7 | | | | | | | |

# EXERCISE 6.2

## ALLOCATION OF HOURS

When allocating time for a weekly schedule, it is suggested that students who want to use the 168 hours of their week productively follow the guidelines below. Determine how closely the time recommended for each activity matches the number of hours you actually spend in each of these categories (based on your time record from the previous exercise) by filling in the blanks on the left-hand side under "Your Hours."

| Category | Your Hours | Ideal # of Hours |
|---|---|---|
| Classes | _____ | 15 (in class) |
| Study | _____ | 38 (2 1/2 hours per class) |
| Meals | _____ | 14 (2 hours a day) |
| Exercise | _____ | 7 (1 hour a day) |
| Sleep | _____ | 49 (7 hours a night) |
| Personal Tasks | _____ | 10 (dressing, laundry, etc.) |
| Work | _____ | 10 (No more than 20 for a full-time student) |
| Social Activity | _____ | 10 (extra-curricular activities, partying, etc.) |
| Free Time | _____ | 15 (for whatever) |
| | | |
| Total Hours | _____ | 168 |

Compare the ideal number of hours for each category and "your hours" for the week. What does this comparison suggest you value most among these categories? What does it suggest you value least? If a discrepancy exists between the way you spend your time and your values, can you explain it?

## VALUES CLARIFICATION

In the left-hand column of the grid below, list eight things that you enjoy doing.

| ACTIVITY | PLACE | PERSON | TYPE | PHYSICAL | MENTAL |
|---|---|---|---|---|---|
|  |  |  |  |  |  |
|  |  |  |  |  |  |
|  |  |  |  |  |  |
|  |  |  |  |  |  |
|  |  |  |  |  |  |
|  |  |  |  |  |  |
|  |  |  |  |  |  |
|  |  |  |  |  |  |

Under **Place**, write **S** if the activity occurs at school and **E** if it occurs elsewhere.

Under **Person**, write **F** if the activity occurs with friends, **G** if it occurs with a group, or **A** if it is something you do alone.

Under **Type**, write **R** if the activity is recreation (sports, socializing, etc.), **RL** for relaxation (napping, sleeping, etc.), **AC** for academic, **C** for chores (cleaning, laundry, etc.), and **W** for job-related activities.

Under **Physical**, write **LP** if the activity requires little or no physical exertion, **MP** for moderate, and **HP** for high physical exertion.

Under **Mental**, write **LM** if the activity requires little or no mental activity, **MM** for moderate, and **HM** for high mental activity.

Count the letter symbols for each column. Enter totals below.

S ___          F ___          R  ___          LP ___          LM ___
E ___          G ___          RL ___          MP ___          MM ___
               A ___          AC ___          HP ___          HM ___
                              C  ___
                              W  ___

What does this information reveal about your values?

_____

_____

## EXERCISE 6.4

## IDENTIFYING RESOURCES FOR GOAL ACHIEVEMENT

The relationship of goals and resources to achievement is an important one to establish. The following steps help to make this connection.

1.  List all the things you want to accomplish as a college student— academically, personally, socially, spiritually, etc. Let your mind run freely, and simply list as many outcomes as you can think of that you want to occur during your college career.

    _____

    _____

    _____

    _____

2.  Identify the three primary goals and the date you expect to reach them.

    _____

    _____

    _____

3.  Pick *one* of these three goals that will be your main focus this year. In convincing language, state why this goal is so important to you, why you want to achieve it, and why it is significant at this time in your life.

    Goal: _____

    Significance:

    _____

    _____

    _____

    _____

4.  For the goal you selected, list all the resources you have that will help you achieve it. Resources include your personal ABC characteristics that will enable you to achieve the goal, as well as external resources available such as other people, finances, facilities, equipment, etc.

    Personal ABC Characteristics:

    _____

    _____

    _____

    External Resources/Support:

    _____

    _____

    _____

5a. Think of a past situation when you used these or other resources to achieve a goal you desired. List the personal ABC characteristics and external resources and support that enabled you to achieve it.

Personal ABC Characteristics:

_____

_____

_____

External Resources/Support:

_____

_____

_____

5b. How did you use these resources? What obstacles did you overcome?

_____

_____

_____

6. For your present goal, list the personal ABC characteristics or skills you *need to develop* or acquire to achieve it. Then, list the external resources or outside support you *will need* to reach the goal.

Personal ABC Characteristics:

_____

_____

_____

External Resources/Support:

_____

_____

_____

7a. List any obstacles, personal or otherwise, you might encounter that could interfere with the pursuit of the goal.

_____

_____

_____

7b. How do you intend to overcome these obstacles?

_____

_____

_____

8. Name one thing you can do today to get you started toward your goal.

_____

_____

## GOAL SETTING

Working toward short-term goals that are in keeping with our long-term goals and values does not mean we have our whole life mapped out. For example, we may not know what we want to major in as yet, much less what kind of career we want to pursue. However, establishing and prioritizing goals is, in part, what college is about, and the sooner we begin this process the better.

The pyramid on the next page can be used to organize values, goals, and related activities to facilitate the making of a personally meaningful time schedule. See pages 170-171 and 174 for a sample illustration.

### Directions

1. Think of a value that is very important to you. At the base of the pyramid to the right, record this value. Examples might be: education, career, money, learning, competence in my field, friendship, love, respect from others, self-reliance, etc.

2. Decide on a few long-term goals that relate to this value and record them in the appropriate spaces in the pyramid.

3. Set up some short-term goals that will help you to achieve the long-term goals and record them in the pyramid.

4. Describe the activities that will enable you to achieve the short-term goals and record them in the pyramid.

# TIME SCHEDULE

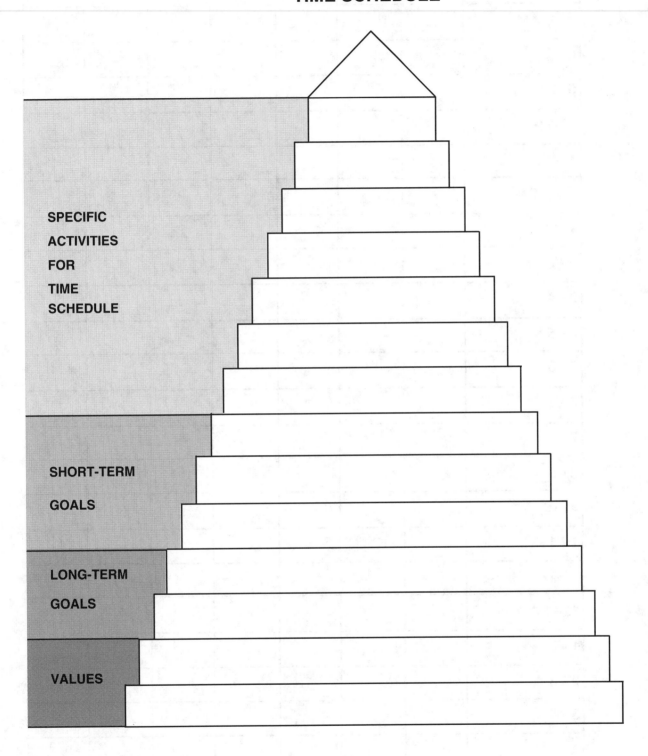

SPECIFIC
ACTIVITIES
FOR
TIME
SCHEDULE

SHORT-TERM
GOALS

LONG-TERM
GOALS

VALUES

# DAILY ACTIVITY SCHEDULE

| | MON | TUE | WED | THU | FRI | SAT | SUN |
|---|---|---|---|---|---|---|---|
| 7 - 8 AM | | | | | | | |
| 8 - 9 | | | | | | | |
| 9 -10 | | | | | | | |
| 10-11 | | | | | | | |
| 11-12 | | | | | | | |
| 12- 1 PM | | | | | | | |
| 1 - 2 | | | | | | | |
| 2 - 3 | | | | | | | |
| 3 - 4 | | | | | | | |
| 4 - 5 | | | | | | | |
| 5 - 6 | | | | | | | |
| 6 - 7 | | | | | | | |
| 7 - 8 | | | | | | | |
| 8 - 9 | | | | | | | |
| 9 -10 | | | | | | | |
| 10-11 | | | | | | | |
| 11-12 | | | | | | | |
| 12- 1 AM | | | | | | | |
| 1 - 2 | | | | | | | |
| 2 - 3 | | | | | | | |
| 3 - 4 | | | | | | | |
| 4 - 5 | | | | | | | |
| 5 - 6 | | | | | | | |
| 6 - 7 | | | | | | | |

*Procrastination is not a modern pastime. For centuries, it has been perceived as "the thief of time."*

# CASE STUDY

Before reading Chapter 7, read the case study below. After completing the chapter, analyze the case study by following steps 1 - 4.

STEP 1   Describe the procrastination problem.

STEP 2   AFFECT:   Identify the feelings that are supporting procrastination.

BEHAVIOR:   Identify the *competing behaviors* contributing to the procrastination.

COGNITION:   Identify the thoughts that are supporting procrastination.

STEP 3   Describe the firing order.

STEP 4   What methods would be most effective in helping the student resolve his procrastination problem?

"Well, I've got a month until my term paper is due. Now's the time to get started," Jason thought. But, he was too excited about making the baseball team to settle down to work at that time. He also had to exercise daily to get in shape for the first game. Besides, he figured that working under stress would be good training for a future career. So here it is 3 a.m. one month later and Jason is frantically writing a ten-page research paper that is due in a matter of hours. Bleary-eyed and exhausted, with just five more hours to work, he is determined to get this paper done because he knows that he cannot afford to hand in another paper late in this class. Then Jason looks at the computer screen and panics. "Six more pages to go! I'll never get this paper finished," he thinks. What else can I possibly write about?" Two more hours pass. Jason wasn't sure what he wrote, but he feels elated as he types up the last of three references. "Hmm, we were supposed to have six references — she won't notice. It's done and that's all that counts!" he thinks. On his way to class, he runs into one of his friends who inquires sympathetically: "Did you manage to get it done?" "Yeah, I had to stay up all night to get ten pages, but you know me," Jason responds, "I do my best work under pressure."

# 7 PROCRASTINATION

Procrastination is the thief of time.
Year after year it steals, till all are fled.

Edward Young (1683-1765)
English poet

## APPLYING THE ABCs TO PROCRASTINATION

Procrastination is not a modern pastime. For centuries, it has been perceived as "the thief of time." In fact, some rather unusual images of procrastination have been put forth. A nineteenth century caricature of a procrastinator personified procrastination as a fool with a parrot sitting on his head and a magpie on each hand, crying "cras, cras, cras." The caricature makes little sense to us today, unless we interpret the bird calls. "Cras," which means "tomorrow" in Latin, is the root of the word "pro*cras*tination," which means "to put forward until tomorrow."

Putting off until a tomorrow that never comes is a phenomenon that is more or less common to us all. Many students complain that procrastination is a major difficulty in their personal and academic lives. It is usually seen as a motivation problem because students say they cannot get themselves to move in the direction they would like. The following statements are somewhat typical:

I put off starting my term paper until a week before it was due, and then had to rush like crazy to get it done. I just wasn't motivated to get started earlier.

I know I should clean the room now before my roommate gets on my case, but I don't feel like it. Knowing me, I'll wait until she starts yelling, and then I'll do it.

It would be smart to put my snow tires on before it snows, but right now I'd rather watch TV. Maybe it won't snow much this winter.

Students contend that they would be less "stressed out" and more productive if they could just stop procrastinating.

This chapter will show how the ABCs, motivation, and methods for change can be applied to the practical problem of procrastination, which will also help in time management. Concepts and methods we have already covered will be integrated in order to provide a systematic approach for dealing with procrastination. We will begin with a brief explanation of what procrastination is, discuss how to identify it, and conclude with an exercise that will help in resolving a specific procrastination problem. To get the most benefit from this chapter, it will be helpful to focus on a particular activity that we procrastinate about.

## PROCRASTINATION: A WORKING DEFINITION

Before determining how procrastination can be managed, we first need to establish what it is. The dictionary offers these definitions:

- to put off intentionally and habitually

- to put off doing something to a future time

- to postpone or delay needlessly

All of these definitions are somewhat misleading. The third definition comes close to how procrastination works, but it is still not specific enough to be of much use. To "delay needlessly" must be qualified further, for *needless delay* only presents a procrastination problem if the delay hurts us in some way. At times it is smart to postpone an action, as for example getting married to someone after the first date.

*Procrastination* is to delay needlessly something that we believe would be to our benefit. We know when procrastination is presenting a problem by its effect on us; we anticipate a procrastination problem by recognizing this effect in advance. For example, if we know that by beginning a research project early in the semester, we are more likely to get the results we want, then a delay of this research would signal that we are experiencing a procrastination problem. Furthermore, if by delaying the paper, we place ourselves under a lot of stress a few days before it is due, this delay is causing us still greater harm emotionally and physically. We prevent procrastination by guarding against such effects ahead of time.

## SPECIFYING A PROCRASTINATION PROBLEM

Now that we know what procrastination is, we are in a position to determine what it is we procrastinate about. If we determine that a delay or postponement of some action is creating or will create difficulties for us, then we have a procrastination problem. We obviously do not postpone doing everything. We may procrastinate in our personal but not our professional life, do things for ourselves but not others, start certain things but not stop other things. We need to specify the problem by identifying the conditions under which procrastination occurs. Consideration of the 4Ws ( who, what, where, and when) discussed in Chapter 4 can assist us with this.

## SOLVING A PROCRASTINATION PROBLEM

Why do we delay the things we say we want or need to do? No doubt some of us could provide complex explanations, but this is not necessary to resolve a specific procrastination problem. If the ABCs of self-management in general and of motivation and time management in particular are valid, they should be applicable to procrastination problems and provide the means to solve them. Let us see how this might be done.

### First: Identify the ABCs of Procrastination

*What feelings are contributing to the procrastination*?

We may delay an activity because we experience anxiety, tension, or nervousness as we try to initiate it or even think about it. We are negatively motivated to do something else in order to avoid or escape these feelings.

We may be angry about having to do an assignment or fulfill a commitment, and to lessen the anger or perhaps spite the other person, we procrastinate.

We may be too lethargic, depressed, or tired to engage in a task now, and get some temporary relief by putting it off. Or, we may bring ourselves down emotionally so that we will have an excuse for not doing something we are anxious or angry about. We may even gain some sympathy in the bargain.

The *feelings that support* procrastination are endless. Procrastination can be a way of handling negative affect associated with doing something. We need to find a better way to deal with negative feelings, other than simply delaying action, if we want to stop procrastinating.

*What cognitions are contributing to the procrastination?*

We may be motivated to procrastinate because we do not believe any immediate or long-term payoffs are associated with the activity, even though others (parents, professors, friends, etc.) keep telling us there are. Or, perhaps the payoffs available (increased knowledge, a paper completed, a clean room) are not worth much to us considering the cost.

We may delay because we are convinced that we work best under stress, and so it is necessary to wait until the last moment before taking action. When we finally reduce this self-imposed stress, we feel a surge of pleasure, which serves as a reinforcer for future procrastination.

We may be motivated to postpone because we do not believe we have the ability to succeed at the task, and fear the results of failure.

We may procrastinate to avoid learning that we are less than perfect or that we may be rejected by others, if we do succeed.

It is apparent that many of these cognitions are based on distortions and dysfunctional beliefs. Nonetheless, such thoughts occur because the procrastination they support helps us avoid something we believe to be of little or no value. As with affect, the *cognitions that support* procrastination actually serve us in the short term, even though they interfere with long-term goals.

*What behaviors are contributing to our procrastination?*

We may engage in a behavior as a substitute for some other activity we need to do. These are called ***competing behaviors***. Competing behaviors may occur because they are easier to perform, receive immediate reinforcement, or satisfy some other goal we have.

We may even procrastinate on a particular task because engaging in the desired behavior is discouraged by others. For example, friends may label us a "nerd" for starting a term paper six weeks before it is due. They may then reward a competing behavior such as leaving the library to go swimming.

Since we are doing something else when we are not doing what we need to do, competing behaviors are obviously a major component of procrastination. Our task is to identify the "something else" and change this behavior.

### Second: Describe ABC Interactions

After identifying the specific ABCs involved when we procrastinate, we should observe their interaction and identify the firing order. For example, if we immediately feel uneasy, tense, and nervous as we focus on a project and then delay it, affect may be the trigger. If we find that just before we begin a task we are full of doubt and uncertainty or question its worth and value, cognition is probably the trigger. If we find that starting the task elicits negative reactions from others or we engage in competing behaviors because they are supported by others, behavior itself may be the trigger.

### Third: Change the Trigger of Procrastination

Once we have identified the trigger, we can determine methods and techniques for changing it and the other ABC components that follow and contribute to our procrastination. The approaches discussed in Chapter 4 should prove helpful. For example:

> If affect was found to be the trigger, the specific negative emotions or sensations contributing to procrastination would need to be identified and changed. For instance, if anxiety was the problem, relaxation techniques might be used to counteract it; if anger was the problem, relaxation and assertiveness might help; if lethargy or fatigue was involved, exercise and rest might prove beneficial. Of course, any problems triggered by affect can be helped by cognitive change techniques, if distortions or dysfunctional beliefs are the underlying cause of these feelings.

> If cognition was found to be the trigger, we would attempt to eliminate our procrastination by first examining our thought processes for distortions that are contributing to the problem. Next, we determine if any dysfunctional beliefs underlie these distortions. The use of corrective self-talk, the DIE Model (reframing, disputation, exchange), or thought stopping could then be used to change any thoughts that are triggering procrastination.

> If behavior was found to be the trigger and it was discovered that little or no reinforcement occurred immediately after the desired behavior, the contingent use of rewards could be used to strengthen the behavior. If competing behaviors are contributing to our procrastination, we need to find deterrents for them or use rewards for the desired behavior after it occurs.

## ACTING ON THE SOLUTION

The foregoing discussion may seem to be an oversimplified analysis of a complex problem, but in reality all problems we experience are going to have ABC components and it is these components that we have to work on to overcome procrastination. There are only a limited number of ways that we can change ourselves and most of these changes will have something to do with affect, behavior and cognition. Thus, once we have a clear picture of what changes are needed, it is up to us to determine the most effective way to bring them about.

An ABC analysis is helpful because it provides useful information on the causes of our procrastination and the purpose it serves in our lives. This information will alert us to when we are procrastinating and may prompt action. We can then keep track of how often it occurs and how successful we are in overcoming it. In short, by paying close attention to the ABCs of our procrastination, we can begin to manage it.

Understanding the reasons for our procrastination and knowing how to overcome it does not mean we will always act on this knowledge. To take action means we are motivated, which requires certain thoughts and feelings (A x C = B). To generate the thoughts and feelings necessary to overcome procrastination, we have to be positively motivated. The irony here is that to overcome procrastination we have *to be motivated to be motivated.* Thus, we are led full circle back to the ABC components of positive motivation. Since we already understand these basic components and their interactions, we have everything in place to begin working on any procrastination problem we wish. Exercise 7.1 will help us toward this end.

### KEY WORDS AND CONCEPTS

**cognitions that support procrastination**
**competing behaviors**
**feelings that support procrastination**
**needless delay**
**procrastination**

**201**

## SUGGESTED READINGS AND TAPES

**Procrastination (General)**

Burka, J.B., & Yuen, L.M. (1989). *The procrastination cure.* Chicago: Nightingale-Conant (audio cassettes).

Dyer, W. (1976). *Your erroneous zones.* New York: Avon Books (Chap. 9).

Ellis, A. (1979). *Overcoming procrastination or how to think and act rationally in spite of life's inevitable hassles.* New York: Signet.

Ellis, D. (1991). *Becoming a master student.* Rapid City, SD: College Survival , Inc. (Chap. 2).

Woodring, S.W. (1990). *Overcoming procrastination.* Boulder, CO: Careertrack Publications (audio cassettes).

# EXERCISE 7.1

## RESOLVING A PROCRASTINATION PROBLEM

The following exercise is intended to help you identify what you procrastinate about, why you procrastinate, and how you can resolve it.

1. Identify one activity you are currently putting off needlessly and want to start doing.

   _____
   _____
   _____
   _____

2. Identify where, when, and with whom you would like the activity to occur.

   Where?          _____

   When?           _____

   With whom?      _____

3. What do you do instead of the activity that you are putting off?

   _____
   _____
   _____
   _____

   Where does this competing activity occur?

   _____
   _____

   When does this competing activity occur?

   _____
   _____

   With whom?

   _____
   _____

   What is gained from this competing activity?

   _____
   _____
   _____

4. Explain why you procrastinate in ABC terms by identifying the ABCs that support or contribute to your procrastination.

Affect:

_____

_____

_____

Behavior:

_____

_____

_____

Cognition:

_____

_____

_____

5. Describe the firing order of your procrastination.

_____

_____

_____

_____

6. Describe how you plan to change the ABC component that triggers your procrastination.

_____

_____

_____

_____

7. Describe how you will change the other two ABC components that contribute to your procrastination.

_____

_____

_____

_____

*Assertiveness is a way of life that influences our interactions with others and our approach to dealing with the problems and injustices we perceive.*

# CASE STUDIES

Before reading Chapter 8, read the case studies in the boxes below. After completing the chapter, analyze the case studies by following Steps 1 through 5. (Do each case study separately.)

STEP 1     Describe whether the student is passive or aggressive.

STEP 2     AFFECT:     Identify the feelings contributing to the problem.

BEHAVIOR:  Identify the behaviors contributing to the problem.

COGNITION: Identify the thoughts contributing to the problem.

STEP 3     Which ABC component listed in STEP 2 is the trigger of the firing order? Describe the firing order. Explain why there is the potential for a downward spiral.

STEP 4     What methods described in this text could be used to alter or change the trigger?

STEP 5     What methods described in this text could be used to alter or change the other components?

---

**Every Monday, Terry sits through another philosophy lecture without a clue as to what the professor is talking about. He takes notes, but the professor is always using vocabulary that Terry has never heard before. Terry figures that everybody else understands what is going on so he is too embarrassed to ask the professor any questions. Besides, this teacher only looks for input at the end of class, and Terry doesn't want to inconvenience the other students by asking a question that might keep them longer. A few days before a test, he thought about asking the professor to define an important term, but when another student raised a question, some students seemed annoyed, so Terry decided to let it go. After getting a 'D' on that exam, Terry knew that he would have done better had he participated in class, but he feels uncomfortable when other students look at him and think he is trying to score points with the teacher. Nonetheless, he still *feels* it is the professor's fault for not being able to figure out that he is lost.**

---

**Tanya is in the same class as Terry and has a similar problem with the vocabulary. Because she is annoyed at the professor, to spite him she rarely asks questions or participates. She, too, is doing poorly on tests. After failing one, she got angry and stormed out of class in a huff. Ever since that day she walks into class and makes it known that she doesn't want to be there. She typically drops her books down on the desk, slumps into her chair, and sits in class with a scowl on her face. During lectures, she sometimes makes snide comments about the professor while talking to the student next to her. Whenever other students ask questions at the end of class, Tanya sighs loudly to show her annoyance and shuffles her books to interrupt. Since the professor doesn't take the hint to let the class out on time, Tanya has been known to get halfway up from her seat as if ready to charge out of the room.**

#  ASSERTIVENESS

> Democracy arises out of the notion that those who are equal in any respect are equal in all respects.
>
> Aristotle (384-322)
> Greek philosopher

## ASSERTIVENESS IN PRINCIPLE AND PRACTICE

*Assertiveness* is a way of life that influences our interactions with others and our approach to dealing with the problems and injustices we perceive. It is an outward display of inward security and self-confidence, and a way of relating to others that reflects a belief in human rights. From a philosophical perspective, assertive people could be said to embody and uphold the principles upon which a democracy is founded, namely principles of equal rights.

From a purely practical point of view, assertiveness is a skill that enables us to prevent and resolve problems that are interfering with the achievement of our goals. When motivated to study and manage our time efficiently, we quickly become aware of the impact other people can have on us. Friends, family, and classmates can unintentionally interfere with our best efforts to follow a study or time schedule, and we learn that we need to influence their behavior in order to direct our own. An effective way to solve this and related problems is to be assertive.

The situations in which assertiveness is useful are not limited to time management and study skills — they are many and varied. How many times have we kept ideas to ourselves when our needs or the needs of others would have been better served had we spoken up? We may have missed a chance to make a new friend for fear of rejection. Perhaps we failed to address a problem with a roommate until it reached crisis proportions. Or, we may have flown off the handle and hurt someone we care about. Maybe we have gotten into fights because we did not know how to deal effectively with conflict. Each of these scenarios describes a situation in which assertiveness would be useful.

When we fail to act assertively, we usually pay a price. This price can have severe personal and societal implications. An understanding of assertiveness, passivity, and aggression will help us better appreciate the implications of making a personal choice among these options.

## The ABCs of Assertiveness

Assertiveness is commonly defined as the ability to see that our needs are met and our rights respected without infringing upon the rights of others. It is traditionally discussed in the literature as an effective approach to interacting with others (Alberti & Emmons, 1978).

The ABC characteristics of assertiveness can be outlined as follows:

**Affect**  Feeling relatively comfortable when stating needs, rights, and ideas.

**Behavior**  Speaking up for oneself and others when necessary. Expression is clear and nonthreatening. Use of assertive communication skills (I messages and active listening) in confrontational situations and in response to aggressive attacks from others.

**Cognition**  Believing that one's own needs and ideas are as important as those of others, and that the rights of self and others are to be respected.

People who attempt to interact with others assertively are apt to become involved in activities and relationships that will foster personal and professional growth. They are also likely to establish relationships with others that are based upon mutual respect.

## The ABCs of Passivity

We are being *passive* when we want our needs to be met, but fail to make them known, or when our rights or those of others are violated, but we do nothing. People who act passively often believe that their needs, rights, or ideas are not important enough to be voiced or they feel too nervous or fearful to express themselves. Rather than doing something about a problem they want resolved, they may hope that someone else will take care of it or that the problem will go away by itself.

Sometimes we may act in a passive manner because we think other people should be able to read our minds and know what we want without our telling them. If they do not respond accordingly, we may feel upset. Instead of speaking directly to the person with whom we are having difficulty, we may complain to someone else or let the problem go unresolved. Both courses of action are ineffective. In using a passive approach, we place our own needs second to those of others, and in doing so, show a lack of respect for ourselves.

The ABC characteristics of passivity can be outlined as follows:

**Affect**      Feeling nervous or anxious when expressing needs, rights, or ideas, particularly if there is any possibility of conflict or rejection.

**Behavior**   Failing to speak up or take decisive action to see that one's own needs and rights are met, and that the rights of others are respected. Avoidance of eye contact and a tendency to speak in a low voice when expressing ideas to others.

**Cognition**  Believing that one's own needs, rights, or ideas are less important than those of others.

People who tend to be passive miss many academic and personal opportunities for growth because they do not assert themselves or they allow others to take advantage of them. They may have difficulty addressing the source of a problem, or if they do confront a problem directly, may apologize needlessly for their actions.

## The ABCs of Aggression

We are aggressive when we infringe upon the rights of someone else to meet our own needs. *Aggression* denies the rights of others in favor of our own desires and is often characterized by the use of intimidation or force. Aggression is also typified by a confrontational communication style. Name calling (global labels) and accusatory *you messages* are typical of this communication style.

*You messages* place blame on others: "*You* always leave all your junk around the room. *You* are such a slob! If *you* have to smoke, *you* could at least clean the ashtrays!" By opening the dialogue with the pronoun "you," the speaker makes an accusation that can immediately put the other person on the defensive. This communication style may be effective in gaining the short-term objective, but it frequently results in a long-term loss because in time other people will simply ignore or avoid the aggressor.

The ABC characteristics of aggression can be outlined as follows:

**Affect**    Feeling very angry or frustrated when things do not go one's own way.

**Behavior**    Attacking others verbally or physically. Use of *you messages* or derogatory labels.

**Cognition**    Believing that one's own needs, wishes, and rights are more important than those of others.

## So Where Do I Fit?

How do we deal with situations that have the potential for conflict? Consider this situation:

> Four students are working on a group research project. Angelo is not pulling his weight. Although he volunteered to find five journal articles for the project, he came to two meetings empty-handed. Angelo said he would have brought the articles, but couldn't because of a family emergency. The last time the students met, Angelo came to the meeting with one article. The other students are concerned that the quality of the project will suffer unless the work Angelo is supposed to do gets done.

Our personal response to such a situation can give us clues as to whether we tend to be assertive, passive or aggressive with our peers in academic situations. A student who responds assertively to this situation would approach Angelo, address the problem directly, remain calm, and initiate a discussion aimed at a resolution. A passive response might be to complain to the other students and avoid any discussion of the problem with Angelo. An aggressive response would be to yell at Angelo or make snide comments and accusations in his presence without attempting to reach an amicable resolution. A quick way to determine if we are responding assertively in the midst of any conflict is to ask ourselves: *To what extent am I contributing to a resolution of the problem as opposed to making no contribution or making the problem worse?"*

Learning new ways of feeling, behaving, and thinking will contribute to assertiveness in a variety of situations, but no one always functions in an assertive manner. For that matter, no one is always passive or aggressive either. We may be assertive with our friends, aggressive with our parents, and passive with our professors and employers. Or, we may be any combination of these three styles depending upon where we are, whom we are with, and what we are doing. Thus, the question is not so much where we fit, but how do we want to interact, with whom, under what circumstances, and for what reasons.

## BECOMING ASSERTIVE: HOW TO GO ABOUT IT

A systematic approach to assertiveness requires changing the affect, behavior, and cognition that promote passivity or aggression. Three general ABC principles apply to being assertive in any situation.

- If we are unable to manage our feelings, such that anxiety or anger are experienced frequently, then we are likely to behave passively or aggressively. Conversely, if these emotions are infrequent and we are often relaxed and upbeat, we are more apt to behave assertively.

- If we are unable to manage our behavior, such that we allow negative interpersonal habits to persist, then we are likely to behave passively or aggressively. Conversely, if we practice and reward positive interpersonal behaviors, we are more apt to act assertively.

• If we are unable to manage our thoughts, such that we often think of ourselves as worse or better than others, then we are likely to act passively or aggressively. Conversely, if these self-perceptions are infrequent, and we think of ourselves and others as having equal worth and value, we are more apt to act assertively.

The remainder of this chapter outlines methods for change that parallel these principles. Some of the difficulties we can expect as we attempt to become more assertive will be discussed, as will some of the rewards that accompany assertiveness.

## Changing Affect to Become Assertive

When we are passive or aggressive because of inappropriate negative emotions, we can reduce or eliminate these feelings by identifying and changing the thoughts that underlie them. In situations where negative emotions or sensations come on quickly and interfere with our ability to be assertive, we can diminish these feelings by "turning on" positive affect. The systematic use of relaxation can serve to counteract the negative feelings that prompt aggressive or passive responses. Exercise can also be used as an outlet for anger, anxiety, and tension that might interfere with assertive behavior. (See Chapter 4, Methods for Changing Affect.)

## Changing Behavior to Become Assertive

To become more assertive, we may want to change specific behaviors. Once we know what we want to start or stop doing, our task is to practice assertive responses until they become habit. To do this, we can use the principles of behavior modification or replace aggressive and passive behaviors with assertive responses through the contingent use of rewards. Imagined rehearsal can prepare us for the actual assertive behaviors we want to engage in. (See Chapter 4, Methods for Changing Behavior.)

## Assertive Communication

While we can all think of assertive behaviors that we would like to initiate or strengthen, a good place to begin is with behaviors that improve communication with others. This approach is referred to as assertive communication. *Assertive communication* is a way of speaking and listening to others that attempts to keep the lines of communication and understanding open. It is not whiny, apologetic, or accusatory, nor is it speaking one's mind just for the sake of being heard. Assertive communication avoids the accusatory verbal attacks and derogatory labels of aggressive communication. It is achieved in part through the use of *I messages* and *active listening*.

### I Messages

An *I message* is a clear and specific statement of the problem from the speaker's perspective with a suggested resolution. The use of *I messages* as opposed to *you messages* is an effective means of communicating when addressing a problem that could turn into an argument. It begins with a statement of our personal feelings and concludes with a request for a specific change in the other person's behavior. The steps for I messages follow:

1. Describe your feelings.

   Example:

   I get upset...

2. Describe in specific terms the behavior of the other person or the situation you want to address.

   Example:

   ...when I come back to our room to study and your friends are here partying.

3. Describe in concrete terms how the other person's behavior is impacting your life.

   Example:

   > It is difficult for me to study when they are here.

4. Offer a resolution to the problem by describing precisely what you would like the other person to do differently.

   Example:

   > I would appreciate it if you would not bring your friends to our room after dinner because that is when I like to get my work done.

Note that the problem is addressed directly and that the emphasis is on the *problem*, not the other person. The use of I messages does not guarantee that other people will not get angry nor does it guarantee that they will change their behavior. However, others are less likely to become defensive or respond aggressively, and they may be more sensitive to our needs in the future.

## Active Listening

Sometimes all the I messages in the world only provoke an aggressive response from some individuals. When this happens, assertive communication can break down immediately if we allow ourselves to be provoked. *Active listening* is a way of dialoguing with others that attempts to understand and reflect their feelings and attitudes while helping us remain in control (Gordon, 1983). It can be used as an assertive response to an aggressive outburst or in any situation that has the potential for conflict. When we listen actively, the goal is to try to empathize with the other person to prevent or resolve a conflict. It requires that we do the following:

1. Listen without interrupting as the other person speaks.

2. Rephrase what the other person said, reflecting an understanding of his or her feelings and point of view. Avoid advising, preaching, patronizing, etc.

3. Wait for a response.

4. Ask the other person to explain anything that was unclear.

5. Repeat steps 1 through 4 if necessary.

In adhering to the principles of active listening, we refrain from trying to think of a "come back" while the other person talks. Instead, we try to put ourselves in his or her shoes. The steps of active listening are demonstrated below by Lee.

Pat:   You've got some nerve! I lend you my good sweater and you return it with a stain on it.

Lee:   (Remains quiet and listens to what Pat is saying.)

Pat:   You're a real slob! I can't believe how inconsiderate you are!

Lee:   I take it you're pretty ticked off at me about the sweater. Are you... (Pat interrupts.)

Pat:   You're darn right I am! How could you be so care-less? How'd you like it if I did that with your stuff?

Lee:   Are you thinking that I'd just blow it off? Is that why you're mad at me?

Pat:   What do you mean? Yeah, of course that's why I'm mad.

Lee:   Well, if I get it dry cleaned and replace it if the stain doesn't come out, will that be okay?

Pat:   Are you serious?

Lee:   Yes. I'll have it dry cleaned and if the stain is still there, I'll replace it.

Pat:   You'd do that?

Lee:   Sure.

Lee responded to the verbal attack by trying to understand (not simply mind read) what Pat was thinking and feeling, and then reflecting this understanding back for clarification and resolution. In the event that Pat had continued to respond aggressively, Lee could have ended the conversation by using a brief I message: *"I'm starting to get upset*

*and instead of arguing, I'd rather talk to you about it later."* Such a response (which may have to be repeated like a broken record to someone who is very angry or upset) indicates an unwillingness to be goaded into an aggressive reaction.

Assertive responses to aggression give the other person a chance to calm down. Quite often people will recognize the civility of our assertive responses and be willing to work out the problem once they have had time to think about it calmly.

## Changing Cognition to Become Assertive

A cognitive skill essential to assertive communication or any other assertive behavior is the ability to interrupt and stop thoughts about ourselves, others, or the situation that might lead to passive or aggressive behavior. Visualizing the positive outcomes of being assertive can also spur us on to act assertively because it enables us to "see" the benefits ahead of time. (See Chapter 4, DIE Model and Methods for Changing Cognition.)

## WHY ARE PEOPLE AGGRESSIVE?

As students often say, "let's get *real*." Assertiveness is a nice idea, but it is tough to put into practice. So while we may pay lip service to the notion of individual rights, when push comes to shove, we may often choose to be aggressive. Why?

## Aggression Seems to Work

Aggressive behavior seems to work. That is, by intimidating or threatening others, we can often get what we want, when we want it. Such immediate gains can make aggression a difficult habit to break, especially when the more we use verbal or physical aggression, the better we get at it. In the words of American author Washington Irving: "A sharp tongue is the only edged tool that grows keener with constant use." The allusion could just as well apply to the clenched fist.

## Aggression Feels Good

Acting assertively toward people we like is difficult enough, but it is all the more difficult with people we label jerks, idiots, nerds, etc. or anyone with whom we are annoyed. We have a knack of justifying aggression toward someone who we think deserves our wrath. The release of pent-up anger or frustration can even feel good. As George Santanya, an American philosopher, so aptly points out: "To knock a thing down, especially if it is cocked at an arrogant angle, is a deep delight to the blood."

## Aggression is Promoted by Society

Not only does aggression seem to work for us and sometimes feel good — society promotes a belief in its value. Let's not be fooled. Being assertive is not a popular position. We may admire a Mahatma Ghandi, a Martin Luther King, or an Eleanor Roosevelt, but such assertive leaders are few and far between. Furthermore, their skill at being assertive does not gain widespread attention in today's society. Popular attention is focused more on the Rambos and the Terminators. The modern hero of the box office, the media, and popular sports is more often aggressive than assertive. As a society, we have come to see aggression as a way to get ahead. Leo Durocher, the fiery and popular manager of the old Brooklyn Dodgers, captured this sentiment well when he said: *"Nice guys finish last!"*

## Aggression is Easy

Being aggressive is easier than being assertive and sometimes appears to be the simple solution to a problem. Passive people may recognize the personal benefits of being assertive, but in their attempt to become assertive, they may become aggressive instead. This can happen because it is easier to go from one extreme to the other than to learn the skills of assertiveness, which require specific affective, behavioral, and cognitive changes.

## Aggression Allows Us the Comfort of Our Prejudices

Aggressive people may also find it difficult to become assertive because freeing themselves of the negative emotions and the cognitive distortions that accompany aggression is hard work. Our anger or hatred toward others may be so strong that it is easier to hold on to distorted perceptions and aggressive behaviors than to change them. This is a serious problem on a personal and societal level. Distortions abound in the judgments we make about individuals and about entire groups of people.

Using a derogatory label in reference to a person or a group is an obvious distortion in that it reduces people to stereotypes. But, as obvious as they are, many stereotypes are the basis for arguments between individuals and wars between nations. Some distortions about other people are very subtle, as for example, when groups of individuals are discussed as if they were all alike. Expressions that are common in this regard are: "it's *those* people, *that* group, the whole lot of *them*." Lumping people together is easier than recognizing differences among individual members of a group. Overgeneralizations, polarized thinking, filtering, and blaming are all distortions that fuel prejudice. This prejudice may take the shape of personal disdain for people who differ from us or it may take on the form of a group that shares in our distorted view.

To become assertive means to engage in the ongoing battle of freeing our minds of distorted thoughts that are at the heart of discrimination and stereotypes of all kinds, including racial, ethnic, sexist, and religious prejudices. It also means that we see benefit in being open-minded.

## Aggression is Motivated Behavior

Whether the motivation is positive or negative, many forces act on or within an individual to initiate aggression and give it direction. In light of what has been said about motivation in Chapter 3 and all the apparent advantages of aggression just mentioned, we can see why so many people are positively motivated to be aggressive.

Although positive motivation for aggression may seem to be a contradiction in terms, positive motivation has little to do with moral or ethical judgments. It has to do with the positive cognitions and feelings that motivate us toward aggression. We may believe that

**219**

aggressively controlling others is beneficial (it works), worth the cost (as the media suggests), and achievable (it is easy). In addition, we may find aggression feels good. Given this scenario, all the elements are in place to support positive motivation for aggression.

Negative motivation may also prompt aggression because of our thoughts and feelings regarding assertiveness. We may believe assertiveness does not work, is too difficult, or unachievable. In addition, we may feel uncomfortable being assertive. These thoughts and feelings could lead us to avoid assertiveness and resort to aggression. This can happen, for example, if assertiveness is viewed negatively by our peer group and mistaken for a lack of strength or toughness. Sometimes people act aggressively because of peer pressure, cognitive distortions, and fears of being seen as a "wimp," not because they feel good being aggressive and believe it is worthwhile. In such instances, they are negatively motivated to act aggressively.

## WHY BE ASSERTIVE?

*If aggression seems to work, feels good, is promoted by society, is so easy, and there is motivation for it, why be assertive?* Weighing the dangers of aggression against the advantages of assertiveness will be instructive in answering this question.

### The Societal Price of Aggression

The societal and personal consequences of aggression are serious ones. A fine line separates verbal aggression from physical aggression, and an even finer line separates physical aggression from violence. Many an argument turns into a physical conflict and many a fight into a homicide. Aggression can and does lead to violence — to assault, rape, murder, and a host of other violent crimes. Most of us see violence as a threat to society and our personal safety; however, we may never have considered that violence easily becomes a way of life in a society that uses aggression to solve its problems. When viewed as a contributor to a serious societal problem, aggression becomes a very unattractive option.

## The Personal Price of Aggression

On a personal level, aggression can hurt us and people we care about. It discourages communication and intimacy, and therefore can hinder our relationships. Screaming at a friend to turn down the radio may get the desired result, but perhaps at the expense of that friendship. Aggression can lead others to lose their respect for us. People tire rather quickly of aggressive outbursts and come to recognize aggression as the immature form of behavior that it is. For this reason, aggression is detrimental to the maintenance of satisfying personal and professional relationships over the long term.

## The Payoffs of Assertiveness

The benefits of living in a utopian society populated with assertive people are quite apparent. In such a society, people would listen to one another, express their ideas freely, and refrain from attacking others. Opportunities for self-fulfillment and societal growth would be abundant.

Yet, in reality, some people are assertive because they truly believe in the rights and dignity of all people, while others are motivated to be assertive because they learn that it has personal payoffs. People who opt to be assertive understand that assertiveness really does work.

By refusing to sacrifice long-term benefits for short-term gains, assertive individuals come out ahead. They generally experience less anxiety and stress than nonassertive people because they are better able to deal with difficulties and to prevent conflicts from arising in the first place. They tend to think well of themselves, and by acknowledging the rights of others, gain the respect of those around them. This in turn makes it easier for them to work with others and have their support when needed.

The mutual respect that assertive individuals foster in their relationships is also conducive to sustaining those relationships. While assertiveness does not guarantee immediate success or popularity, it is more effective than aggression and passivity in the long term because it guarantees our integrity as we pursue our goals and objectives. Thus, in response to Leo Durocher's comment about nice guys finishing last, we can say with confidence : *Nice guys finish first — by the end of the season!*

# ASSERTIVENESS IS A CHOICE

As was already mentioned, people who are just beginning to become more assertive can lapse into aggression unintentionally. Sometimes this occurs because people mistakenly think that being assertive means they *must be* or *should be* assertive in all situations, at all times. However, assertiveness, like any aspect of self-management, is a free choice. One can freely choose to place the needs of others ahead of oneself or to postpone an assertive response until the time is right. For example, if someone continually interrupts us before we have finished speaking in class, we may choose not to draw this to the other person's attention because we have decided that asserting ourselves will create an unwanted conflict. Our failure to be assertive might be based on the premise that right now we can better tolerate the interruptions than the possible consequences of addressing the problem. Or, we might determine that our comments are very important ones and that we do not want to be interrupted in the future. In this instance, we decide it is best to discuss our concerns with the other student after class.

## Weighing the Outcomes

The choice of whether or not to act assertively is best decided only after weighing the possible outcomes of being assertive in a given situation. Consider the following:

> Arnie would like to tell his boss that he doesn't want to work overtime anymore. He is worried, however, that his boss will yell as he is known to do. As Arnie ponders this problem, he thinks about the other employees who are eager and willing to work longer hours. Since it is important for Arnie to keep his position and he believes that confronting his boss might jeopardize his job, he decides that he will say nothing for now and continue working overtime for a while longer.

The outcomes of an assertive encounter with another person are important factors to consider before deciding to act. In this case, although the employee might have achieved the desired outcome by confronting his boss, he decided that the chance of losing his job was too great a risk to take in order to state his position.

Once we are practiced at being assertive, we recognize that assertiveness is a skill that we choose to exercise when we decide it is appropriate.  As such, deciding not to speak up or act in a particular situation could very well be an assertive response.  So long as we know we have thought about the outcomes and *could have* asserted ourselves *if we wanted to*, then restraint from taking action is an assertive option.

**KEY WORDS AND CONCEPTS**

**active listening**
**aggression**
**assertive communication**
**assertiveness**
**I messages**
**passive**
**you messages**

## SUGGESTED READINGS AND TAPES

### Assertiveness

Alberti, R., & Emmons, M. (1978). *Your perfect right.* San Luis Obispo, CA: Impact Publishers.

Fensterheim, H., & Baer, J. (1978). *Don't say yes when you want to say no.* New York: Dell Press.

### Assertiveness for Students

Ellis, D. (1991). *Becoming a master student.* Rapid City, SD: College Survival Inc. (Chap. 8).

Friday, R.A. (1988). *Create your college success.* Belmont, CA: Wadsworth (Chap. 20).

Gardner, J. N., & Jewler, A.J. (1992). *Your college experience: Strategies for success.* Belmont, CA: Wadsworth (Chap. 14).

Starke, M.C., (1993). *Strategies for college success.* Englewood Cliffs, NJ: Prentice-Hall (Chap. 9).

Yates, B.T. (1985). *Self-management: The science and art of helping yourself.* Belmont, CA: Wadsworth (Chap. 10).

## EXERCISE 8.1

## COMMUNICATION STYLES

Review the following conversations and identify whether the individuals are communicating in a passive, assertive, or aggressive manner.

### Conversation 1

Ramon: You did a great job for the team today!

John: No, I wasn't as good as I should've been.

Ramon: You've got to be kidding! You really turned the game around with those last two shots.

John: I just got lucky.

Would John's communication style best be described as passive, assertive, or aggressive? Why?

_____

_____

_____

_____

_____

### Conversation 2

Jane: I think we need to get this room in shape. I'll try to keep my part of the room neat . I 'd appreciate it if you'd do the same by hanging up your clothes.

Cynthia: You know, you aren't any bargain when it comes to neatness! You're always leaving your junk around!

Jane: Well, I think that the room could be kept neater and I wanted you to help me get it in shape.

Cynthia: Just because you decide you want to do something, you expect everyone to jump.

Jane: Are you saying that you would like to leave it as is?

Cynthia: You worry about your business — I'll worry about mine! All right?

Jane: I really don't want to argue with you. I'm just asking you to help me get the room straightened.

Would the communication style Jane used be labeled passive, assertive, or aggressive? Why? What about Cynthia? Why?

_____

_____

_____

_____

_____

## Conversation 3

Jeremy:   I can't believe that Dwayne isn't doing a stitch of work on our group project.

Sue:   Yeah, I know. It's not fair. We're all going to get the same grade and  Dwayne hasn't done a thing. He better have something for us tonight when we meet.

(Dwayne runs up to Sue and Jeremy)

Dwayne:   Jeremy! Sue! How's it going?

Jeremy:   OK, I guess.

Dwayne:   I'm glad I caught up with you guys — I can't meet tonight, but you two go ahead and meet without me.

Sue:   But Dwayne, you might not like what we come up with. We're almost finished with the project.

Dwayne:   Hey, you know me. I'm easy to please — whatever you do is fine. Oh, I've got to run — catch you later!

(Dwayne runs off)

Jeremy:   Can you believe that guy!

How would you describe Sue and Jeremy's communication styles in dealing with Dwayne? Were they effective? Explain why.

_____

_____

_____

_____

_____

## EXERCISE 8.2

## ABCs OF ASSERTIVENESS

For each of the 13 situations described below, do the following:

1. Write down what you would probably do (B) in that situation (not what you think you are supposed to do).

2. Indicate what feelings (A) and thoughts (C) would have contributed to this behavior.

3. Specify whether your response was passive, assertive, or aggressive. Then, explain why.

---

**Sample Answer**

**Situation:** My roommate brings friends into our room when I want to study.

**Behavior:** I would tell them that I was trying to study and politely ask them to leave.

**Feelings:** I would be a bit annoyed.

**Cognition:** I would think: "This is my room. I have a right to some privacy."

**Explanation:** This is an assertive response because the problem was addressed directly without using "you messages" or directing anger or annoyance toward the other person. The thoughts focused on my personal rights without "distorting" the magnitude of the problem.

---

**Situation 1:** I have five minutes to get to class and someone I don't know cuts ahead of me in the lunch line.

**Situation 2:** I am telling an interesting story to my friends and just as I am about to get to the main point, one of them interrupts me and changes the subject.

**Situation 3:** I am doing a group project with two other students that I do not know very well and one of the students is not doing the work.

**Situation 4:** I am at a party and I see someone I'd like to meet.

Situation 5:     A friend calls me and I really don't want to talk on the phone.

Situation 6:     My roommate changes the TV channel while I'm watching a good movie.

Situation 7:     My friends ask me to go out and I have a lot of work that I want to get done.

Situation 8:     I order a hamburger "rare" in a diner, but it is served "well done."

Situation 9:     The class period is almost over, everyone is packing up to go, and I have a question about the lecture.

Situation 10:    My friends are saying nasty things about someone that I like.

Situation 11:    A clerk denies that he shorted me five dollars when giving me my change.

Situation 12:    A lively classroom debate is taking place and I have a point of view that no one has raised.

Situation 13:    All the students in the class agree on a particular issue that I strongly disagree with.

**PROFESSOR INTERVIEW AND PRESENTATION**

In learning to become more assertive in the classroom and with professors, many students have found this exercise to be extremely helpful.

**Interview**

<u>Directions</u>:

Make an appointment to interview one of your professors in his or her office. You should call to make the appointment at least two weeks in advance and schedule a meeting for approximately 30 - 45 minutes. Explain to the professor that the interview is part of a class assignment.

Prior to the meeting, prepare an outline of the questions you will ask during the interview. Your questions could focus on the reasons why this professor became a teacher, what he or she believes constitutes good teaching or a good class. You might ask what this teacher sees as the most and least rewarding aspects of teaching. Learning about why your professor became a teacher and his or her expectations of students could also be interesting. Perhaps you might ask for a brief description of an ideal student or teacher.

After you have conducted your interview, write three to four typed, double-spaced pages discussing what you learned about this professor and what your personal experience was in doing this assignment. Instructions for the paper follow:

- The first part of the paper should focus on information you gathered during the interview. What did you find out about this person that you did not know before?

- The second part of your paper should focus on the ABCs of this experience. In this section, discuss your thoughts, feelings, and behaviors before, during, and after the interview, noting any interesting changes in the ABCs that occurred.

- The third part of your paper should include advice you would give to other students on what they must do to succeed in this professor's classes.

Before handing in your paper be sure to revise it using the checklist for revision on pages 160-161.

**Presentation**

<u>Directions</u>:

Your presentation to the class should summarize the information collected from the interview, as well as your ABC reactions before, during, and after the interview. You should plan to present for at least 5 minutes.

Prepare your presentation well in advance and practice it beforehand (in front of a small audience if possible).

If your teacher has the presentation videotaped, watch the tape and note your ABC reactions as you view your presentation. Then, write a two-page paper (typed, double spaced) on your presentation, focusing on the content and style. Be sure to note those aspects of your presentation that you were pleased with, as well as those aspects you would change for a future presentation.


This exercise was adapted from Jewler and Gardner (1987).

9

For some people self-esteem connotes an air of conceit; for others it is key to success. Still others will argue that self-esteem only helps people feel good when they are doing poorly.

# CASE STUDY

Before reading Chapter 9, read the case study below. After completing the chapter, analyze the case study by following steps 1 through 4.

STEP 1      Describe Brenda's initial problem.

STEP 2    AFFECT:     Identify the feelings that contribute to low self-esteem. Then identify those that contribute to high self-esteem.

           BEHAVIOR:    Identify the behaviors that contribute to low self-esteem. Then identify those that contribute to high self-esteem.

           COGNITION: Identify the thoughts that contribute to low self-esteem. Then identify those that contribute to high self-esteem.

STEP 3      Identify the trigger of the firing order for the low self-esteem problem. Then identify the trigger for Brenda's improved self-esteem. Describe the upward spiral that reflects this improvement in Brenda's self-esteem.

STEP 4      What methods or techniques described in this text could have been used to change the trigger of the low self-esteem problem?

Brenda has always known that she lacks coordination and that she is not the athletic type. She is therefore very upset that she is required to take a three-credit phys. ed. course next semester. To make matters worse, a horseback riding class is all that will fit in her schedule, and Brenda's been afraid of animals since she was a kid. Even when just talking to her friends about riding a horse, she finds herself stammering a bit, which further signals to her how physically inept she is.

Since she needs the course to graduate and sees no other alternative, Brenda grudgingly signs up for the course. Yet, to Brenda's surprise, in the first class she discovers that other students are also scared and she begins to feel a little better. Then she learns that she is not expected to get in the saddle right away, but rather to walk around the stables, pat a few horses, and learn how to bridle them. Brenda is surprised how gentle they are and how her self-confidence is improving as she becomes more familiar with horses. She has actually become attached to Victor, a beautiful palomino. As the day she was expected to mount a horse approached, Brenda used self-talk to encourage herself. Once in the saddle, she was pleased to hear the instructor comment that she sits on the horse well. She was singled out as a model of good posture and balance. After that, walking the horse came easily, and to her amazement, weeks later she was able to gallop.

Brenda's horseback riding experience was an extremely positive one. She now sees herself as more coordinated and athletic than she thought, and is less fearful of other animals. She feels so good about herself that she is thinking of joining a horseback riding club and might even try something she has always shied away from — skiing.

# SELF-ESTEEM

> You've no idea what a poor opinion I have of myself — and how little I deserve it.
>
> W. S. Gilbert (1836-1911)
> English librettist
> (writer of opera text)

> Remember, no one can make you feel inferior without your consent.
>
> Eleanor Roosevelt (1884-1962)
> American diplomat,
> humanitarian

## WHAT DOES IT MEAN TO ESTEEM ONESELF?

For some people, self-esteem connotes an air of conceit; for others, it is key to success. Still others will argue that self-esteem only helps people feel good when they are doing poorly.

Self-esteem is not exaggerated self-praise, nor is it feeling comfortable when performance is poor. The once common meaning of the word esteem — to evaluate or estimate — gives us our starting point. *Self-esteem* will be defined as our overall evaluation of our worth as individuals. To esteem oneself is to evaluate oneself.

## ABCs OF SELF-ESTEEM

We all have opinions about our physical, mental, and social abilities and as these opinions change or stabilize over time, so does our self-esteem. *Low self-esteem* is a negative evaluation of oneself that frequently results from cognitive distortions and dysfunctional beliefs. *High self-esteem* is a positive evaluation of oneself that frequently results from accurate, functional, and balanced thoughts.

Self-esteem is primarily a cognitive process of self-evaluation, but affect and behavior also significantly influence it. In this chapter we will see that by managing affect, behavior, and cognition, we evaluate ourselves more realistically, and as a result, increase the opportunities to enhance our self-esteem.

**233**

## Affect and Self-esteem

As discussed in earlier chapters, our thoughts can influence our feelings and our feelings can have a direct and immediate impact on our thinking. If we think about ourselves while we are feeling bad, we are more likely to evaluate ourselves negatively; if we think about ourselves while we are feeling good, we are more likely to evaluate ourselves positively.

When we are feeling down, it is not easy to think positively about anything, including ourselves. Feelings of sadness, depression, and despair not only help to filter out pleasant thoughts, but also may trigger counterproductive thoughts about our worth and value as individuals. The same is true regarding negative sensations such as tension and fatigue.

Inappropriate negative emotions and sensations make us more vulnerable to distorted thoughts and dysfunctional beliefs. They have a sneaky way of making distortions in thinking believable, and therefore, we are more likely to act upon them. In the following example, a student taking an exam is so anxious that it triggers a series of negative self-evaluations.

> Rachel has finals this week and has been cramming for days. She is feeling so pressured and stressed from studying constantly that she is about ready to give up. She begins to think that it will be an impossible task to get through the material for computer science. Worrying about the work she has yet to do, she says to herself "I just can't handle this stress. I'm going to fail anyway so why bother putting myself through all this." The more upset she becomes, the more thoughts about failing and dropping out of school begin to preoccupy her mind.

During exam week, many students feel scared and may evaluate this feeling as an indication of incompetence. Thinking negatively when we are feeling stressed is commonplace, but accepting an erroneous perception such as "I can't do this" as fact only intensifies the affect and may lead us to act as if it were true.

Some *negative emotions* trigger distorted self-evaluations almost instantaneously, while others can have this effect several hours, weeks, or years later. Anger is an emotion that may trigger a low opinion of ourselves long after the reasons for the anger have been forgotten. Since most of us do not evaluate ourselves positively after losing control, our self-esteem can suffer when we later recall an angry outburst. Emotional trauma experienced years ago can have a lasting impact on our self-esteem if we still associate the emotion with a lack of ability or worth. Past fears or anxieties are often mistakenly used as a basis for evaluating ourselves in the present. Perhaps we believe that we cannot give a class presentation because we judge the experience of once having had stage fright as proof of our inadequacy as a public speaker. When "I can't do it" is based on a feeling from the past, we give lasting credibility to a temporal emotion, and it can have a prolonged negative impact on our self-evaluation.

Positive feelings have the opposite effect. Thoughts such as "I'm pretty good at this!" are much easier to come by when we are happy and feeling good. Being excited and "turned on" can lead us to think more positively about ourselves than when we are emotionless.

Because our affective state influences our self-esteem, it is wise to refrain from evaluating ourselves when we are experiencing extreme emotion, whether positive or negative. We need to be particularly cautious not to judge ourselves harshly when upset.

## Changing Affect to Enhance Self-esteem

Since we run the risk of lowering self-esteem whenever we experience inappropriate negative emotions and sensations, we might want to use methods such as relaxation and reframing to counteract the effects of such feelings. By relaxing in those situations associated with negative affect, we are less likely to do or say things that we will later evaluate negatively. For example, we may anger ourselves a lot over some things that our friends or parents do. To deal with the situation more effectively, as soon as we begin to get annoyed, we could slow down our breathing by inhaling deeply while focusing on letting go of the tension. Or, by *reframing* we can focus on some of the positive or humorous aspects of an otherwise negative event. Sometimes a combination of methods is most effective. The more we work at reducing inappropriate negative affect, the less significant its role becomes in forming our self-evaluation. (See Chapter 4, Methods for Changing Affect.)

# Behavior and Self-esteem

Generally, we evaluate ourselves positively when our actions reflect our values and goals, and negatively when our actions deviate from the standards and objectives we have set.

## Competence and Effort

Competent behavior is a potent force in raising self-esteem. It involves initiating action, making sacrifices, and completing tasks successfully, among other things. However, ***competence*** as it relates to self-esteem is a matter of our own judgment; we set the ground rules in terms of our own standards and objectives. If our standard calls for diligent effort in the pursuit of an objective, then we can justifiably evaluate ourselves positively when we put forth our best effort. Therefore, in part, completing tasks successfully means that the outcome we achieve reflects our best attempt. Although we cannot guarantee that every effort will result in the desired outcome, *we can guarantee our effort*. In this sense, we can be at least partially successful at every task we undertake, and these successes will serve to enhance our self-esteem.

Consider how the two young men described in the following examples might evaluate their behaviors.

### Example One:

David was determined to make the college track team. He set as a short-term goal a two-mile run every morning at 6:00 a.m. for four weeks. To motivate himself to do it, he bet his best friend that he could pull it off. One morning, he barely managed to get up because he was tired from staying out late the night before. After suffering through his morning run, David avoided staying out late from then on. He stuck to his plan for four weeks, tried out for the team, but didn't make it. Over the summer, he put himself through an intense regimen to build up his stamina and endurance, tried out for the cross country team in the fall, and made it.

**Example Two:**

Jason wanted to raise his grade in chemistry by getting a 'B' on the final exam. He detailed a plan to achieve this goal and began to put it into action by going to the library every afternoon for two hours, but instead of studying as planned, he talked away the hours with his friends. As the day of the chemistry final drew near, he tried to stick to his plan, but wasn't sure it was worth the effort and couldn't resist talking to his buddies. When he took the final, Jason was not well prepared, but luckily guessed the correct answers to most of the objective questions. He got the 'B' he wanted.

In each example the outcome is a favorable one. Yet, these two students would probably evaluate their behaviors quite differently. David set a goal and did what he set out to do. Although he did not make the track team, his effort was diligent and eventually paid off. In addition, his performance would likely prompt positive accolades from others because persistence in face of adversity is a quality most people admire. In the second example, Jason accomplished his goal of a 'B' grade, but it had little to do with his best effort or competency in chemistry. While he might be pleased with the grade, thinking about the behaviors that produced it would probably not lead him to take any personal pride in having acquired it.

*Personal effort* that results in the achievement of a desired goal enhances self-esteem because we begin to see ourselves as self-directed and capable individuals. Also, since our actions are evaluated by a wider audience than ourselves, praise and recognition from others are rewards that often follow competent behavior. Rewards raise self-esteem still another notch because receiving the reward itself is evaluated as a positive accomplishment.

### Effort and "Failure"

What happens to our self-esteem when our immediate efforts are not that competent and consistently result in "failure"? Many individuals who maintain high self-esteem in the face of failure do so because they do not label the result a failure. They simply label it an *undesired outcome*, learn from it, and keep working diligently until they achieve the outcome they want. Since their behavior is not labeled a failure, neither are they, and their self-esteem does not suffer.

**237**

This is not merely a matter of semantics, but rather a realistic and functional way of perceiving behavior that enhances our self-esteem and motivation. Thomas Edison can be cited as an example. Someone once asked Edison how he motivated himself to keep trying when he had failed in approximately 50 attempts to find the right filament for the first light bulb. Surprised by the comment, Edison explained that he had not failed, but had simply discovered 50 ways not to invent a light bulb!

### Changing Behavior to Enhance Self-esteem

Increasing our achievements in any area requires a change in some aspect of our behavior. Once we have decided to initiate a change in our behavior, we might decide to modify the antecedents and consequences of that behavior to make the change easier. For example, we might want to increase study time an additional hour each morning, but find that most mornings we watch television instead. To get ourselves to study more, we could place a note on our desk as a reminder to study and, after we have studied for an hour, use television as a reward. (See Chapter 4, Methods for Changing Behavior.)

## Cognition and Self-esteem

As previously mentioned, our self-evaluation is more constructive when it is accurate, functional, and balanced. An *accurate and functional self-evaluation* attempts to be free from distortions and dysfunctional beliefs. A *balanced self-evaluation* focuses as much on effort as on results, and as much on assets as on deficits. Therefore, if low self-esteem is a problem, we need to consider *how* and *what* we are thinking about ourselves.

### Distortions in Self-evaluations

When we distort information about ourselves, our self-evaluation will be based on erroneous conclusions (McKay & Fanning, 1987). Several *distorted self-evaluations* are illustrated below.

### Filtering

My hair is wind blown. I look like a complete wreck!

### Catastrophizing

I failed the mid-term. I don't have what it takes to get a college degree.

### Global labeling

I made a mistake. What a stupid jerk I am.

### Overgeneralizing

She doesn't like me — probably no woman will ever find me attractive.

### Mind reading

I didn't know what to say when I first met him.  He must think I am a real bore.

Thinking that lowers self-esteem often underestimates or negates positive qualities and exaggerates weaknesses.  However, overestimating and exaggerating the significance of our attributes or abilities is a form of distorted thinking as well.  We all recognize the "anything you can do I can do better" mentality in others, but sometimes fail to see it in ourselves.  Examples of distorted thinking that reflect an inflated view of oneself (but may actually mask low self-esteem) are as follows:

### Overgeneralizing

Getting an 'A' on that paper makes me a shoo-in for a 3.5 this semester.

### Filtering out areas for improvement and focusing exclusively on good qualities

Since I'm such a great athlete, I really don't have to put much effort into getting good grades.

### Global labeling based on an accomplishment

That award proves that I'm "numero uno." Nobody can outdo me.

Exaggerations like these can detract from positive qualities that we really do possess and set us up for disappointment. Generally people with high self-esteem are realistic and balanced in their judgments about their abilities. They usually avoid overestimating or underestimating themselves and tend not to be preoccupied with comparing their abilities to those of others.

## Changing Distortions to Enhance Self-esteem

In their book, *Self-Esteem*, McKay and Fanning (1987) claim that one of the most important characteristics that distinguishes humans from other animals is an awareness of self. They describe this awareness as "the ability to form an identity and then attach value to it" (p. 1). The value we place on our own identity is often reflected in our self-talk. *Self-talk* is an extremely important part of our self-evaluation because it usually reveals what we really think about ourselves. Therefore, we need to pay close attention to it and change it when it is inaccurate.

Eliminating distortions in self-talk is the first step toward thinking more accurately about ourselves. We can do this by getting in the habit of correcting imprecise and unbalanced thinking as in the following examples.

|  | Distortion | Correction |
|---|---|---|
| **Global Labeling** | | |
| | I am a fat slob. | I am 15 pounds over-weight and annoyed with myself. |
| | I am a failure, a real jerk. | I failed the last two quiz-zes and am concerned that I might get a 'F' in the course. |
| **Overgeneralizing** | | |
| | I never do anything right. | This is the second time I missed the deadline for an assignment; I need to set up a time schedule. |
| | I always lose my tem-per; I just have no self-control. | This week I got angry at my friend on three dif-ferent occasions. We need to talk. |
| **Mind reading** | | |
| | If I speak up in class, my friends will think I'm just trying to impress the teacher for a grade. | If I really want to know what my friends think about me, I need to ask them. |
| | I could tell she didn't like me from the look on her face. | I don't know if she likes me or not, we just met. |
| **Catastrophizing** | | |
| | My presentation was a total disaster. I must have looked like a fool. I'll never be able to show my face again. | During my presentation I was shaking, said "um" a lot, stammered, and forgot half the speech. However, I got a good discussion going after-wards. |

## Dysfunctional Beliefs in Self-evaluations

When directed at ourselves, dysfunctional beliefs such as perfectionism, approval, fairness, determinism, and avoidance can lower our self-esteem.

### <u>Perfectionism and Self-esteem</u>

If we believe we must be *perfect* at everything we do, our opinion of ourselves will suffer each time we fall short of this unrealistic standard. We have all heard the old adage, "If you can't do it right, don't do it at all." While doing a great job is commendable, some people believe anything short of perfection is totally unacceptable.

*Perfectionism* means we place emphasis solely on the end result and give ourselves little, if any, credit for our efforts, for partial success, or for what we learned from an experience. When people believe a goal must be achieved flawlessly, they are intolerant of

mistakes and setbacks that may be part of the process of achieving a goal. Take for example the student who wanted to make the track team, but ended up joining the cross country team instead. Had he believed that he must be perfect, his failure in achieving his original goal might have deterred him from trying out for the cross country team. Even though his conditioning regimen prepared him for cross country, a desire for perfection would suggest anything short of making the track team was a failure.

The belief in perfection sets us up for disappointment and defeat because it generates distortions by focusing our attention only on what has not been achieved. Because of this, perfectionists perceive themselves as having failed much more often than others. The net result may be a lowering of self-esteem.

A variation on the theme of perfectionism is the inflated, and equally unrealistic, belief that "I am perfect the way I am. There is no room for improvement." In this instance, perfectionism is not something to aspire toward, but rather a state already acquired. People who believe they are perfect may miss opportunities for growth by neglecting areas where they might otherwise improve.

## Approval and Self-esteem

Another dysfunctional belief that contributes to low self-esteem is the belief that we must have constant *approval* from all the important people in our life. It is not easy to avoid this dysfunctional belief because we are bombarded continually by messages that promote it. Many popular song titles equate a person's worth and reason for living with acceptance by others rather than self-acceptance. A few examples would be:

> *You're Nobody 'til Somebody Loves You*
> *I Can't Live if Living is Without You*
> *You are the Sunshine of My Life*
> *You Make Me Feel Like a Natural Woman*

More realistic and accurate thinking is reflected in the following song titles:

> *I'm Still Standing*
> *I Will Survive*
> *Got Along Without You Before I Met You —*
> *Gonna Get Along Without You Now*

Linking evaluations of ourselves too closely to the opinions of others is to relinquish control over our self-esteem. By placing the judgments of others above our own, we evaluate ourselves negatively whenever others fail to respond positively to us.

### Fairness and Self-esteem

Fairness is an ideal state that is free from bias and injustice. People who are fair-minded are admired because they strive hard to be balanced and nonjudgmental in dealing with others. The difficulty is that opinions about what is fair or unfair vary widely. A functional belief in fairness takes this into account, but a dysfunctional one is intolerant of an opposing point of view.

A dysfunctional belief in *fairness* has to do with our reactions to situations that do not turn out the way *we* think is fair. When we believe that life is supposed to be fair, we are hard hit whenever our version of fairness is violated. If we draw the inference that something is wrong with us because things have not gone our way, we may begin to wonder why what we judge to be fair is so often ignored. Under such circumstances, we may choose to give up because we see ourselves as lacking the ability to make things turn out fairly. Over time, we may evaluate ourselves negatively for our inability to do anything about all these injustices.

What begins as a rigid belief in fairness can lead us to personalize our plight and lower our self-esteem. Therefore, when we catch ourselves getting overly worked up over a perceived injustice, we want to be sure that the "injustice" is not really a disguised form of simply wanting our own way.

### Determinism and Self-esteem

The effects of a dysfunctional belief in *determinism* on self-esteem are similar to those mentioned in our discussion of fairness. A belief in determinism becomes dysfunctional and detrimental to self-esteem when it is used as an excuse for not making an effort to improve or learn new skills. It can prevent people from making changes in their lives that would further their development.

When we blame fate for our problems or use it to explain daily events, personal responsibility and self-management take a back seat. We may find ourselves waiting a lifetime for our ship to come in because we never realized that we command that ship. *"That's just the way it was meant to be"* can become an excuse for not learning new skills or for remaining in a negative situation. We can come to believe that we cannot manage ourselves or any aspect of our future. Our self-esteem suffers as a result.

Even if our lot in life is relatively pleasant and trouble-free, a dysfunctional belief in determinism can have a negative impact on self-esteem because we may not credit ourselves for our accomplishments. We might fail to recognize the important role we play in achieving a particular goal by attributing our success to sheer luck or "good genes." We may even believe the envious comments of others, who attribute our successes to simply being in the right place at the right time or being born with a "silver spoon" in our mouths. Fate receives the credit and an opportunity to enhance our self-esteem is lost.

## Avoidance and Self-esteem

*Avoidance* is another dysfunctional belief that can eat away at self-esteem. It may prevent us from experiencing success in something we think is worthwhile, but too risky to try. It can have the insidious effect of draining our lives of the excitement of new challenges and opportunities. The negative effects of avoidance on self-esteem are subtle and indirect. It lowers our self-esteem when we draw the inference that we have missed out on something for fear of failure, and as a result, label ourselves a "loser." The safe and narrow path that avoidance holds us to can stifle us academically, professionally, and personally.

## Changing Dysfunctional Beliefs to Enhance Self-esteem

As discussed in Chapter 2, dysfunctional beliefs can easily be overlooked. However, in becoming aware of our illogical thoughts and negative self-talk, we may begin to realize that they are rooted in beliefs that foster *distorted self-evaluations*. When we put ourselves down, a dysfunctional belief might be at work. A few examples follow.

### Perfectionism

> I don't take a course unless I can get an 'A' or 'B' because anything less means I'm a failure.

> After this much practice, if I miss a putt inside of three feet I should give up golf.

### Approval

It is clear that I can't succeed in business since my management professor doesn't respect my ideas.

Since I don't have a boyfriend/girlfriend, my life is meaningless.

### Fairness

Nothing ever goes my way. I do one little thing wrong and really get "reamed out," while everyone else seems to get away with murder.

When I have a group project, I don't bother working very hard because I wouldn't get credit anyway.

### Determinism

Oh, it's no big deal, just luck, that I won the game. I got a lot of lucky breaks.

If I'm meant to get the job, I will; if not, I won't. My interviewing skills won't have anything do with it. They already know who they want to hire.

### Avoidance

I could never give a speech to a large audience. I would die of nervousness.

If I'm still having trouble after two drafts of an essay, it means I'll never be able to write an 'A' paper, so why put myself through this?

Once we are in the habit of recognizing errors in thinking, we will have a better chance of preventing them and correcting them when they do occur. However, since some thinking habits are tough to break, we will still need to rely on practical methods such as *disputing, reframing,* or *thought stopping* to change illogical beliefs that lower self-esteem.

# ABC INTERACTIONS AND SELF-ESTEEM

We have focused primarily on the relationship of each ABC component to self-esteem as well as on how to enhance self-esteem by changing these components. However, it is also important to understand how ABC interactions can influence self-esteem. When our self-esteem spirals upward, ABC interactions contribute to a series of experiences that we would evaluate positively, as in the following example:

> Barbara stops by to see her history teacher (B) and their talk leads her to think (C) more positively about the professor. Now that she understands (C) what he expects from students, she feels more comfortable (A) in class and she begins to participate (B) more often. One day, the professor asked if anyone would like to give a presentation on his or her paper topic. Barbara decides (C) to volunteer. When she delivers (B) the presentation to the class, she realizes (C) afterward that she actually enjoyed it (A). A few months later, Barbara decides (C) to join the debate team. She never really thought of herself (C) as a public speaker, but now sees (C) herself differently.

Note how each ABC component influences another in a progressively upward spiral that leads to a positive self-evaluation.

When our self-esteem spirals downward, a series of ABC interactions culminate in experiences that we evaluate negatively. Consider the following example:

> Angela drank (B) a couple of six packs last night and has a hangover. She feels tense and irritable (A). She finds it difficult to concentrate (C) on her homework and begins to think about (C) having a beer in order to feel better. After all, she says to herself (C), "I'm not going to get work done anyway." She goes out drinking (B) with a few friends, and the next day she wakes up and feels (A) worse than ever. She pulls the covers over her head and falls asleep (B). After missing her classes (B), she is angry (A) with herself, gets in her car, pushes it to 70 miles per hour (B), and gets a ticket for reckless driving. "Now I have really blown it," she thinks (C). "How could I have been so stupid. What a jerk I am..."

Note how each ABC component influences another in a progressively downward spiral that leads to a negative self-evaluation.

It is important to realize that when we find ourselves sliding along a downward ABC spiral, we can intervene at any point and at least halt, if not reverse, its direction. Because of the nature of ABC interactions, a change at any point in a downward spiral could eventually lead to a more positive self-estimate.

If we learn how to promote upward spirals and how to alter the course of a downward turn, we can manage our self-esteem as we do other aspects of our life.

## ABC CHARACTERISTICS OF SELF-ESTEEM

In terms of the ABCs, a person with high self-esteem could be characterized as follows:

**Affect**      Has feelings that are more positive than negative. Experiences a full range of emotions and sensations, but extreme affect rarely clouds thinking or directs behavior inappropriately.

**Behavior**    Directs actions toward realistic goals. Acts assertively with others, spends time on activities that are meaningful, and often achieves goals that are set.

**Cognition**   Perceives strengths and weaknesses in accurate, functional, and balanced terms. Recognizes distorted thinking and dysfunctional beliefs about him/herself and refutes them. Often thinks positively about him/herself.

Obviously, these are general ABC characteristics, but knowing them allows us to evaluate ourselves quickly. If we find an absence of these characteristics, we can use the ABCs of self-management to develop them and in the process raise our self-esteem.

**KEY WORDS AND CONCEPTS**

**accurate and functional self-evaluation**
**balanced self-evaluation**
**distorted self-evaluations**
**high self-esteem**
**low self-esteem**
**self-esteem**
**undesired outcome**

**influences on self-esteem:**

> **ABC interactions**
> **approval**
> **avoidance**
> **competence**
> **determinism**
> **fairness**
> **negative emotions**
> **perfectionism**
> **personal effort**
> **self-talk**

## SUGGESTED READINGS AND TAPES

**Self-esteem**

Barksdale, L.S. (1972). *Building self-esteem.* Idyllwild, CA: The Barksdale Foundation.

Brandon, N. (1986). *The psychology of high self-esteem.* Chicago: Nightingale-Conant (Audio cassettes).

Coopersmith, S. (1967). *The antecedents of self-esteem.* San Francisco: W.H. Freeman.

Dyer, W. (1991). *Pulling your own strings.* New York: Harper Perennial.

McKay, M., & Fanning, P. (1987). *Self-esteem.* Oakland, CA: New Harbinger Publications.

Robinson, B.E. (1991). *Heal your self-esteem.* Deerfield Beach, FL: Health Communications.

Zimbardo, P.G. (1977). *Shyness.* Reading, MA: Addison-Wesley.

## EXERCISE 9.1

## RECOGNIZING COGNITIONS THAT INFLUENCE SELF-ESTEEM

Each of the following thoughts can influence one's self-esteem. Match each statement with the distortion or dysfunctional belief it best represents.

| | |
|---|---|
| ____ 1. I'd never take statistics— it's too difficult for me. | A. Global label |
| ____ 2. If I can't get at least a 'B' grade in a course, I don't take it. | B. Avoidance |
| ____ 3. I'm such a "klutz." | C. Filtering |
| ____ 4. I wasn't cut out to do anything athletic. | D. Fairness |
| ____ 5. I have no limitations; I can do anything I put my mind to. | E. Polarized thinking |
| ____ 6. I can tell she thinks I'm a jerk. | F. Overgeneralization |
| ____ 7. My poor foul shooting will cost us a lot of games and probably keep us out of the playoffs; I should quit the team now. | G. Determinism |
| ____ 8. Given the money I'm paying, it's not right that I get stuck with an inexperienced teacher. | H. Catastrophizing |
| ____ 9. With my communication skills, I don't have to prepare or know the facts, I can just "wing it" in any situation. | I. Mind Reading |

## EXERCISE 9.2

## SELF-ESTEEM INVENTORY

This exercise is divided into three parts. Each part builds upon your answers to the previous section, so be sure to complete each part before moving on to the next.

**Part I**

List as many words and phrases as you can to describe yourself with respect to each word or phrase below. Try to give a complete picture of yourself for each item.

Describe yourself as...

a student:

_____
_____
_____
_____

an employee or worker:

_____
_____
_____
_____
_____

a friend:

_____
_____
_____
_____
_____

a citizen:

_____
_____
_____
_____
_____

a family member:

_____
_____
_____
_____

a roommate:

_____
_____
_____
_____

Describe your...

athletic ability:

_____
_____
_____
_____

communication skills:

_____
_____
_____
_____

physical appearance:

_____
_____
_____
_____

strengths:

_____
_____
_____
_____

areas for improvement:

_____
_____
_____
_____

**Part II**

Review all the words and phrases used to describe yourself in each category in Part I of this exercise. Identify any distortions or dysfunctional beliefs in your self-evaluation and list them on the left-hand column below. Pay particular attention to language that is imprecise, inaccurate, unbalanced. In the right-hand column, rewrite the words and phrases in language that is specific, accurate, balanced, and distortion free.

_____          _____
_____          _____

_____          _____
_____          _____

_____          _____
_____          _____

_____          _____
_____          _____

_____          _____
_____          _____

_____          _____
_____          _____

_____          _____
_____          _____

_____          _____
_____          _____

_____          _____
_____          _____

_____          _____
_____          _____

## Part III

Now that you have completed a more accurate inventory of yourself, write a short paragraph describing yourself. Incorporate characteristics identified in the right-hand column of Part II of this exercise. Emphasize characteristics that you view positively, without ignoring areas for improvement.

_____

_____

_____

_____

_____

_____

_____

_____

_____

_____

_____

_____

_____

_____

_____

_____

_____

_____

_____

_____

_____

_____

_____

_____

_____

This exercise was adapted from McKay and Fanning (1987).

## 10

*"Seek for truth in the groves of Academe."* We might not be inclined to take the advice..., but those who have immersed themselves in his poetry have come to know...Horace as a man of good reason with a passion for living and learning from life.

# CASE STUDY

After reading Chapter 10, fill in the box below with your own case-study dialogue. Assume that you are a faculty member advising a student who has lost his or her motivation for academics. Write a conversation between the two of you that reveals the reasons for the student's loss of motivation and the specific things you suggest this student do to regain academic motivation.

# 10 ACADEMIC MOTIVATION

> Your reason and your passion are the rudder and the sails of your sea-faring soul.
>
> Kahil Gibran (1883-1931)
> Syrian poet, mystic

> Seek for truth in the groves of Academe.
>
> Horace (65 BC-8 AD)
> Roman poet

## REASON AND PASSION

*"Seek for truth in the groves of Academe."* We might not be inclined to take the advice of a Roman poet who lived nearly two thousand years ago, but those who have immersed themselves in his poetry come to know and love Horace as a man of good reason with a passion for living and learning from life. Edith Hamilton (1973), a scholar of ancient Greek and Roman culture, describes him as the kind of person we "wish could have lived forever," one who had "that most delightful gift of enjoying keenly all life's simplest pleasures" (p. 123). She calls it wisdom. We can call it motivation. To borrow Gibran's metaphor, Horace's "reason and passion" were the "rudder and sails" that led him to the "groves of academe." While our discussion of motivation in Chapter 3 was much less poetic, the metaphor reflects the principles of motivation laid out in that chapter and the spirit of the pages that conclude this text. All the general principles for steering one's reason and passion toward any pursuit were previously discussed, but no systematic application was made to academic motivation — a topic of considerable importance to college students.

All college students are motivated to be in college. Their motivation may be high, medium, or low, positive or negative, but there is some motivation for being in college. Otherwise they would not be there. If we wish to manage this motivation systematically, we must first decide whether positive or negative motivation primarily directs us as college students. Both may actually support our actions, but it is imperative to determine which one is primary.

The aim of this final chapter is: 1) to bring together the information necessary to complete a personal assessment of our academic motivation; 2) to aid in developing a personal plan for maintaining academic motivation; 3) to provide an approach for restoring academic motivation if it is ever lost. The first part of the chapter will focus on assessing and maintaining our motivation. The second part will focus on regaining lost motivation. Exercises at the end of the chapter will be used to collect personal data needed to structure and implement a plan to maintain motivation for academics.

A review of Chapter 3 is recommended before reading this final chapter. This review will help in deciding which type of motivation is primary and in identifying the ABC components .

## ASSESSING AND MAINTAINING ACADEMIC MOTIVATION

If we want to assess and maintain our motivation, whether positive or negative, for short- or long-term objectives, we need to do the following:

- Identify the ABC components of our academic motivation.

- Identify the firing order of these ABC components.

- Identify and use methods to maintain academic motivation.

### Identifying the ABC Components

Identifying the *ABCs of academic motivation* requires self-observation and serious reflection on each separate component that comprises it. Because cognition and affect are the key elements in motivation, it is helpful to focus on them first before addressing specific behaviors.

With respect to *cognition*, we need to assess the benefits and costs of trying to achieve our academic goals, as well as the personal skills that will enable us to reach them. With respect to *affect*, we need to identify the emotions and sensations we experience in college that keep us motivated academically. With respect to *behavior*, we need to identify the things we do and say that contribute to these thoughts and feelings.

After reading this chapter, we can gather the personal information needed to understand the ABC components of our academic motivation by doing the concluding exercises. If our motivation for academics is primarily positive, we should complete Exercise 10.1 and then complete Exercises 10.3 and 10.4. If it is primarily negative, we should complete Exercise 10.2 before doing the other exercises. If unsure whether we are more positively or negatively motivated, doing both Exercises 10.1 and 10.2 will help clarify the matter before doing the others.

## Identifying the Firing Order

As was discussed in Chapter 1, identifying a firing order reveals which component serves as the *trigger* that sets off the ABC interaction and specifies the order in which the components follow one another. By determining which ABC component of our motivation is the trigger, we know which component is primary, and therefore which one to address first in trying to maintain motivation for a particular goal or objective.

From years of experience in school, we may already know which ABC component is the "ignition key" that starts our motivation for academics. We may know that we are only motivated to learn when we perceive a meaningful payoff that we are confident we can obtain at minimal cost. In such a case, *cognition is the trigger.* Or, we may only be motivated when we are "revved up" or very relaxed, after which we focus on a specific academic objective. In such a case, *affect is the trigger.* Or, we may only be motivated when we are actively engaged in doing something, which then leads us to think and feel positively or negatively about some school-related objective. In such a case, *behavior is the trigger.* If we do not know the firing order of our academic motivation, we can determine it by doing Exercise 10.3 at the end of this chapter.

## Identifying and Using Methods

Once we have assessed the ABC components and their firing order, we can use specific methods to strengthen these components. To do this, we apply the appropriate methods directly to problems related to the particular benefits, costs, beliefs, emotions, sensations, and activities that comprise our academic motivation. These methods will be discussed under the appropriate ABC heading.

### Methods Applied to Cognition

To sustain academic motivation, we need to strengthen the belief that the benefits of the college education we are receiving outweigh the costs. We also have to continually reinforce a belief in our ability to achieve our educational goals. A variety of techniques can be used to strengthen these cognitions such as visualizing rewards, supportive self-talk, imaging success, recalling past achievements, attaining goals, and attributing causes.

### <u>Visualizing Rewards</u>

To maintain the expectation of receiving the long-term payoffs associated with a college education, these future payoffs must be brought into the present to support ongoing academic behaviors and activities. *Visualizing future rewards* after engaging in an academic task is one way of doing this. For example, to stay motivated when writing a term paper, we can vividly picture ourselves handing it in, receiving a good grade, and smiling as we walk on stage to receive our diploma at graduation. When studying, we could envision ourselves using our knowledge on the job and receiving praise from a manager. We should *not* visualize any negative scenes that relate to the costs of being a college student. For example, we would not focus on missing parties or on all the work that remains to be done to achieve our goals. Instead, we would remind ourselves that highly motivated people focus on the rewards for success, not the costs.

## Supportive Self-Talk

To maintain the expectation of receiving the benefits of a college education, our self-talk after completing each academic activity related to our goal must be supportive, as well as descriptive of the payoff we expect to receive. For example, after participating in a class discussion, our self-talk should be congratulatory and state how this behavior will help us achieve in college  and in our career. Some specific examples might be:

- Good for me, I'm speaking up more. This will help  me get a decent grade  in this class.

- I'm actually learning how to do something that will help me get a job.

- I'm getting better at speaking up and working with others.

- These skills will help me in any career after I graduate.

Our self-talk can be used to remind us that according to Jeweler and Gardner (1987), college graduates compared to non-graduates usually:

- have more control over their personal lives and careers

- have higher self-esteem

- adapt better to life's changes

- find life more interesting and less  boring

- make more money

We can also use our self-talk to emphasize the temporary nature of the personal and financial  costs of going to college.  For example, we could tell ourselves that a party missed during a school night will allow time to party on the weekend;  the money now spent on tuition will be returned many times over by a high paying job in the future; the books purchased each semester will build a valuable personal library, etc. If thoughts or images of costs keep coming to mind, thought stopping can block them out. If cognitive distortions or dysfunctional beliefs exaggerate the costs, we can use disputation, reframing, and other methods described in Chapter 4 to change them.

There are costs associated with being a college student, but reminding ourselves continuously that the short-term costs are significantly outweighed by the long-term benefits will help to motivate us to do the immediate tasks related to our long-term objectives. It may even help to recall the somewhat caustic bumper sticker slogan: "If you think education is expensive, try ignorance."

*Supportive self-talk* is positive and reinforcing, and it is also phrased in such a way that it suggests what to do rather than what not to do. For example, before giving a speech it is better to think: "relax and stand up straight," rather than "don't tense up and don't slouch." By continually talking to ourselves in positive terms, we can strengthen a belief in our ability to engage in goal-oriented behaviors and achieve our objectives.

## Imaging Success

Successful athletes believe that they can win any competition they enter and this belief is fortified by the *success images* they create for themselves before and during the event. Jack Nicklaus attributes much of his self-confidence to picturing in his *mind's eye* the ideal swing, ball trajectory, and final result on every shot in practice and in each tournament. Mary Lou Retton believed she could score a perfect ten in her last gymnastic event in the 1984 Olympics because she had *mind-scripted* her performance so many times before the event; Greg Louganis visually rehearsed his final Olympic dive 40 times before "going for the gold" (Waitley, 1990). If imagery techniques helped these athletes achieve world class success, they most certainly can help students achieve a college education.

To keep ourselves motivated for college, we need to reinforce a belief in our ability to attain our goals and receive the desired rewards. Believing that we can achieve a college degree can be strengthened by imagining ourselves actually engaging successfully in the necessary academic tasks. For example, we could envision ourselves making a successful class presentation, meeting with our advisor, contributing to a class discussion, and any other behaviors relevant to a particular academic situation. Whenever we actually do engage in these activities successfully, we need to observe our behavior carefully and try to impress the image of this activity in our mind's eye immediately, so we can use it in the future.

If we have difficulty imagining ourselves engaging in a particular academic activity, we can strengthen this skill by practicing the visualization exercises in Chapter 4. It may also help to observe others who are proficient in these activities and emulate them in our imagination.

## Recalling Past Achievements

Belief in ourselves can be strengthened by regularly *reflecting on past achievements* as well as the problems that have been encountered and overcome. Calling to mind problem-solving methods that have worked before bolsters self-confidence because we reinforce the expectation that they will work for us again. Having available a list of our past achievements enables us to focus on them quickly, further helping to sustain belief in our ability to achieve.

## Attaining Goals

Our self-confidence increases through the attainment of meaningful or challenging goals, whether they be short- or long-term. Because the *achievement of short-term goals* provides immediate feedback and reinforcement, we should set out to achieve a number of short-term goals. All these goals do not have to relate to academics, since self-confidence gained in one area can generalize to others. The more we encounter success, the more we believe that we will have "successful encounters" (Waitley, 1990).

The attainment of short-term goals is satisfying, but it will not be as rewarding as the *achievement of long-term goals*, which requires patience and persistence. Belief in our ability to persevere toward a long-term goal increases as we perceive ourselves capable of tolerating the discomfort that accompanies delays in achieving our objectives. To strengthen our ability to endure frustration, we can practice delaying gratification in some area of our life each day. For example, instead of eating dessert immediately after a meal, we can delay it for a half-hour; or instead of taking a nap at the first sign of fatigue, we could do some homework first. Eventually, this ability will strengthen, and we will come to see ourselves as a person who can tolerate discomfort and persevere toward our goals.

## Attributing Causes

To maintain and strengthen belief in ourselves it is important to attribute any success we achieve, at least in part, to our ability and effort, not solely to luck, external events, or other people. *Taking credit where credit is due* is simply acknowledging our role in accomplishing our goals. This increases self-confidence and enhances self-esteem, which serves to keep us positively motivated.

*Attributing causes* refers to the process of "attributing" or assigning cause for something that has occurred. It relates to belief in oneself, and therefore to motivation, because the conclusions we reach about the causes of problems we encounter can determine whether we will be motivated to solve them.

When the causes are seen as *temporary*, *external*, and *specific* to the problem at hand, we are more apt to remain motivated to address them, than when the causes are perceived as permanent, internal, and having a broad, general impact on our life. For example, suppose we set as our goal an 'A' grade in a class. If we perceive receiving a poor grade on a test as a temporary, rather than a permanent setback that can be overcome by additional effort, we will probably remain motivated to achieve our original goal. Or, if we perceive the cause of the grade as due in part to the noisy room, poor lighting, excessive heat, etc., rather than an intellectual deficit, we are more apt to remain motivated, believing we can do better next time when the external conditions improve. Similarly, if we perceive that the poor grade reflects our lack of knowledge regarding the specific test questions, rather than the course content in general, we will probably stay motivated believing we can do better on future tests. Since it is often difficult to determine beforehand the causes for a lack of success, it is to our *advantage* to view the causes as temporary, external, and specific — if we want to stay motivated (Waitley, 1991).

History is replete with examples of individuals who believed they could overcome obstacles that others thought impossible to surmount. For this reason they remained motivated when others gave up. Roger Bannister, the first man to break the four-minute mile barrier in 1954, did so at a time when the leading physiologists said that it was physically impossible for a human being to run the mile in under four minutes. Bannister obviously believed that the causes of previous failures to crack this barrier were *temporary* (records are meant to be broken), *external* (poor track conditions, wind resistance, etc.), and *specific* to the other individuals who had tried (negative thinking, physical condition, etc.). Thus, he believed that with appropriate training and perseverance, he could accomplish what no human being had done before him. As significant as his achievement was, it is even more interesting to note that within six months after Bannister's feat, several other runners broke the four-minute mile. Of course, human physiology did not change during that time, but beliefs about what humans could accomplish certainly did!

To stay motivated, we need to think about the causes of the problems we encounter in ways that support a belief in our ability to overcome them. This is not to suggest that we distort reality or simply adopt a "pollyanna" view of life; however, when the reality is uncertain, as it often is, it is better to attribute successes and "failures" to causes that support positive motivation, than to causes that undermine it.

## Role Models

Belief in ourselves can be strengthened by learning what other people who have struggled to maintain their motivation have been able to accomplish. ***Role models*** who display the skills we admire can provide good examples. Reading biographies of high achievers, listening to motivation tapes, watching movies and videos of positive role models, hanging out with optimistic, proactive people, and avoiding "gloom and doom" cynics and "nay sayers" who continually look on the negative side of life can help. Such activities over time will reinforce the notion that "if others can do it, so can I."

## Methods Applied to Affect

If positive cognitions are maintained by the methods described above, positive feelings will most likely result. The combination of positive cognition and affect is, of course, the basis for positive motivation.

To help maintain positive feelings for academic tasks, the techniques discussed in Chapter 4 can be applied as follows:

- Get adequate rest, particularly when classes are scheduled the following day.

- Exercise regularly and eat a balanced diet. This will keep our energy level high for doing concentrated work and minimize the negative effect of fatigue, tension, and illness that can cause us to "tune out" or miss classes.

- Take ***positive imagery*** breaks from studying several times a day. That is, create a mental picture of anything that contributes to positive feelings, which in time will strengthen the association between studying and positive affect.

- Practice relaxation daily, but particularly at the first sign of stress during exam time.

- Spend at least part of each day engaging in some enjoyable activity, unrelated to academic requirements.

## Methods Applied to Behavior

A common sense approach to academic motivation argues that when the appropriate thoughts and feelings are in place, we are motivated to behave in ways that bring us closer to our educational goals. While this statement is true, behaviors can also influence thoughts and feelings, as was emphasized in Chapter 3. By acting in a way that is consistent with being positively motivated toward academics, motivation for academic tasks can be maintained. Thus, by acting as a motivated college student, we can remain one. Some of these actions might be:

- Dressing for class as a student (differently than we dress for lounging around, partying, etc.)

- Sitting in the front row in class

- Asking questions and participating in class discussions

- Talking to friends socially about course readings, class topics, history, philosophy, literature, etc. and limiting conversations on nonacademic subjects (dating, work, sports, etc.)

- Reading a newspaper each day and a news magazine each week

- Watching a TV news program each day

- Watching educational programming each week

- Attending college-wide cultural events several times a month

- Talking to professors outside of class

- Joining a campus club or society

- Visiting historical sites, museums, art galleries, etc.

To see to it that these behaviors are repeated and become habit, we need to reinforce them each time they occur, at least verbally to ourselves.

**269**

# REGAINING LOST ACADEMIC MOTIVATION

When the techniques for maintaining motivation described above are used regularly, motivation for academics is not likely to be lost. If this happens, however, the following ABC analysis can guide us in restoring it.

## Cognitive Changes:  Perception of  Benefits

If we no longer believe there is value or benefit in the goal being sought, our motivation for the goal will be lost or at least reduced.  For example, we may no longer value a career in business, and therefore have diminished motivation for an advertising course. To regain our motivation for the course, we need to restore our "old" values or establish new values that relate to advertising.  It is also possible that we still value a business career,  but no longer see the connection between the goal of being a stock broker, for example, and learning advertising. Until this connection is reestablished, motivation for studying advertising will be minimal.

If we no longer know what we value in terms of our education or see little benefit in studying anything, we may need to clarify our values in general, and with respect to academics in particular. *Values clarification* can be quite helpful in this regard.  (See Suggested Readings for Chapter 6 and Exercise 6.3.)

If we have less motivation for a goal and related activities because we no longer value it (our major, for example), but decide we want to try to reach the objective anyway, we will need to find some benefit in the goal and the activities in order to remain motivated. Finding benefits can be accomplished by reframing, seeking advice, establishing incentives, reading biographies, and using rewards.

## Reframing

We can gain renewed motivation for a goal and its related tasks by reframing the activities so that they are not seen as a waste of time, but rather as beneficial to us (see reframing, Chapter 4). For example, the activities may be seen as applicable to another career, or helpful in developing perseverance, or an aid in strengthening our tolerance for frustration, etc.

## Seeking Advice

By asking others who have objectives similar to ours what value they see in their ultimate goals and how they personally benefit from what they are doing, we may learn of values and benefits we might never have known about. Speaking to a practicing stock broker, for example, may help restore motivation for a business major or an advertising course.

## Establishing Incentives

We can *establish incentives* for a former goal by associating it with one that is currently valued. For example, we may want to learn how to cope in situations that are unappealing or difficult to change because we know that such coping skills will help us in any situation. Learning to cope with our present difficulties regarding our major could be viewed as a good preparation for dealing with problems in a future profession. Seeing this relationship can provide an incentive to keep striving toward the goal in spite of the difficulties.

### Reading Biographies

Reading about individuals whose values changed often during their lifetime and learning how they coped during the transition period can help us adjust when our values are in the process of changing. People like Billy Joel, Jane Fonda, and Malcolm X underwent major life changes, which gave new shape and direction to their lives. Much can be learned from the experiences of such individuals.

### Using Rewards

We can use external rewards temporarily to reinforce activities leading to a goal, when the activity or goal is no longer valued in itself. For example, if we find that we no longer value doing the required readings for a course, we might provide tangible reinforcers for the activity so that some immediate benefit is obtained.

## Cognitive Changes: Perception of Costs

If motivation has been lost or diminished for a goal because the cost (compared to the payoff) is perceived as too high, we either need to reduce the cost or increase the benefit of the goal and the activities related to achieving it.

### Reducing Costs

The cost of anything is based in part on our perception of cost, so one way to reduce the cost is to change our perception. If we focus on the cost too much, thought stopping might prevent this from occurring. Also, there may be some practical steps that can be taken to counteract the cost of pursuing a goal. For example, if the cost of studying is less "party time" with friends, it would be important to schedule some future recreation, before our motivation for studying is lost entirely.

### Increasing Benefits

The payoff we expect to receive can become more attractive by making the image of this reward as vivid as possible. *Vividness of images* will increase by enlarging the size of the image, making it more colorful, bringing the image closer to us in our mind's eye, and imagining the payoff frequently. For example, as we approach graduation, we can motivate ourselves each day by picturing right in front of us a large diploma in a colorful frame hanging on our office wall. The benefit of achieving our goals can also be enhanced by adding images of other payoffs associated with our objectives. For example, imagining the smiling face of someone we love or the "toys" we can buy when we are successful.

## Cognitive Changes: Perception of Self

If motivation is lost or diminished because we no longer believe in our ability to achieve our academic goals, the following suggestions should prove helpful.

1. Check to see if cognitive distortions or dysfunctional beliefs are contributing to this change in attitude. If so, eliminate them.

2. Check to see if negative affect is contributing to the problem. For example, being overtired, stressed, sick, etc. If so, be sure to attribute the change in attitude to its proper source, and then address that problem.

3. Check to see if personal liabilities are being focused on to the exclusion of personal assets. If so, *refocus.*

4. Concentrate on what can be accomplished short term, not long term. *Do* something quickly to restore self-confidence.

5. Review the positive thoughts, images, and self-talk that originally supported the belief that the academic goal could be achieved. Determine whether these cognitions were in error. If not, concentrate on these strengths daily.

6. Focus on past accomplishments and relate them to the present.

7. Use thought stopping for doubts that keep coming to mind.

## Affective Changes:  Decrease in Positive Affect

Motivation can be  lost  because the *positive feelings* related to the activity or goal have  faded.  When positive cognitions have diminished and  positive affect is reduced as a result, then restoring these cognitions will  restore the affect.

If positive feelings have diminished due to the passage of time, as for example when the excitement of something new has worn off, we can try to reestablish the conditions under which the positive feelings were first experienced. For instance, if we lose our motivation for romance  with a boyfriend or girlfriend because we have gotten used to the relationship, we could again  do some of the things that were fun when the relationship was fresh and exciting.  Reliving these events may stir up the old feelings of excitement and passion.  This method can apply as well to restoring the good feelings experienced when first entering college.

We can also practice positive feelings or relaxation in the presence of  the event or person toward which motivation needs to be restored.  By consistently pairing positive affect in this manner, positive feelings will be reassociated with the event or person, and motivation can return.  This method can apply to even the most rigorous academic task.

## Affective Changes: Increase in Negative Affect

Loss of motivation can occur because negative feelings related to the activity or goal have developed. If  the negative affect has developed as a result of  certain cognitions, we should work on changing these cognitions.  However, if negative feelings have developed because negative experiences have occurred in pursuit of the goal, we can counteract these feelings by generating positive affect as we strive for the goal. For example, we may begin our college career full of excitement and enthusiasm.  Over time, however, we are bound to encounter negative events that contribute frustration and annoyance. As these negative feelings develop, they can block out the initial positive feelings, resulting in a loss of positive motivation. By turning on positive affect (such as excitement, enthusiasm, or even relaxation) at the *first sign* of negative affect — *before* it takes a strong hold — the negative feelings can be eliminated.

## Behavioral Changes: Lack of Success

Motivation can be lost when the behaviors we engage in no longer bring about the desired results. If motivation is lost or diminished because goal-oriented activities have been unsuccessful, practicing the behavior apart from the actual situation in which it needs to occur can help. For example, if motivation for participation in class

has been lost because we stumble over our words, we could practice speaking out loud at home. We should refrain from volunteering comments in class until improvement has occurred in this "safe place."

By setting several short-term goals that we are capable of achieving, we avoid the potentially demoralizing effect of "failure" and its impact on our motivation. Stringing together short-term successes optimizes the chances for reaching our long-term goals because these successes help to keep us motivated.

Finding a role model and emulating those actions we want to develop to reach our own goals can also work. For example, some students have improved academically by modeling the behavior of successful students, just as many golf pros have improved their game by modeling themselves after Jack Nicklaus or Arnold Palmer.

275

## Behavioral Changes: Competing Behaviors

Motivation for academics can also be lost if behaviors that compete with academic achievement have increased. When behaviors that interfere with academics outnumber the behaviors that would generate success in college, the following steps can be taken to decrease these competing behaviors.

1. Identify the antecedent conditions for these behaviors and eliminate them.

2. Identify the reinforcers, rewards, or payoffs for these behaviors and eliminate them.

3. Identify deterrents or penalties for competing behaviors and apply them.

For example, we may find that our "academic" behaviors (reading, writing, class attendance) have decreased in part because our "socializing" behaviors have increased. As a result our motivation for academics may have diminished. Determining why our socializing has increased may reveal that there are certain antecedents that encourage us to socialize. These antecedents might be urgings from friends, having a few beers, loud "party time" music in the dorm, etc. Whatever the antecedents that precede our socializing, we need to reduce them. We also need to eliminate any rewards for socializing if we want to socialize less. Perhaps the positive reactions from friends serve to reinforce it, while their "put downs" discourage studying. Avoiding these friends for a time may minimize their influence over us. If we cannot think of any rewards for socializing that can be eliminated, we can arrange some deterrents or penalties for socializing so that this option is less attractive to us. It should be apparent that much of what has been outlined above reflects the principles of behavior modification discussed in Chapter 4.

## SUMMARY

In this chapter, we applied the ABCs and the general concepts of motivation to the specific topic of academic motivation. We saw that academic motivation can be understood in terms of its ABC components and their interactions. We also saw that it can be maintained or regained by applying specific techniques to each of these components. Conceptually, we should find little that is new in this last chapter. Practically every topic in this book has been approached in this way to provide students with a systematic approach to better manage any aspect of their lives. This detailed illustration of the ABCs of motivation applied to academics is both a guide and an invitation to students to try their own creative hand at applying this systematic approach to other areas of interest.

## A FINAL WORD

And, so we conclude this text where we began — with the basic principles of the ABCs. Yet at the same time, we are undoubtedly much further from where we started if we have gained some fresh ideas about who we are and how we can get to where we want to be. Using the ABCs as our common denominator, a general approach to self-management established the interconnections among a number of different areas for intellectual, personal, and professional growth. No doubt there are countless areas of application that could still be explored. With enough positive motivation, we will surely find them.

### KEY WORDS AND CONCEPTS

**ABCs of academic motivation**
**achievement of short-term goals**
**achievement of long-term goals**
**attributing causes**
**establish incentives**
**positive imagery**
**reflecting on past achievements**
**role models**
**success images**
**supportive self-talk**
**values clarification**
**visualizing future rewards**
**vividness of images**
**temporary, external, and specific (causes)**

**277**

## SUGGESTED READINGS AND TAPES

**Achievement Motivation**

Atkinson, R.C., & Raynor, J.O. (1974). *Motivation and achievement*. New York: Halstead.

**Applied Self-Talk**

Waitley, D. (1990). *The power of self-talk*. Chicago: Nightingale-Conant (Audio cassettes).

**Imagery in Athletics**

Garfield, C. (1984). *Peak performance: Mental training techniques of the world's greatest athletes*. Los Angeles: Tarcher.

Murphy, M. (1973). *Golf in the kingdom*. New York: Dell.

Nicklaus, J. (1974). *Golf my way*. New York: Simon and Schuster.

Schwarzenegger, A., & Hall, D. (1982). *The education of a bodybuilder*. New York: Pocket Books.

**Attribution and Motivation**

Barr-Tal, D. (1978). Attribution analysis of achievement-related behavior. *Review of Educational Research, 48,* 259-271.

**Values and Motivation**

McClelland, D.C. (1985). How motives, skills, and values determine what people do. *American Psychologist, 40,* 812-825.

**EXERCISE 10.1**

## ASSESSING THE ABCs OF POSITIVE ACADEMIC MOTIVATION

Positive academic motivation means that we engage in academic tasks because we experience more positive thoughts and feelings with respect to academic tasks than negative ones. In other words, we do not engage in academic tasks as a means of avoiding negative consequences, but rather because we envision positive consequences related to the academic tasks we do. Complete this exercise if you are primarily **positively motivated** for academic tasks. If you are unsure, do this exercise and Exercise 10.2. Then do Exercises 10.3 and 10.4.

1. Identify the *cognitions* that contribute to your positive **academic** motivation by responding to each of the following questions:

   a. What are the benefits, rewards or payoffs that you expect to receive from your college education? List them.

   _____     _____
   _____     _____
   _____     _____
   _____     _____

   b. What are the costs, penalties, or losses you expect to encounter as a result of pursuing a college education? List them. (See Chapter 3, Cognition and Positive Motivation, for discussion of costs related to motivation and Chapter 5, Cognition and Motivation for Learning.)

   _____     _____
   _____     _____
   _____     _____
   _____     _____

   c. What skills, talents, or abilities do you believe you have that will enable you to achieve your goal of a college education? List them.

   _____     _____
   _____     _____
   _____     _____
   _____     _____

   d. Do the benefits outweigh the costs? Circle your answer.

   yes     no     uncertain

e. Do you have the abilities needed to succeed academically in college? Circle your answer.

yes    no    uncertain

f. If you answered **no** to 1d or 1e, what can you do to overcome this problem?

_____

_____

_____

g. If you answered **uncertain** to 1d or 1e, what can you do to resolve this uncertainty?

_____

_____

_____

2. Identify the *feelings* that contribute to your positive motivation for college by responding to the following:

a. Describe the positive feelings (emotions and sensations) you experience in college with respect to **academic** activities (reading, writing, studying, class discussions, etc.).

_____

_____

_____

b. Describe the positive thoughts, if any, associated with these feelings.

_____

_____

_____

c. Describe the positive feelings you experience in college with respect to personal or social activities (parties, clubs, sports, conversations, etc.).

_____

_____

_____

d. Describe the positive thoughts, if any, associated with each of these feelings.

_____

_____

_____

e. Do academic tasks or the personal/social aspects of college prompt more positive feelings? Circle your answer.

academic tasks    personal/social    uncertain

f. If academic tasks do not prompt more positive feelings, what can you do to increase these positive feelings?

_____

_____

_____


3. Identify the *behaviors* that contribute to your positive motivation for *academics* by responding to each of the following:

a. What specific behaviors do you engage in as a college student that contribute to the positive thoughts associated with achieving academically?

_____

_____

_____


b. What specific behaviors do you engage in as a college student that contribute to the positive feelings associated with achieving academically?

_____

_____

_____


c. What other behaviors might you engage in to increase positive thoughts and feelings associated with achieving academically?

_____

_____

_____

# EXERCISE 10.2

## ASSESSING THE ABCs OF NEGATIVE ACADEMIC MOTIVATION

Negative academic motivation means that academic tasks are done primarily to avoid or escape from something (e.g. criticism from others, a low grade, dismissal from school, etc.), rather than to accomplish something in a positive sense. Complete this exercise if you are often **negatively motivated** with respect to academic tasks. If you are unsure, do Exercises 10.1 and 10.2 before going on to the next two exercises.

1. Identify the *cognitions* that contribute to your negative **academic** motivation by responding to each of the following:

   a. List the benefits you believe you receive by being negatively motivated for academic learning in college. That is, when you engage in academic tasks as a means of avoiding or escaping something unpleasant, what are the benefits?

   _____     _____
   _____     _____
   _____     _____
   _____     _____

   b. List the costs you believe you experience by being negatively motivated. That is, what does it cost you academically? What do you **not** get out of academics when you do academic tasks only to avoid something unpleasant? (See Chapter 3, Cognition and Negative Motivation and Chapter 5, Cognition and Motivation for Learning.)

   _____     _____
   _____     _____
   _____     _____
   _____     _____

   c. To remain negatively motivated over a long period of time, we develop certain skills, talents, or abilities so we can continue to avoid or escape unpleasant consequences. What skills do you believe you have that will enable you to continue to pursue academics in this way? List them and explain.

   _____
   _____
   _____

   d. Are the benefits of your negative academic motivation greater than the costs? Circle one.

yes     no     uncertain

e. If the benefits of negative academic motivation are not greater than the costs, what can you do to change this? Explain.

_____
_____
_____

2. Identify the *feelings* that contribute to your negative **academic** motivation by responding to each of the following:

a. Describe the negative feelings that are reduced or avoided by pursuing academics in college.

_____
_____
_____

b. List the negative cognitions, if any, associated with these negative feelings that are being reduced or avoided.

_____
_____
_____

3. Identify the *behaviors* that contribute to your negative **academic** motivation by responding to each of the following:

a. List the behaviors that contribute most to the negative cognitions that support your negative academic motivation. (See Chapter 5, Behaviors That Motivate To and Fro.)

_____
_____
_____

b. List the behaviors that contribute to the negative feelings that support your negative academic motivation.

_____
_____
_____

c. What specific behaviors occur *only* to avoid failure, but enable you to encounter success nonetheless? (These are called "fear of failure" behaviors because their primary purpose is to keep you from failing, not to help you achieve academically in a "positive" sense.) List them.

_____
_____
_____

## EXERCISE 10.3

## ASSESSING THE FIRING ORDER FOR ACADEMIC MOTIVATION

To determine the ABC firing order for academic motivation, follow the procedures outlined in Parts I and II of Exercise 3.4. In doing this exercise, be sure to recall a time in your life when you had high motivation for **academic achievement**. To gain additional information on each ABC component of your academic motivation, do Part III of Exercise 3.4 and again be sure to focus on your motivation for academics in answering these questions.

## EXERCISE 10.4

### DETERMINING METHODS FOR MAINTAINING ACADEMIC MOTIVATION

1. Rank the following methods for maintaining the *cognitive* aspects of positive motivation in order of personal preference.  Place  1 next to your first preference,  2 next to your second preference, etc.

   ___ a.  Visualizing rewards
   ___ b.  Supportive self-talk
   ___ c.  Imaging success
   ___ d.  Recalling past achievements
   ___ e.  Attaining goals
   ___ f.  Attributing causes

2. Rank the following methods for maintaining the *affective* aspects of academic motivation in order of personal preference. Place  1 next to your first preference, 2 next to your second preference, etc.

   ___ a.  Getting adequate rest
   ___ b.  Exercising regularly
   ___ c.  Maintaining a balanced diet
   ___ d.  Practicing relaxation
   ___ e.  Taking positive imagery breaks
   ___ f.  Engaging in non-academic recreation

3. Rank  the following methods for maintaining the *behavioral* aspects of academic motivation in order of personal preference.  Place 1 next to your first preference,  2 next to your second preference, etc. Cross out any behavior that you refuse to do to maintain your academic motivation. Do not include these behaviors in your ranking.

   ___ a.  Dressing appropriately for class
   ___ b.  Sitting in the front of the class
   ___ c.  Asking questions and participating in class discussions
   ___ d.  Talking to friends about course readings, topics, etc.
   ___ e.  Reading a newspaper each day
   ___ f.  Reading a news magazine each week
   ___ g.  Watching a news program on television every day
   ___ h.  Watching educational programming each week
   ___ i.  Attending cultural events on and off campus
   ___ j.  Talking to professors outside of class
   ___ k.  Participating in a campus club or society
   ___ l.  Visiting historical sites, museums, art galleries, etc.

| | |
|---|---|
| **ABC** | Letters that stand for affect, behavior, and cognition. |
| **ABC approach to time management** | An assessment of how affect, behavior, and cognition contribute to or interfere with using time in a personally meaningful way. |
| **ABC interaction** | A cause-and-effect relationship among affect, behavior, and cognition. |
| **accuracy** | (In thinking and language) Describing people and events based on available evidence while refraining from conjecture. |
| **accurate and functional self-evaluation** | An evaluation of oneself that is precise, correct, and free of distortions and dysfunctional beliefs. |
| **active listening** | A way of communicating with others that attempts to understand and reflect verbally the feelings and point of view of another person. |
| **affect** | Another word for feelings that refers to emotions and sensations. It is a physical state that we experience in response to an internal or external stimulus. (See **emotion** and **sensation**.) |
| **aggression** | Feelings, behaviors, and thoughts that meet one's own needs, but interfere with or deny the rights of others. |
| **antecedents** | Conditions (4Ws: who, where, what, when) present before a behavior occurs. |
| **appropriate negative emotion** | An unpleasant physical state of arousal that is a beneficial response to an external or internal stimulus. |
| **appropriate negative sensation** | An unpleasant internal physical response that is a beneficial reaction to sensory stimulation. |

**GLOSSARY**

**approval**

A dysfunctional belief that acceptance by others is a necessary condition for happiness and contentment.

**assertive communication**

The use of I messages and active listening when interacting with other people in situations with the potential for conflict. (See **I messages** and **active listening**.)

**assertiveness**

Feelings, behaviors, and thoughts that support one's own needs without interfering with or denying the rights of others.

**attributing causes**

The process of assigning the cause or determining the reason for something that happens.

**avoidance**

A dysfunctional belief that there is benefit in avoiding anything unpleasant, risky, or challenging.

**balanced self-evaluation**

An evaluation of oneself that focuses realistically on strengths as well as on areas for growth or improvement.

**balanced thinking**

(In thinking and language) Focusing equally on the positive and the negative and avoiding a one-sided point of view.

**behavior**

Observable acts or activities people engage in. Things people do, say, or the responses people make.

**behavior modification**

A change technique that alters antecedents and consequences to manage behavior.

**being right**

A distorted thinking process in which a person refuses to acknowledge personal fallibility or error.

**beliefs**

(See **functional** and **dysfunctional beliefs**.)

**blaming**

A distorted thinking process in which a person insists upon holding someone or something at fault for a problem or difficulty.

| | |
|---|---|
| **catastrophizing** | A distorted thinking process in which future disaster is anticipated based on a single incident. |
| **cognition** | Refers to any mental activity — thoughts, beliefs, self-talk, images, ideas, perceptions, judgments, reasoning, recollections, etc. |
| **competing behaviors** | Behaviors that substitute for, and thus interfere with, actions a person wants to occur. |
| **computer literacy** | A basic understanding of how computers work, their uses, and their limitations. |
| **consequences** | Conditions present after a behavior occurs. |
| **coping** | (In Part Three of the DIE Model) Adjustment to negative data. |
| **Cornell System** | A specific method of taking class notes in which notebook pages are divided into two parts. The left-hand side is used for key terms and questions; the right-hand side is used for class notes. |
| **data** | The 'D' of the DIE Model. Objective facts that provide an occasion for a positive or negative emotional response. The data might refer to circumstances, people, or other external events. (See **DIE Model**.) |
| **deep breathing relaxation** | A breathing pattern that reduces negative affect by using the lower part of the lungs. |
| **determinism** | A dysfunctional belief in which a person maintains that present thoughts, feelings, and behaviors are caused and controlled by events or other people. |

**GLOSSARY**

**DIE model**

The letters DIE stand for data, interpretation, and emotional response. Part One of this model (DIE) illustrates how emotional responses (and sometimes behaviors that follow) come from how and what people think. Parts Two and Three of the model provide a method for changing an emotional response by changing distorted thinking and dysfunctional beliefs or by learning to cope and reframe. (See **coping** and **reframing**.)

**dispute**

(In Part Two of the DIE Model) Challenging distorted thinking and dysfunctional beliefs in order to diminish a negative emotional response.

**distorted thinking**

A thinking process that is based upon illogical, erroneous, or faulty reasoning, which can result in negative emotions.

**downward ABC spiral**

A progressive series of ABC interactions that lead to a negative outcome or experience.

**dysfunctional belief**

A belief that has no basis in fact or reason, leads to inappropriate negative emotions, sensations, or behaviors, and undermines a person's happiness or personal goals.

**effective writers**

Writers who convey their ideas in an organized, clear, and concise manner by revising their drafts repeatedly while keeping the reader in mind.

**emotion**

Affect that is experienced as either pleasant or unpleasant. An internal physical state that can be initiated by one's thinking. Happiness, sadness, anger, frustration, and joy are all examples of emotions.

**emotional reasoning**

A distorted thinking process in which a person draws inferences about reality based on a personal emotional state.

| | |
|---|---|
| **emotional response** | The 'E' of the DIE Model, which stands for emotional response. An emotion that results from an interpretation of the data. (See **DIE Model**, **affect**, and **emotion**.) |
| **exchange** | (In Part Two of the DIE Model) Distorted thinking and dysfunctional beliefs are replaced by specific, accurate, and balanced thoughts in order to diminish a negative emotional response. |
| **execution stage** | (Of time management) Acting on the planned activities of a schedule, after having determined values, goals, and related activities. |
| **expectations** | A dysfunctional belief that one should always receive a personal payback for a good deed. |
| **external control** | A dysfunctional belief that people are not personally responsible for and in control of their feelings and behaviors. Other people or outside events are seen as causing one's personal reactions. |
| **external senses** | Sight, hearing, touch, taste, and smell. |
| **fairness** | A dysfunctional belief that only one's personal view of right and wrong is correct. People who hold strongly to this belief are intolerant of, and angered by, any person or event that does not conform to what they believe is right. |
| **filtering** | A distorted thinking process that screens out the positive aspects of a situation, while focusing exclusively on the negative. |
| **firing order** | Specifies the trigger as well as the order in which a person experiences the ABC components of an ABC interaction. (See **trigger** and **ABC interaction**.) |

**GLOSSARY**

| | |
|---|---|
| **functional analysis of behavior** | An analysis of antecedents and consequences that determines their influence on a behavior one wants to change. (See **antecedents** and **consequences**.) |
| **functional belief** | A belief that is based on evidence or logical thinking and results in affect and behavior that assists one in achieving a goal. |
| **global labeling** | A distorted thinking process that generalizes a few details about people or events into an overall evaluation. |
| **goals** | Objectives to be attained that relate to personal values. |
| **high motivation** | Actions that result from intense feelings and strong beliefs. |
| **high self-esteem** | A predominately positive overall evaluation of one's worth. |
| **imagined rehearsal** | Rehearsing a desired behavior in one's mind using images and self-talk to perfect a skill. |
| **I message** | A form of assertive communication that is a clear and specific statement of a problem from the speaker's perspective with a suggestion for a resolution. |
| **imperative should(s)** | (See **shoulds**.) |
| **inappropriate negative emotion** | An unpleasant physical state of arousal that is a harmful response to an external or internal stimulus. |
| **inappropriate negative sensation** | An unpleasant internal physical response that is a harmful reaction to sensory stimulation. |
| **internal senses** | Physical sensations that relate to motion and balance. |

| | |
|---|---|
| **interpretation** | (In Part One of the DIE Model) The 'I' of the DIE Model stands for interpretation. It is a person's subjective thoughts and beliefs about the objective facts (data). |
| **long-term goals** | Objectives that relate to one's personal values and are attainable only after a series of short-term goals are met. |
| **low motivation** | Actions that result from weak feelings and ambivalent beliefs. |
| **low self-esteem** | An predominately negative self-evaluation of one's worth. |
| **mind reading** | A distorted thinking process in which a person assumes to know what other people are thinking. |
| **motivated learner** | One who has positive feelings and thoughts while engaging in academic pursuits. |
| **motivation** | An internal state that compels movement in a specific direction (A x C = B). |
| **negative behaviors** | Counterproductive behaviors that result from negative thoughts and feelings. |
| **negative cognitions** | (See **negative thinking**.) |
| **negative motivation** | To move away from a person, situation, or event that is associated with negative affect and cognition. |
| **negative thinking** | Thinking that focuses primarily on one's liabilities and weaknesses. |
| **nonjudgmental** | (In thinking and language) Focusing on how people and events "are" rather than on how they "should" be. |
| **on-the-spot thought stopping** | A procedure for diminishing the effects of negative thoughts by blocking them out as they occur. |

**GLOSSARY**

| | |
|---|---|
| **overgeneralizing** | A distorted thinking process that reaches a general conclusion based on a single piece of evidence. |
| **passivity** | Feelings, behaviors, and thoughts that deny or negate one's own needs in favor of others. |
| **perfectionism** | A dysfunctional belief that one should never make a mistake or be flawed in any way. |
| **personalization** | A distorted thinking process in which individuals attribute events or other people's reactions to themselves. |
| **planning stage** | (Of time management) Identifying one's personal values, the long-and short-term goals that relate to these values, and the specific activities that will bring about these goals. |
| **polarized thinking** | A distorted thinking process that puts people, situations, or events in extreme categories, not allowing for a middle ground or compromise. |
| **positive behaviors** | Behaviors that result from positive thoughts and feelings. |
| **positive imagery** | A mental picture or sensory representation of anything that contributes to positive feelings. |
| **positive motivation** | To move toward an objective or goal that is associated with positive affect and cognition. |
| **positive thinking** | Thinking that is realistic, proactive (as opposed to reactive), and free from distorted thoughts and dysfunctional beliefs. Focusing on personal assets and strengths as well as on what is good in others. |
| **practice** | (In Part Three of DIE Model) A step in the DIE Model in which exchanged thoughts are rehearsed. (See **exchange**.) |
| **practice method of thought stopping** | A procedure for eliminating persistent or recurrent negative thoughts by focusing on and blocking them out. |

| | |
|---|---|
| **procrastination** | Needless delay in initiating or completing activities that cause problems for oneself. |
| **progressive relaxation** | A procedure for reducing stress and muscle tension by contracting, tensing, and relaxing various muscle groups throughout the body. |
| **proofreading** | Rereading and correcting the final draft of a revised paper for errors in spelling, punctuation, and grammar. |
| **realistic goals** | Objectives that can be achieved by indi-viduals given their own efforts and abilities. |
| **reframing** | Focusing on the positive aspects or benefits of negative data. |
| **revision** | A process by which writers critically read and rework their written material, making conceptual, content, and organizational changes as their view of the material changes. |
| **rewards** | (In behavior modification) The systematic use of something a person enjoys to strengthen a behavior. (See **contingent use of rewards**.) |
| **short-term goals** | Objectives that can be achieved by activities or behaviors that occur within a limited period of time. |
| **self-esteem** | A person's overall evaluation of him- or herself. |
| **self-management** | Directing one's affect, behavior, and cognition in a purposeful manner in order to attain a specific goal. |
| **self-talk** | Speaking to oneself in one's mind as a way of thinking about or giving advice and directions to oneself. |
| **sensation** | Affect experienced primarily as a physical response that results from our external and internal senses. |

**GLOSSARY**

| | |
|---|---|
| **shoulds** | A distorted thinking process that is based on a list of uncompromising rules on how people must or ought to act. Not every use of the word should represents distorted thinking, as for example when it describes a contingent relationship: "If you want to achieve a high gpa, you should study often." |
| **specificity** | (In thinking and language) Focusing on the particular and relevant aspects of the situation or circumstance without drawing a general conclusion. |
| **success images** | Mental pictures or sensory representations of oneself achieving desired goals and objectives. |
| **thought stopping** | A method of curtailing negative thinking. (See **on-the spot** and **practice method**.) |
| **time savers** | (In time management) Feelings, behaviors, and thoughts that contribute to the efficient use of time. |
| **time wasters** | (In time management) Feelings, behaviors, and thoughts that interfere with the efficient use of time. |
| **trigger** | The ABC component that begins (triggers) the firing order. |
| **undesired outcome** | The unintended result of a person's effort to achieve a goal (often referred to as "failure"). |
| **upward ABC spiral** | A progressive series of ABC interactions that contribute to a positive outcome or experience. (See **ABC interaction** and **downward ABC spiral**.) |
| **values** | That which is personally important or meaningful to an individual. |
| **values clarification** | The process of discovering and understanding what is important and worthwhile in one's own life. |

| | |
|---|---|
| **visualization** | The process of picturing in our minds activities we want to engage in as a means of strengthening a belief in our ability to achieve. |
| **you message** | An aggressive form of communication that uses the pronoun "you" in an accusatory manner. |

**GLOSSARY**

# BIBLIOGRAPHY

Abel, R. (1976). *Man is the measure.* New York: The Free Press.

Alberti, R., & Emmons, M. (1978). *Your perfect right.* San Luis Obispo, CA: Impact Publishers.

Bandura, A. (1977). *Social learning theory.* Englewood Cliffs, NJ: Prentice- Hall, Inc.

Boorstin, D. (1985). *The discoverers.* New York: Vintage Books.

Bry, A. (1978). *Visualization: Directing the movies of your mind.* New York: Barnes & Noble Books.

Davis, M., Eshelman, E.R., & McKay, M. (1988). *The relaxation and stress reduction workbook* (3rd ed). Oakland, CA: New Harbinger Publications.

Ellis, A. (1969). *The essence of rational psychotherapy: A comprehensive approach to treatment.* New York: Institute for Rational Living.

Ellis, A., & Harper, R. (1975). *A new guide to rational living.* Englewood Cliffs, NJ: Prentice-Hall.

Fensterheim, H., & Baer, J. (1975). *Stop running scared.* New York: Dell Publishing Co., Inc.

Fisher, C. (1992). An empirically based model for the development and retention of listening skills in information systems college students. *Proceedings of the International Academy of Information Manage-ment* (pp. 81-102). Dallas: Academy of Information Management.

Gerald M., & Eyman, W. (1981). *Thinking straight and talking sense.* New York: Institute for Rational Living.

Gordon, T. (1983). *Leadership effectiveness training.* New York: Putnam.

Hamilton, E. (1973). *The Roman way.* New York: Avon Books.

Hirsch, E.D. (1987). *Cultural literacy: What every American needs to know.* Boston: Houghton Mifflin Company.

Ivers, M. (1991). *The Random House guide to good writing.* New York: Random House.

Jeans, J. (1981). *Physics and philosophy.* New York: Dover Publications, Inc.

Jewler, A.J. & Gardner, J.N. (1987). *Step by step to college success.* Belmont, CA: Wadsworth.

Lange, A., & Jakubowski, P. (1976). *Responsible assertive behavior: Cognitive/behavioral procedures for trainers.* Champaign, IL: Research Press.

Lazarus, A. (1977). *In the mind's eye: The power of imagery for personal enrichment.* New York: Rawson Associates Publishers, Inc.

Lazarus, A. (1989). *The practice of multimodal therapy.* Baltimore: Johns Hopkins University Press.

Lazarus, A., & Fay, A. (1975). *I can if I want to.* New York: Warner Books.

McKay, M., Davis, M., & Fanning, P. (1981). *Thoughts & feelings: The art of cognitive stress intervention.* Oakland, CA: New Harbinger Publications.

McKay, M., & Fanning, P. (1987). *Self-esteem.* Oakland, CA: New Harbinger Publications.

McKay, M., & Fanning, P. (1988). *Combatting distorted thinking.* [Audio recording]. Oakland, CA: New Harbinger Publications.

McKeown, P.G. (1988). *Living with computers.* New York: Harcourt Brace Jovanovich, Inc.

Peale, N.V. (1952). *The power of positive thinking.* New York: Prentice-Hall.

Robbins, A. (1986). *Unlimited power* [Audio recording]. Chicago: Nightingale-Conant .

Rudestam, K.E. (1980). *Methods of self-change.* Monterey, CA: Brooks/Cole.

Seligman, M.E. (1991). *Learned optimism.* New York: Alfred A. Knopf.

Waitley, D. (1990). *The new dynamics of winning* [Audio recording]. Chicago: Nightingale-Conant.

Waitley, D. (1991) *The psychology of human motivation* [Audio recording]. Chicago: Nightingale-Conant.

Walter, T., & Siebert, A. (1993). *Student success.* Fort Worth, TX: Holt, Rinehart, Winston.

Watson, D., & Tharp, R. (1989). *Self-directed behavior. Self-modification for personal adjustment* (5th ed). Monterey, CA: Brooks/Cole.

# INDEX

Positive cognition. *See* Cognition
Positive imagery, 268
Positive motivation. *See* Motivation
Positive thinking. *See* Cognition
Positive thoughts. *See* Cognition
Practice, 93. *Also see* DIE Model, Part Two
Practice test, 150-151
Procrastination, 195-201
 and ABC interactions, 199-200
 affect that supports, 197-198
 cognitions that support, 198
 competing behaviors, 199
 definition of, 196
 and motivation, 197, 198, 201
 solving the problem of, 197-200
 specifying the problem of, 197
 trigger of, 199-200
Progressive relaxation, 97-98
Proofreading, 152

**R**

Reframing. *Also see* DIE Model, Part Three
Revision, 151-153
Rewards, 105-106
Role models, 268, 275

**S**

Self-esteem, 233-248
 and ABC interactions, 246-249
 accurate and functional self-evaluation, 238, 240-241
 and affect, 234-235
 balanced self-evaluation, 238, 240-241
 and behavior, 236-238
 changing affect to enhance, 235
 changing behavior to enhance, 238
 changing dysfunctional beliefs to enhance, 245-246
 and competence, 236-237
 definition of, 233
 distorted self-evaluation, 234-235, 238-241, 245-246
 and downward spiral, 247-248
 and dysfunctional beliefs, 242-246
 and effort, 236-238
 and failure, 237-238, 241, 275
 high, 233, 236-238, 240, 248-249
 inflated self-evaluation, 239-240, 243
 low, 233, 234-235, 242-247
 and self-talk, 240-241
 and undesired outcomes, 237-238
 and upward spirals, 247-248
Self-evaluation. *See* self-esteem
Self-management, 3-17
Self-motivated learner, 131, 133
Self-talk, 7, 73-75, 240-241, 263-264
 positive, 74-75
 and self-esteem, 240-241
 supportive, 263-264

Sensation. *See* Affect
Shaping, 106-107
Short-term goals. *See* Goals
Shoulds, 36, 133-134
Specificity, 115
SQ4R, 148-150
Stress, 139-140, 198
Study habits, 144
Study skills, 145-154
Success images, 264-265

**T**

Test-taking, 150-151
Thought stopping, 109-112
 examples of on-the-spot method, 110-111
 on-the-spot method, 109-111
 practice method, 111-112
Thoughts. *See* Cognition
Time management, 165-181
 and affect, 167-168
 and assertiveness, 168, 179-180
 and behavior, 168
 and cognition, 169-177
 creating a schedule, 170-171, 181
 and decision-making, 178
 definition of, 167
 execution stage of, 169, 177-180
 following a schedule, 177-180
 and goals, 169-176
 planning stage of, 169-177
 problems with, 179-180
 steps for, 181
 time savers, 168
 time wasters, 168
 and values, 169-176
Time savers, 168
Time schedule, 170-171, 177-180, 181
Time wasters, 168
Topic format, 148
Trigger, 11-13

**U**

Undesired outcome, 237-238
Upward spiral, 15-16, 75-76, 247-248

**V**

Values, 169-176
 conflict with goals, 172
 and goal setting, 169-174, 176, 270-272
 of high achievers, 176
 and motivational problems, 70-71, 270-272
 related to activities, 170-171, 173-174
 related to goals, 170-171, 173-174
 related to schedule, 170-171, 173-174